CHARTER OF THE

MW00425842

Basic Documents in World Politics

CHARTER OF THE UNITED NATIONS

Together with Scholarly Commentaries and Essential Historical Documents

Edited and with an Introduction by

IAN SHAPIRO AND JOSEPH LAMPERT

Yale UNIVERSITY PRESS/NEW HAVEN & LONDON

Published with assistance from the foundation established in memory of Amasa Stone Mather of the Class of 1907, Yale College.

Yale University Press books may be purchased in quantity for educational, business, or promotional use. For information, please e-mail sales.press@yale.edu (U.S. office) or sales@yaleup.co.uk (U.K. office).

Designed by Mary Valencia.
Set in Joanna and Eureka Sans types by Westchester Book Group.
Printed in the United States of America.

Library of Congress Cataloging-in-Publication Data

Charter of the United Nations : together with scholarly commentaries and essential historical
    documents / Edited and with an Introduction by Ian Shapiro and Joseph Lampert.
      pages cm. — (Basic documents in world politics)
    Includes bibliographical references and index.
    ISBN 978-0-300-18043-5 (pbk. : alk. paper)
      1. United Nations. Charter.   2. United Nations.   3. International law.   I. Shapiro, Ian,
editor.   II. Lampert, Joseph, editor.
    KZ4991.C43 2014
    341.23—dc23
                                                                                    2013036265

A catalogue record for this book is available from the British Library.

This paper meets the requirements of ANSI/NISO Z39.48–1992 (Permanence of Paper).

10 9 8 7 6 5 4 3 2 1

Contents

Introduction
Ian Shapiro and Joseph Lampert, **vii**

Documents

From the Joint Statement of Winston S. Churchill, Franklin D.
Roosevelt, and Josef Stalin at the Yalta Conference,
February 11, 1945 **3**
From the Address to Congress Reporting on the Yalta Conference,
Franklin D. Roosevelt, March 1, 1945 **5**
Address to the United Nations Conference on International
Organization at San Francisco, Harry S. Truman, April 25, 1945 **10**
Charter of the United Nations **14**
Statute of the International Court of Justice **46**

**Part I The United Nations Charter: Structure, Origins, and
Institutional Change**

1 The UN Charter: A Global Constitution?
Michael W. Doyle, **67**
2 Lost in Transition? The League of Nations and the United Nations
M. Patrick Cottrell, **91**
3 Has the UN Lived Up to Its Charter?
Stephen Schlesinger, **107**
4 Change and the United Nations Charter
Edward C. Luck, **121**

Part II Early Impact and State Formation

5 The United Nations and the Emergence of Independent India
Srinath Raghavan, **143**
6 Palestine and Israel at the United Nations: Partition, Recognition,
and Membership
Debra Shushan, **157**

7 Namibian Independence: A UN Success Story
Jean Krasno, 174

Part III The United Nations in the Contemporary World

8 A History of UN Peacekeeping
James Dobbins, 195
9 Fighting the Last War: The United Nations Charter in the Age of the
War on Terror
Oona A. Hathaway, 210
10 Science and Politics on a Warming Planet: The IPCC and the
Representation of Future Generations
Joseph Lampert, 225

List of Contributors 243

Index 245

Introduction

Ian Shapiro and Joseph Lampert

The Charter of the United Nations was agreed to in April 1945 at a founding conference attended by delegations from fifty nations and held at the San Francisco Opera House, and was subsequently signed on June 26, 1945. Enacted in the wake of the horrors of World War II, the result of negotiations begun in the midst of the fight, the Charter and the body it created aimed to secure lasting peace and security after the second cataclysmic war of the twentieth century. To do so would require achieving and maintaining consensus among the great powers, which, while keen to avoid the mistakes of the past, were looking forward and attempting to shape the postwar world. The document forged in San Francisco and the new global organization it established faced challenges from the outset, and as the world changed and new global threats emerged, a central question facing the UN would be how well it could adapt and respond to issues the Charter framers could not have anticipated.

The creation of a new world organization to maintain peace and security was among the stated war aims of the Allied nations, but serious negotiations did not begin until the summer of 1944, in the form of the Dumbarton Oaks Conference in Washington, DC. There, representatives from the "Big Four"—the United States, Great Britain, the USSR, and China—gathered to discuss how the organization should be structured and what its powers and duties should be. The tensions and disagreements of Dumbarton Oaks presaged the difficulties the UN project would face. The USSR and China did not attend at the same time (the Soviets had not entered the war against Japan, and they were suspicious of the Chiang Kai-shek regime). The growing mistrust between the US and Great Britain on one side and the USSR on the other that would eventually grow into the Cold War stoked disagreements over issues like membership in the organization (the Soviets at first insisted that all sixteen nations of the USSR be represented in the General Assembly). Most crucially, the delegates were unable to agree on the voting procedure for the Security Council, in particular the veto power of the five permanent members. It is remarkable that in the face of such disputes, the parties were able to produce a set of guiding principles for the eventual Charter, released as "Proposals for the Establishment of a General International Organization," on October 9, 1944.[1]

Resolving the remaining disagreements, in particular the scope of the veto power, was left to the heads of state meeting at the Yalta Conference in February 1945, where Churchill, Roosevelt, and Stalin were able to come to a resolution. That the process for creating the new organization was dominated by the great powers, and that they fully intended to guard their power and interests in the Charter is evident in the oblique reference to the "voting procedure" issue in the Yalta Statement issued by the three leaders, which stated that the foundations for a general international organization "were laid at Dumbarton Oaks. On the important question of voting procedure, however, agreement was not there reached. The present Conference has been able to resolve this difficulty. . . . As soon as the consultation with China and France has been completed, the text of the proposals on voting procedure will be made public."

The Yalta Statement also announced the San Francisco Conference, which was to be held "to prepare the charter . . . along the lines proposed in the informal conversations at Dumbarton Oaks." At this founding conference, small nations and outside groups got the chance to enter the conversation, though the imperative to keep the US, the USSR, Great Britain, China, and France in the organization resulted in significant pressure to reach and maintain consensus and to accede to the prerogatives the great powers reserved for themselves in the Security Council.[2] If Dumbarton Oaks and Yalta hosted the hard-nosed negotiations among the great powers, in San Francisco the proceedings gained some of the idealism that attaches to the idea of a general international organization for keeping the peace. In his opening address to the conference President Harry Truman (Roosevelt had died two weeks earlier) helped set the tone, telling the delegates "in your hands rests our future" and asserting that "We must build a new world—a far better world—one in which the eternal dignity of man is respected." It was not until the San Francisco meeting that the lofty language of the Preamble, with its call "to reaffirm faith in fundamental human rights, in the dignity and worth of the human person, in the equal rights of men and women and of nations large and small" and "to promote social progress and better standards of life in larger freedom" was decided upon.[3]

From its origins, then, the United Nations was an amalgam of idealist aspirations for world peace and progress and realist assertions of great power dominance, a dynamic that has characterized the organization ever since. The contributors to this volume pick up on this theme in a variety of ways. Organized into three sections, the essays gathered here assess the significance of the Charter and the organization it established in the context of their creation, subsequent legacy, and role in addressing contemporary problems. The first set of essays addresses how the Charter structures global authority, the purpose of the UN as it was conceived at the time of the Charter's adoption, and to what degree the subsequent history of the body lives up to the Charter's vision. The second section discusses the role of the UN in the early stages of new or newly independent countries that have emerged since its founding—India, Palestine/Israel, and Namibia—both as an institutional arena for new states and other actors to pursue their goals, and as a possible facilitator of political transitions. The final section addresses the role and influence of the UN and its Charter today, as the organization encounters a changing global political landscape, with essays examining the role of the UN in peacekeeping, the use of force after 9/11, and the problem of climate change.

THE UNITED NATIONS CHARTER: STRUCTURE, ORIGINS, AND INSTITUTIONAL CHANGE

The opening chapter by Michael Doyle provides a framework for thinking about the place of the UN Charter in structuring power and authority on a global scale by asking the question: How constitutional is the Charter? Doyle argues two points. First, the Charter is not like a national federal constitution (e.g., the US Constitution), but neither is it an ordinary contract-like treaty. Its key constitutional features are three: supranationality, inequality, and an "invitation to struggle," which leads to inevitable pushback from states when UN authority expands. Second, Doyle argues, unlike that of many domestic constitutions, the pushback more than holds its own. The UN, unlike the EU and the United States, has neither integrated its parts nor centralized authority. In support of this view, Doyle compares the Charter both to domestic constitutions and to conventional treaties, and examines the nature of the supranationality and inequality provided for in the Charter, as well as the Secretariat and its neutrality and independence. He then considers the movement toward "global legislation" signaled by the Security Council's counterterrorist resolutions and the experience of the Millennium Development Goals (MDGs) as examples of the tension between supranationality and state sovereignty, drawing on his experience as special adviser to Secretary-General Kofi Annan in 2001–3.

In the next essay the focus shifts to examining the establishment of the UN and how the body has changed and performed since the Charter was adopted. M. Patrick Cottrell reminds us that the UN Charter was negotiated not only in the context of the calamity of World War II but also under the shadow of the failed League of Nations. Although the architects of the Charter were keen to avoid the pitfalls that scuttled the first attempt at a global organization for protecting the peace, many of the core principles of the League made their way into the new institution in one form or another, particularly in the areas of collective security, multilateralism, and self-determination. Indeed, as Cottrell argues, it is striking that ideas associated with the League, so widely discredited by its critics, reappeared even stronger in the UN framework. The UN that emerges from this account is a world body attempting to reconcile the Wilsonian ideals of the League with the realist notion that such aspirations are undermined when the prerogatives of the great powers are not preserved.

As Cottrell emphasizes, the UN project, like the League of Nations, is a temporally contingent achievement, informed by the concerns and experiences of the moment. How did this new organization, founded in a Charter forged in the lessons of World War II and the experience of the League experiment, confront the changing global landscape of the tumultuous second half of the twentieth century? The next two chapters examine the establishment of the UN from the perspective of how the body has changed and performed, exploring to what degree the institution has measured up to the goals of the Charter. Stephen Schlesinger evaluates the UN in terms of how the organization has fulfilled, veered from, or surpassed the original vision of its founders. His essay reviews the conflicting goals of the diplomats at the 1945 San Francisco meeting and the compromises they agreed on. Tracing how the provisions of the Charter have changed and, on occasion, atrophied over the course of the twentieth century and into the twenty-first, Schlesinger finds that the UN has stayed relevant in world affairs by employing an unusual mix of realism and idealism in its operations.

In his essay, Edward C. Luck turns the focus to the Charter's relationship to forces of change, analyzing the ways the Charter tends to preserve the global status quo and to what degree it allows for and perhaps promotes change both within the UN itself and in the broader world. He identifies the core elements of the "conservative" Charter as those that grant the great powers permanent seats and veto authority on the powerful Security Council, while also tracing a "progressive" Charter concerned with human rights and the promotion of social and economic well-being. Exploring the strategic and political factors that contributed to these different aspects of the Charter during the negotiations leading up to its adoption, Luck observes that the organization it created has historically been remarkably slow to reform structurally—as its architects intended in 1945—but quick to adapt to or to anticipate shifts in global values and opportunities. The essay concludes by assessing how the UN and the global political landscape have been served by this dynamic, suggesting that although the conservative and progressive aspects of the Charter have both been beneficial, some change to its conservative elements—in particular to the membership and the functioning of the Security Council—may be necessary to preserve the legitimacy and success of the UN project in the long term.

EARLY IMPACT AND STATE FORMATION

How would the text of the Charter translate into political practice? Whereas the essays of part 1 address this question by focusing largely on how the Charter structures international authority and how the Charter is implicated in processes of institutional change, the essays in part 2 examine the UN in the context of the concrete political challenges brought about by the emergence of new and newly independent states around the world, one of the great political developments of the postwar era. The UN played a key role in many of these transitions, helping to integrate these new states into the international order. The three chapters of part 2 examine this dynamic, exploring the relationship between the UN and a newly independent India, its attempt to partition Palestine into Arab and Jewish states, and its involvement in the establishment of Namibia.

Though the drafting and adoption of the Charter was driven largely by the agendas of the great powers, less powerful states sought to influence the new world body and to use it to advance their interests and ideals. Just what kind of influence such states could exert was an open question in the UN's early history. Prime Minister Jawaharlal Nehru, in particular, looked to the UN not only as a potential facilitator of a new form of postwar internationalism, but also as an arena where a newly independent India could make its mark on the world. This account emerges from Srinath Raghavan's examination of India's early interaction with the UN. Raghavan begins by considering debates in both Britain and India about the UN during the run-up to independence and partition, then examines India's early attempts not just to register its presence in the UN but also to alter the character of the organization—particularly in the context of the General Assembly motion against the "Ghetto Act" in South Africa and the debate over the future of South West Africa. Raghavan then traces the change in India's stance toward the UN by looking at the Kashmir dispute, arguing that this transition was not as stark as some scholars have suggested.

Raghavan observes that Britain considered referring the issue of Indian independence to the UN, but ultimately decided against it. This stands in contrast to the case of Palestine/Israel, where the UN found itself embroiled in the conflict-ridden process of establishing new states from the European-administered mandates created during the interwar period. Debra Shushan investigates the role of the young organization in recommending the partition of Palestine and subsequently recognizing the state of Israel. Although the Arab-Jewish dispute over Palestine predated the UN, the fledgling body concluded that it was necessary to impose a solution. In opting for the partition of mandatory Palestine into an Arab state, a Jewish state, and a UN trusteeship for Jerusalem, all within an economic union, the United Nations Special Committee on Palestine privileged prior international commitments to creating a Jewish "national home" over Arab arguments that Jews were foreign interlopers who lacked any claim to Palestine. The resulting UN General Assembly resolution 181 was not entirely pleasing to the Zionist movement, particularly because it called for drastic restrictions on Jewish immigration, and it was even less satisfactory to Arab states and organizations, which had rejected partition outright. The UN attempted to broker an end to the ensuing war, and UN mediator Count Folke Bernadotte was assassinated by the Zionist militant group Lehi for his efforts. Ultimately, in May 1949, the UN voted to recognize Israel, calling on the new member state to fulfill the dictates of prior UN resolutions by enabling the UN to administer Jerusalem and allowing Palestinian refugees to return home. Focusing throughout on features that distinguish the UN's early approach to the Palestine/Israel question, Shushan concludes her chapter by reflecting on the dilemma over the UN's consideration of Palestinian statehood and membership status from the perspective of the organization's historic mission to bring peace and independence to the Jewish and Arab peoples who inhabit this contested land.

The recognition of Israel was not the only time the UN proved influential in the establishment of a new state. As Jean Krasno shows, the UN was central to achieving Namibia's independence and democratic governance. Krasno examines UN involvement in Namibia, which began as far back as 1949, the year South Africa initiated its policy of Apartheid, not only in South Africa but also in South West Africa (now Namibia), which was under its control. Beginning in 1949, the General Assembly attempted a series of actions to wrest control of Namibia from South Africa and grant the Namibian people their independence, which had been promised under the League of Nations' mandate system. When several legal attempts failed, in 1966 the General Assembly passed resolution 2145, terminating South Africa's mandate. Shortly afterwards, the UN created the UN Council for South West Africa, made up of eleven member states, to begin a process of administering the territory from a distance. Martti Ahtisaari of Finland became the commissioner for South West Africa in 1977, and the council and the commissioner did much to train Namibians for leadership and to plan for independence. The South West Africa People's Organization (SWAPO) was given observer status at the UN as the sole representatives of the Namibian people. In 1978 the Security Council, now actively involved, passed resolution 435, creating the United Nations Transition Assistance Group (UNTAG), which was supposed to oversee the transition to independence. But it was not until the Cold War began to thaw and South African intransigence weakened that UNTAG could be deployed, in 1989. The work of the Council for South West Africa in preparing for independence was a significant factor in the success of the 1989 elections, the writing of the new constitution, and creating what has been a stable democratic system in Namibia.

THE UNITED NATIONS IN THE CONTEMPORARY WORLD

Since the UN Charter was negotiated and adopted, many of the problems it was meant to resolve have evolved, and new challenges have sprung up. The final section of this book turns attention to the Charter's long-term impact, focusing on how the UN has shaped global affairs and responded to contemporary problems, including peacekeeping, the post-9/11 use of force, and climate change.

The principal reason for founding the UN was to prevent further armed conflict. James Dobbins's chapter on UN peacekeeping returns to this issue, tracing the evolution of UN military interventions from the defense of South Korea in the early 1950s, through the emergence of inter-positional peacekeeping in the decades thereafter, to the much more frequent and more expansive nation-building missions that have characterized UN (and US) military operations since 1989. Dobbins assesses the efficacy of UN peace-keeping; compares its capacity and record to that of other international force providers, such as NATO, the EU, and the African Union; and contrasts the UN's approach with the more muscular approach to "peace enforcement" taken by coalitions under American leadership.

Oona A. Hathaway continues this exploration of the UN's role in keeping the peace, shifting the focus to security issues not anticipated by the Charter's architects by examining the challenges to the Charter's prohibitions on the use of force in the post-9/11 era—and how the UN has responded. Noting that the Charter aimed to prohibit warfare between nation-states and to vest the Security Council with the authority to respond to threats to the peace, Hathaway argues that this framework did not address the insipient emergence and spread of new weapons technologies—especially weapons of mass destruction—nor did it address threats to states by non-state actors. The spread of increasingly destructive weapons technology and the emergence of non-state actors with a global reach since the Charter's adoption has laid bare the gaps in its framework and raised questions about how to interpret the prohibition on aggressive use of force by states. Since the attacks on the United States on 9/11, for example, many have argued that states' inherent right to self-defense–preserved in Article 51 of the Charter–permits states to use force to preempt the extreme threats posed by such weapons. As the 2002 US National Security Strategy Memo controversially put it, "The greater the threat, the greater is the risk of inaction–and the more compelling the case for taking anticipatory action to defend ourselves, even if uncertainty remains as to the time and place of the enemy's attack." Hathaway also examines the recurring and increasingly salient tension between the Charter's protection of state sovereignty and prohibition on the use of force (except for self-defense) on one hand, and the increasing pressure for intervention to protect human rights since the Charter was adopted on the other.

Armed conflict is not the only threat to global security and progress. In the final chapter Joseph Lampert looks at how the UN has addressed climate change, an issue not on the minds of those who crafted the Charter but one that is emerging as a pressing challenge of the twenty-first century. Lampert's essay describes the creation and history of the Intergovernmental Panel on Climate Change (IPCC), one illustration of how the UN can provide a framework for states, specialized agencies, and other actors to address global problems. Though there have been some successes in the effort to limit climate change–motivated in part by the work of the IPCC—setbacks in the formulation of a successor to the Kyoto Protocol suggest that a new framework for global climate politics is needed. Lampert's essay suggests that a significant factor preventing the development of a global policy that seriously addresses climate change may be traced to a legitimacy gap in the ongoing negotiations over a binding climate agreement: the fact that future generations are not represented in the discussion means that those whose interests will be most vitally affected are not included in the policy-making process. Lampert argues that recasting the IPCC as a reviewing agency, charged with trusteeship over the interests of future generations affected by climate change, will bring climate change politics into better accord with this democratic principle of legitimacy and perhaps spur the negotiation of a meaningful climate treaty.

REALISM, IDEALISM, AND UN EFFICACY

The prominent theme that emerges from these essays is that the mix of realist power politics and idealist aspirations that marked the negotiations at Dumbarton Oaks, Yalta, and San Francisco has been a defining feature of the Charter and the UN ever since—and often in surprising ways. Lest critics dismiss the Charter as little more than a set of well-intentioned exhortations, Cottrell's account of the transition from the League of Nations to the United Nations reminds us that one of the central achievements of the Charter has been to tie the pursuit of ideals of peace, human rights, and progress to maintaining the privileges reserved by the great powers. Indeed, part of the rationale for the veto power held by the permanent members of the Security Council was to allow for greater enforcement power in security matters than the League's unanimity rule permitted—without the veto, the great powers would not agree to a system that empowered the new organization to sanction aggressors against their wishes. From the beginning, then, the Charter linked the lofty principles articulated in the Preamble and elsewhere in its text with realist considerations of great power affiliation and cooperation.

This particular mix of realism and idealism has resulted in remarkable durability for the UN, as Schlesinger's contribution argues, but it has also limited the potential of the UN as an effective hub of global governance. Doyle's account of state "pushback" against UN authority vividly illustrates this. He argues that one feature of the Charter is supranationality—the UN is empowered to make decisions without the continuous consent of its members, and those decisions bind even those members that voted against them. Supranationality, however, is not the same as sovereignty. Sovereign equality of member states is guaranteed by Article 2.1, a realist concession to the primacy of states. The result, then, is that although the Charter grants binding decision-making authority to the UN, the principle of state sovereignty granted by the Charter makes the pushback by states a much more powerful force than it is in other constitutional arrangements, such as those of the US and the EU. State pushback is, of course, often more pronounced and successful when done by a powerful state, particularly one of the permanent five members of the Security Council, but as Doyle shows, all states, large and small, engage in pushback with some success, whether in the realm of UN budget negotiations, arrangements for military forces to enforce Security Council resolutions, or in agreeing to and implementing the MDGs.

In many ways, then, the strength of state pushback against UN authority is a product of the tension between the idealist aim of a world body for the peaceful (and binding) settlement of disputes, on one hand, and realist assertions of state power, on the other. This dynamic has played out in a number of arenas, as illustrated by other contributors to this volume. Some show that state pushback is facilitated by the principles of the Charter itself. For example, not only does the Charter guarantee the sovereign equality of member states, as Doyle emphasizes, but it also preserves, in Article 51, "the inherent right" of states to self-defense. As Hathaway argues, the state assertiveness represented by the post-9/11 rise of the doctrine of preemptive self-defense threatens to expand what was originally intended to be a limited concession to the Article 2.4 proscription against the "threat or use of force," to the point that it could become, as she puts it, the exception that swallows the rule. Other essays explore state pushback that results from weak enforcement mechanisms for UN resolutions. For example, as Shushan demonstrates, state pushback against a young UN had much to do with how the Palestine/Israel partitioning controversy unfolded in the 1940s. The UN partition plan that aimed to resolve the conflict was rejected by a number of Arab states, which refused to recognize the General Assembly resolution that authorized it. The outgoing mandatory power, Britain, declined to enforce it, and Secretary-General Trygve Lie could not persuade the US or Britain to provide troops to enforce it. The war that ensued led to an increase in Israel's territory beyond that allowed in the resolution.

However, while Doyle's account of state pushback illustrates how the tension between realism and idealism present in the Charter can limit the UN's potential governing efficacy, Luck's analysis of the progressive Charter complicates this story by showing how those elements of the Charter aimed at promoting change in the areas of human rights and economic and social progress have been the source of much of the UN's success. In contrast to the conservative provisions of the Charter that attempted to lock in the 1945 status quo, the progressive Charter, as Luck shows, was meant to enable innovation and action in order to adapt to changing circumstances. Against critics who dismiss the rhetoric of "We the Peoples" and references to human rights and social progress as empty proclamations, Luck makes the case that these provisions "allowed interested member states, the international secretariat, and civil society partners to craft institutions, methods, and procedures capable both of responding to immediate challenges and of being modified as conditions and needs changed."

In practice the UN has become an arena within which global actors of various stripes—states, aspiring states, and nongovernmental organizations—could make their claims and pursue their goals and visions. Raghavan's treatment of Nehru's perspective on the UN illustrates this and shows how a Charter premised largely on the idea that preserving great power prerogatives is the key to peace and security also gave rise to an institution that could be shaped and put to use by and for smaller powers. So too does Krasno's account of the long and difficult path toward Namibian independence. Among other factors that contributed to this outcome were the efforts of the Organization of African Unity (OAU), an organization of African states with observer status at the UN—and the members of which, of course, were voting members of the General Assembly. A key development in the struggle for Namibian independence was the OAU's work to obtain observer status for SWAPO at the UN. As Krasno states, this "demonstrated that the UN offered a proactive avenue that otherwise would not have existed." As Luck emphasizes, much of the progressive character of the Charter results from the fact that it established "a framework for action, not a rigid or detailed template," which enabled the development of the UN's functionalist system of programs and agencies for addressing a wide array of problems. Lampert's exploration of the IPCC as a response to climate change illustrates just this. Environmental protection of any kind was decidedly not on the radar of those drafting the Charter, yet they created a body capable of responding to new challenges to human well-being, putting into place an organization aimed at saving "succeeding generations" from more than "the scourge of war," in the words of the Preamble.

As several of the essays gathered here suggest, the relevance of the United Nations and its Charter to global governance depends a great deal on the capacity of the organization to adapt to the new and evolving challenges of the twenty-first century. Even as the end of the Cold War freed the UN to exert its influence on global affairs without being completely shackled by the rivalry between the US and the USSR, UN success still frequently depends on the cooperation of great powers. Thus, whatever role the UN might have as a hub of global governance will inevitably be shaped by the prerogatives of the five permanent members of the Security Council, whose vetoes (or threats of vetoes) continue to have a substantial impact on the organization's agenda—from blocking the Palestinian bid for full UN membership (by the US in 2011) to whether to bring pressure on Syria to halt its crackdown on its civilian population (by both Russia and China in 2011 and 2012).

In addition to navigating the competing agendas of the great powers, the UN has found itself situated amidst other increasingly salient international institutions, a development that may often promote UN objectives but also has the potential to displace the organization as a potential focal point of global governance.[4] For instance, in the realm of peacekeeping—the central concern for those who drafted the Charter—NATO in particular has taken on a more substantial role since the intervention in Kosovo in the 1990s. This was clearly illustrated in the Libya campaign of 2011. While the Security Council passed a resolution (1973) authorizing a no-fly zone, an arms embargo, and other measures to protect Libyan civilians from the Qaddafi regime, operational control was ceded to a coalition of states coordinated by NATO. The roles of the US and the EU in peacekeeping operations have also grown in recent years. So too has that of the African Union, often through the active support of the UN, as it has become "the peacekeeper of last resort for that continent," as James Dobbins notes in chapter 8.

While the architects of the Charter intended for the UN to be an institution slow to evolve (as Luck's essay emphasizes), the central question facing the world body and the legacy of the Charter is whether it can change enough to remain relevant to a global landscape vastly different from the one that emerged after World War II. Thus far the UN has adapted more or less within the confines of the original Charter (amendments passed in the 1960s expanded the size of the Security Council, though this had no impact on the membership or veto power of the five permanent members). But the success that an institution shaped by mid-twentieth-century concerns can have in the twenty-first-century world may depend upon it engaging in much more substantial processes of change than it has attempted in the past. At stake is whether the ideal of a truly global institution, open to all nations and with the stated purpose "to promote social progress and better standards of life in larger freedom," continues to be a live aspiration for those working to bring about a more peaceful and secure world.

Notes

1. For a comprehensive history of the Dumbarton Oaks Conference, see Robert C. Hilderbrand, *Dumbarton Oaks: The Origins of the United Nations and the Search for Postwar Security* (Chapel Hill: University of North Carolina Press, 1990).

2. Bruno Simma, *Charter of the United Nations: A Commentary* (New York: Oxford University Press, 2002), 10.

3. Mark Mazower makes the case that the primary architect of the Preamble was Jan Smuts, then the prime minister of South Africa and a leader of the White settler movement there. Mazower argues that the ideals of the Preamble—and perhaps the UN project itself—are compromised by Smuts's colonialist worldview. See Mark Mazower, *No Enchanted Palace: The End of Empire and the Ideological Origins of the United Nations* (Princeton: Princeton University Press, 2009), 28–65. Edward Luck contests this account in chapter 4 of this volume, showing that Smuts's role was not as central as Mazower claims.

4. Robert Keohane suggests several ways in which the efficacy and legitimacy of UN multilateralism is constrained by reliance on great powers and international institutions, such as NATO, in "The Contingent Legitimacy of Multilateralism," in *Multilateralism under Challenge? Power, International Order, and Structural Change*, ed. Edward Newman, Ramesh Thakur, and John Tirman (Tokyo: United Nations University Press, 2006), 56–76.

DOCUMENTS

FROM THE JOINT STATEMENT OF
WINSTON S. CHURCHILL, FRANKLIN D. ROOSEVELT, AND
JOSEF STALIN AT THE YALTA CONFERENCE
FEBRUARY 11, 1945

. . .

UNITED NATIONS CONFERENCE

We are resolved upon the earliest possible establishment with our allies of a general international organization to maintain peace and security. We believe that this is essential, both to prevent aggression and to remove the political, economic, and social causes of war through the close and continuing collaboration of all peace-loving peoples.

The foundations were laid at Dumbarton Oaks. On the important question of voting procedure, however, agreement was not there reached. The present Conference has been able to resolve this difficulty.

We have agreed that a conference of United Nations should be called to meet at San Francisco in the United States on April 25, 1945, to prepare the charter of such an organization, along the lines proposed in the informal conversations at Dumbarton Oaks.

The Government of China and the Provisional Government of France will be immediately consulted and invited to sponsor invitations to the conference jointly with the Governments of the United States, Great Britain, and the Union of Soviet Socialist Republics. As soon as the consultation with China and France has been completed, the text of the proposals on voting procedure will be made public.

. . .

UNITY FOR PEACE AS FOR WAR

Our meeting here in the Crimea has reaffirmed our common determination to maintain and strengthen in the peace to come that unity of purpose and of action which has made victory possible and certain for the United Nations in this war. We believe that this is a sacred obligation which our Governments owe to our peoples and to all the peoples of the world.

Only with the continuing and growing cooperation and understanding among our three countries and among all the peace-loving Nations can the highest aspiration of humanity be realized—a secure and lasting peace which will, in the words of the Atlantic Charter, "afford assurance that all the men in all the lands may live out their lives in freedom from fear and want."

Victory in this war and establishment of the proposed international organization will provide the greatest opportunity in all history to create in the years to come the essential conditions of such a peace.

Signed:

Winston S. Churchill

Franklin D. Roosevelt

J. Stalin

FROM THE ADDRESS TO CONGRESS
REPORTING ON THE YALTA CONFERENCE
FRANKLIN D. ROOSEVELT
MARCH 1, 1945

. . .

I come from the Crimea Conference with a firm belief that we have made a good start on the road to a world of peace.

There were two main purposes in this Crimea Conference. The first was to bring defeat to Germany with the greatest possible speed, and the smallest possible loss of Allied men.

. . .

The second purpose was to continue to build the foundation for an international accord that would bring order and security after the chaos of the war, that would give some assurance of lasting peace among the Nations of the world.

Toward that goal also, a tremendous stride was made.

At Teheran, a little over a year ago, there were long-range military plans laid by the Chiefs of Staff of the three most powerful Nations. Among the civilian leaders at Teheran, however, at that time, there were only exchanges of views and expressions of opinion. No political arrangements were made— and none was attempted.

At the Crimea Conference, however, the time had come for getting down to specific cases in the political field.

There was on all sides at this Conference an enthusiastic effort to reach an agreement. Since the time of Teheran, a year ago, there had developed among all of us a—what shall I call it?—a greater facility in negotiating with each other, that augurs well for the peace of the world. We know each other better.

I have never for an instant wavered in my belief that an agreement to insure world peace and security can be reached.

. . .

When we met at Yalta, in addition to laying our strategic and tactical plans for the complete and final military victory over Germany, there were other problems of vital political consequence.

For instance, first, there were the problems of the occupation and control of Germany . . .

. . .

Second—again for example—there was the settlement of the few differences that remained among us with respect to the International Security Organization after the Dumbarton Oaks Conference. As you remember, at that time, I said that we had agreed ninety percent. Well, that's a pretty good percentage. I think the other ten percent was ironed out at Yalta.

. . .

Never before have the major Allies been more closely united— not only in their war aims but also in their peace aims. And they are determined to continue to be united with each other—and with all peace-loving Nations—so that the ideal of lasting peace will become a reality.

. . .

Of equal importance with the military arrangements at the Crimea Conference were the agreements reached with respect to a general international organization for lasting world peace. The foundations were laid at Dumbarton Oaks. There was one point, however, on which agreement was not reached at Dumbarton Oaks. It involved the procedure of voting in the Security Council. I want to try to make it clear by making it simple. It took me hours and hours to get the thing straight in my own mind—and many conferences.

At the Crimea Conference, the Americans made a proposal on this subject which, after full discussion was, I am glad to say, unanimously adopted by the other two Nations.

It is not yet possible to announce the terms of that agreement publicly, but it will be in a very short time.

When the conclusions reached with respect to voting in the Security Council are made known, I think and I hope that you will find them a fair solution of this complicated and difficult problem. They are founded in justice, and will go far to assure international cooperation in the maintenance of peace.

A conference of all the United Nations of the world will meet in San Francisco on April 25, 1945. There, we all hope, and confidently expect, to execute a definite charter of organization under which the peace of the world will be preserved and the forces of aggression permanently outlawed.

This time we are not making the mistake of waiting until the end of the war to set up the machinery of peace. This time, as we fight together to win the war finally, we work together to keep it from happening again.

I—as you know—have always been a believer in the document called the Constitution of the United States. And I spent a good deal of time in educating two other Nations of the world in regard to the Constitution of the United States. The charter has to be—and should be—approved by the Senate of the United States, under the Constitution. I think the other Nations all know it now. I am aware of that fact, and now all the other Nations are. And we hope that the Senate will approve of what is set forth as the Charter of the United Nations when they all come together in San Francisco next month.

The Senate of the United States, through its appropriate representatives, has been kept continuously advised of the program of this Government in the creation of the International Security Organization.

The Senate and the House of Representatives will both be represented at the San Francisco Conference. The Congressional delegates to the San Francisco Conference will consist of an equal number of Republican and Democratic members. The American Delegation is—in every sense of the word—bipartisan.

. . .

The structure of world peace cannot be the work of one man, or one party, or one Nation. It cannot be just an American peace, or a British peace, or a Russian, a French, or a Chinese peace. It cannot be a peace of large Nations—or of small Nations. It must be a peace which rests on the cooperative effort of the whole world.

It cannot be a structure of complete perfection at first. But it can be a peace—and it will be a peace—based on the sound and just principles of the Atlantic Charter—on the concept of the dignity of the human being—and on the guarantees of tolerance and freedom of religious worship.

. . .

The Crimea Conference was a meeting of the three major military powers on whose shoulders rested chief responsibility and burden of the war. Although, for this reason, France was not a participant in the Conference, no one should detract from the recognition that was accorded there of her role in the future of Europe and the future of the world.

. . .

She [France] has been invited to join as a sponsor of the International Conference at San Francisco next month.

She will be a permanent member of the International Security Council together with the other four major powers.

. . .

The Conference in the Crimea was a turning point—I hope in our history and therefore in the history of the world. There will soon be presented to the Senate of the United States and to the American people a great decision that will determine the fate of the United States—and of the world—for generations to come.

There can be no middle ground here. We shall have to take the responsibility for world collaboration, or we shall have to bear the responsibility for another world conflict.

I know that the word "planning" is not looked upon with favor in some circles. In domestic affairs, tragic mistakes have been made by reason of lack of planning; and, on the other hand, many great improvements in living, and many benefits to the human race, have been accomplished as a result of adequate, intelligent planning—reclamation of desert areas, developments of whole river valleys, and provision for adequate housing.

The same will be true in relations between Nations. For the second time in the lives of most of us this generation is face to face with the objective of preventing wars. To meet that objective, the Nations of the world will either have a plan or they will not. The groundwork of a plan has now been furnished, and has been submitted to humanity for discussion and decision.

No plan is perfect. Whatever is adopted at San Francisco will doubtless have to be amended time and again over the years, just as our own Constitution has been.

No one can say exactly how long any plan will last. Peace can endure only so long as humanity really insists upon it, and is willing to work for it—and sacrifice for it.

Twenty-five years ago, American fighting men looked to the statesmen of the world to finish the work of peace for which they fought and suffered.

We failed them then. We cannot fail them again, and expect the world again to survive.

The Crimea Conference was a successful effort by the three leading Nations to find a common ground for peace. It ought to spell the end of the system of unilateral action, the exclusive alliances, the spheres of influence, the balances of power, and all the other expedients that have been tried for centuries—and have always failed.

We propose to substitute for all these, a universal organization in which all peace-loving Nations will finally have a chance to join.

I am confident that the Congress and the American people will accept the results of this Conference as the beginnings of a permanent structure of peace upon which we can begin to build, under God, that better world in which our children and grandchildren—yours and mine, the children and grandchildren of the whole world—must live, and can live.

And that, my friends, is the principal message I can give you. But I feel it very deeply, as I know that all of you are feeling it today, and are going to feel it in the future.

ADDRESS TO THE UNITED NATIONS CONFERENCE ON
INTERNATIONAL ORGANIZATION AT SAN FRANCISCO
HARRY S. TRUMAN
APRIL 25, 1945

Delegates to the United Nations Conference on International Organization:

The world has experienced a revival of an old faith in the everlasting moral force of justice. At no time in history has there been a more important Conference, nor a more necessary meeting, than this one in San Francisco, which you are opening today.

On behalf of the American people, I extend to you a most hearty welcome.

President Roosevelt appointed an able delegation to represent the United States. I have complete confidence in its Chairman, Secretary of State Stettinius, and in his distinguished colleagues, former Secretary Cordell Hull, Senator Connally, Senator Vandenberg, Representative Bloom and Representative Eaton, Governor Stassen and Dean Gildersleeve.

They have my confidence. They have my support.

In the name of a great humanitarian—one who surely is with us today in spirit—I earnestly appeal to each and every one of you to rise above personal interests, and adhere to those lofty principles, which benefit all mankind.

Franklin D. Roosevelt gave his life while trying to perpetuate these high ideals. This Conference owes its existence, in a large part, to the vision and foresight and determination of Franklin Roosevelt.

Each of you can remember other courageous champions, who also made the supreme sacrifice, serving under your flag. They gave their lives, so that others might live in security. They died to insure justice. We must work and live to guarantee justice—for all.

You members of this Conference are to be the architects of the better world. In your hands rests our future. By your labors at this Conference, we shall know if suffering humanity is to achieve a just and lasting peace.

Let us labor to achieve a peace which is really worthy of their great sacrifice. We must make certain, by your work here, that another war will be impossible.

We, who have lived through the torture and the tragedy of two world conflicts, must realize the magnitude of the problem before us. We do not need far-sighted vision to understand the trend in recent history. Its significance is all too clear.

With ever-increasing brutality and destruction, modern warfare, if unchecked, would ultimately crush all civilization. We still have a choice between the alternatives: the continuation of international chaos—or the establishment of a world organization for the enforcement of peace.

It is not the purpose of this Conference to draft a treaty of peace in the old sense of that term. It is not our assignment to settle specific questions of territories, boundaries, citizenship and reparations.

This Conference will devote its energies and its labors exclusively to the single problem of setting up the essential organization to keep the peace. You are to write the fundamental charter.

Our sole objective, at this decisive gathering, is to create the structure. We must provide the machinery, which will make future peace, not only possible, but certain.

The construction of this delicate machine is far more complicated than drawing boundary lines on a map, or estimating fair reparations, or placing reasonable limits upon armaments. Your task must be completed first.

We represent the overwhelming majority of all mankind. We speak for people, who have endured the most savage and devastating war ever inflicted upon innocent men, women and children.

We hold a powerful mandate from our people. They believe we will fulfill this obligation. We must prevent, if human mind, heart and hope can prevent it, the repetition of the disaster from which the entire world will suffer for years to come.

If we should pay merely lip service to inspiring ideals, and later do violence to simple justice, we would draw down upon us the bitter wrath of generations yet unborn.

We must not continue to sacrifice the flower of our youth merely to check madmen, those who in every age plan world domination. The sacrifices of our youth today must lead, through your efforts, to the building for tomorrow of a mighty combination of nations founded upon justice for peace.

Justice remains the greatest power on earth.

To that tremendous power alone, will we submit.

Nine days ago, I told the Congress of the United States, and I now repeat it to you:

"Nothing is more essential to the future peace of the world, than continued cooperation of the nations, which had to muster the force necessary to defeat the conspiracy of the axis powers to dominate the world.

"While these great states have a special responsibility to enforce the peace, their responsibility is based upon the obligations resting upon all states, large and small, not to use force in international relations, except in the defense of law. The responsibility of the great states is to serve, and not dominate the peoples of the world."

None of us doubt that with Divine guidance, friendly cooperation, and hard work, we shall find an adequate answer to the problem history has put before us.

Realizing the scope of our task and the imperative need for success, we proceed with humility and determination.

By harmonious cooperation, the United Nations repelled the onslaught of the greatest aggregation of military force that was ever assembled in the long history of aggression. Every nation now fighting for freedom is giving according to its ability and opportunity.

We fully realize today that victory in war requires a mighty united effort. Certainly, victory in peace calls for, and must receive, an equal effort.

Man has learned long ago, that it is impossible to live unto himself. This same basic principle applies today to nations. We were not isolated during the war. We dare not become isolated in peace.

All will concede that in order to have good neighbors, we must also be good neighbors. That applies in every field of human endeavor.

For lasting security, men of good-will must unite and organize. Moreover, if our friendly policies should ever be considered by belligerent leaders, as merely evidence of weakness, the organization we establish must be adequately prepared to meet any challenge.

Differences between men, and between nations, will always remain. In fact, if held within reasonable limits, such disagreements are actually wholesome. All progress begins with differences of opinion and moves onward as the differences are adjusted through reason and mutual understanding.

In recent years, our enemies have clearly demonstrated the disaster which follows when freedom of thought is no longer tolerated. Honest minds cannot long be regimented without protest.

The essence of our problem here is to provide sensible machinery for the settlement of disputes among nations. Without this, peace cannot exist. We can no longer permit any nation, or group of nations, to attempt to settle their arguments with bombs and bayonets.

If we continue to abide by such decisions, we will be forced to accept the fundamental philosophy of our enemies, namely, that "Might Makes Right." To deny this premise, and we most certainly do, we are obliged to provide the necessary means to refute it. Words are not enough.

We must, once and for all, reverse the order, and prove by our acts conclusively, that Right Has Might.

If we do not want to die together in war, we must learn to live together in peace.

With firm faith in our hearts, to sustain us along the hard road to victory, we will find our way to a secure peace, for the ultimate benefit of all humanity.

We must build a new world—a far better world—one in which the eternal dignity of man is respected.

As we are about to undertake our heavy duties, we beseech Almighty God to guide us in building a permanent monument to those who gave their lives that this moment might come.

May He lead our steps in His own righteous path of peace.

CHARTER OF THE UNITED NATIONS

WE THE PEOPLES OF THE UNITED NATIONS DETERMINED

to save succeeding generations from the scourge of war, which twice in our lifetime has brought untold sorrow to mankind, and

to reaffirm faith in fundamental human rights, in the dignity and worth of the human person, in the equal rights of men and women and of nations large and small, and

to establish conditions under which justice and respect for the obligations arising from treaties and other sources of international law can be maintained, and

to promote social progress and better standards of life in larger freedom,

AND FOR THESE ENDS

to practice tolerance and live together in peace with one another as good neighbours, and

to unite our strength to maintain international peace and security, and

to ensure, by the acceptance of principles and the institution of methods, that armed force shall not be used, save in the common interest, and

to employ international machinery for the promotion of the economic and social advancement of all peoples,

HAVE RESOLVED TO COMBINE OUR EFFORTS TO ACCOMPLISH THESE AIMS.

Accordingly, our respective Governments, through representatives assembled in the city of San Francisco, who have exhibited their full powers found to be in good and due form, have agreed to the present Charter of the United Nations and do hereby establish an international organization to be known as the United Nations.

CHAPTER I
PURPOSES AND PRINCIPLES
Article 1

The Purposes of the United Nations are:

1. To maintain international peace and security, and to that end: to take effective collective measures for the prevention and removal of threats to the peace, and for the suppression of acts of aggression or other breaches of the peace, and to bring about by peaceful means, and in conformity with the principles of justice and international law, adjustment or settlement of international disputes or situations which might lead to a breach of the peace;

2. To develop friendly relations among nations based on respect for the principle of equal rights and self-determination of peoples, and to take other appropriate measures to strengthen universal peace;

3. To achieve international co-operation in solving international problems of an economic, social, cultural, or humanitarian character, and in promoting and encouraging respect for human rights and for fundamental freedoms for all without distinction as to race, sex, language, or religion; and

4. To be a centre for harmonizing the actions of nations in the attainment of these common ends.

Article 2

The Organization and its Members, in pursuit of the Purposes stated in Article 1, shall act in accordance with the following Principles.

1. The Organization is based on the principle of the sovereign equality of all its Members.

2. All Members, in order to ensure to all of them the rights and benefits resulting from membership, shall fulfill in good faith the obligations assumed by them in accordance with the present Charter.

3. All Members shall settle their international disputes by peaceful means in such a manner that international peace and security, and justice, are not endangered.

4. All Members shall refrain in their international relations from the threat or use of force against the territorial integrity or political independence of any state, or in any other manner inconsistent with the Purposes of the United Nations.

5. All Members shall give the United Nations every assistance in any action it takes in accordance with the present Charter, and shall refrain from giving assistance to any state against which the United Nations is taking preventive or enforcement action.

6. The Organization shall ensure that states which are not Members of the United Nations act in accordance with these Principles so far as may be necessary for the maintenance of international peace and security.

7. Nothing contained in the present Charter shall authorize the United Nations to intervene in matters which are essentially within the domestic jurisdiction of any state or shall require the Members to submit such matters to settlement under the present Charter; but this principle shall not prejudice the application of enforcement measures under Chapter VII.

CHAPTER II
MEMBERSHIP
Article 3

The original Members of the United Nations shall be the states which, having participated in the United Nations Conference on International Organization at San Francisco, or having previously signed the Declaration by United Nations of 1 January 1942, sign the present Charter and ratify it in accordance with Article 110.

Article 4

1. Membership in the United Nations is open to all other peace-loving states which accept the obligations contained in the present Charter and, in the judgment of the Organization, are able and willing to carry out these obligations.

2. The admission of any such state to membership in the United Nations will be effected by a decision of the General Assembly upon the recommendation of the Security Council.

Article 5

A Member of the United Nations against which preventive or enforcement action has been taken by the Security Council may be suspended from the exercise of the rights and privileges of membership by the General Assembly upon the recommendation of the Security Council.

The exercise of these rights and privileges may be restored by the Security Council.

Article 6

A Member of the United Nations which has persistently violated the Principles contained in the present Charter may be expelled from the Organization by the General Assembly upon the recommendation of the Security Council.

CHAPTER III
ORGANS
Article 7

1. There are established as principal organs of the United Nations: a General Assembly, a Security Council, an Economic and Social Council, a Trusteeship Council, an International Court of Justice and a Secretariat.

2. Such subsidiary organs as may be found necessary may be established in accordance with the present Charter.

Article 8

The United Nations shall place no restrictions on the eligibility of men and women to participate in any capacity and under conditions of equality in its principal and subsidiary organs.

CHAPTER IV
THE GENERAL ASSEMBLY
Composition
Article 9

1. The General Assembly shall consist of all the Members of the United Nations.

2. Each Member shall have not more than five representatives in the General Assembly.

Functions and Powers
Article 10

The General Assembly may discuss any questions or any matters within the scope of the present Charter or relating to the powers and functions of any organs provided for in the present Charter, and, except as provided in Article 12, may make recommendations to the Members of the United Nations or to the Security Council or to both on any such questions or matters.

Article 11

1. The General Assembly may consider the general principles of co-operation in the maintenance of international peace and security, including the principles governing disarmament and the regulation of armaments, and may make recommendations with regard to such principles to the Members or to the Security Council or to both.

2. The General Assembly may discuss any questions relating to the maintenance of international peace and security brought before it by any Member of the United Nations, or by the Security Council, or by a state which is not a Member of the United Nations in accordance with Article 35, paragraph 2, and, except as provided in Article 12, may make recommendations with regard to any such questions to the state or states concerned or to the Security Council or to both. Any such question on which action is necessary shall be referred to the Security Council by the General Assembly either before or after discussion.

3. The General Assembly may call the attention of the Security Council to situations which are likely to endanger international peace and security.

4. The powers of the General Assembly set forth in this Article shall not limit the general scope of Article 10.

Article 12

1. While the Security Council is exercising in respect of any dispute or situation the functions assigned to it in the present Charter, the General Assembly shall not make any recommendation with regard to that dispute or situation unless the Security Council so requests.

2. The Secretary-General, with the consent of the Security Council, shall notify the General Assembly at each session of any matters relative to the maintenance of international peace and security which are being dealt with by the Security Council and shall similarly notify the General Assembly, or the Members of the United Nations if the General Assembly is not in session, immediately the Security Council ceases to deal with such matters.

Article 13

1. The General Assembly shall initiate studies and make recommendations for the purpose of: a. promoting international co-operation in the political field and encouraging the progressive development of international law and its codification; b. promoting international co-operation in the economic, social, cultural, educational, and health fields, and assisting in the realization of human rights and fundamental freedoms for all without distinction as to race, sex, language, or religion.

2. The further responsibilities, functions and powers of the General Assembly with respect to matters mentioned in paragraph 1 (b) above are set forth in Chapters IX and X.

Article 14

Subject to the provisions of Article 12, the General Assembly may recommend measures for the peaceful adjustment of any situation, regardless of origin, which it deems likely to impair the general welfare or friendly relations among nations, including situations resulting from a violation of the provisions of the present Charter setting forth the Purposes and Principles of the United Nations.

Article 15

1. The General Assembly shall receive and consider annual and special reports from the Security Council; these reports shall include an account of the measures that the Security Council has decided upon or taken to maintain international peace and security.

2. The General Assembly shall receive and consider reports from the other organs of the United Nations.

Article 16

The General Assembly shall perform such functions with respect to the international trusteeship system as are assigned to it under Chapters XII and XIII, including the approval of the trusteeship agreements for areas not designated as strategic.

Article 17

1. The General Assembly shall consider and approve the budget of the Organization.

2. The expenses of the Organization shall be borne by the Members as apportioned by the General Assembly.

3. The General Assembly shall consider and approve any financial and budgetary arrangements with specialized agencies referred to in Article 57 and shall examine the administrative budgets of such specialized agencies with a view to making recommendations to the agencies concerned.

Voting
Article 18

1. Each member of the General Assembly shall have one vote.

2. Decisions of the General Assembly on important questions shall be made by a two-thirds majority of the members present and voting. These questions shall include: recommendations with respect to the maintenance of international peace and security, the election of the non-permanent members of the Security Council, the election of the members of the Economic and Social Council, the election of members of the Trusteeship Council in accordance with paragraph 1 (c) of Article 86, the admission of new Members to the United Nations, the suspension of the rights and privileges of membership, the expulsion of Members, questions relating to the operation of the trusteeship system, and budgetary questions.

3. Decisions on other questions, including the determination of additional categories of questions to be decided by a two-thirds majority, shall be made by a majority of the members present and voting.

Article 19

A Member of the United Nations which is in arrears in the payment of its financial contributions to the Organization shall have no vote in the General Assembly if the amount of its arrears equals or exceeds the amount of the contributions due from it for the preceding two full years. The General Assembly may, nevertheless, permit such a Member to vote if it is satisfied that the failure to pay is due to conditions beyond the control of the Member.

Procedure
Article 20

The General Assembly shall meet in regular annual sessions and in such special sessions as occasion may require. Special sessions shall be convoked by the Secretary-General at the request of the Security Council or of a majority of the Members of the United Nations.

Article 21

The General Assembly shall adopt its own rules of procedure. It shall elect its President for each session.

Article 22

The General Assembly may establish such subsidiary organs as it deems necessary for the performance of its functions.

CHAPTER V
THE SECURITY COUNCIL
Composition
Article 23[1]

1. The Security Council shall consist of *fifteen* Members of the United Nations. The Republic of China, France, the Union of Soviet Socialist Republics, the United Kingdom of Great Britain and Northern Ireland, and the United States of America shall be permanent members of the Security Council. The General Assembly shall elect *ten* other Members of the United Nations to be non-permanent members of the Security Council, due regard being specially paid, in the first instance to the contribution of Members of the United Nations to the maintenance of international peace and security and to the other purposes of the Organization, and also to equitable geographical distribution.

2. The non-permanent members of the Security Council shall be elected for a term of two years. In the first election of the non-permanent members *after the increase of the membership of the Security Council from eleven to fifteen, two of the four additional members* shall be chosen for a term of

---

1. In 1965, the Security Council expanded from its original membership of eleven to fifteen members. The italicized text in Articles 23 and 27 reflects an amendment to the Charter that effected this change. The amendment was passed by the General Assembly on December 17, 1963, and went into effect on August 31, 1965.

one year. A retiring member shall not be eligible for immediate re-
election.

3. Each member of the Security Council shall have one representative.

Functions and Powers
Article 24

1. In order to ensure prompt and effective action by the United
Nations, its Members confer on the Security Council primary responsibility for the maintenance of international peace and security, and agree
that in carrying out its duties under this responsibility the Security
Council acts on their behalf.

2. In discharging these duties the Security Council shall act in
accordance with the Purposes and Principles of the United Nations. The
specific powers granted to the Security Council for the discharge of
these duties are laid down in Chapters VI, VII, VIII, and XII.

3. The Security Council shall submit annual and, when necessary,
special reports to the General Assembly for its consideration.

Article 25

The Members of the United Nations agree to accept and carry out the
decisions of the Security Council in accordance with the present
Charter.

Article 26

In order to promote the establishment and maintenance of international
peace and security with the least diversion for armaments of the world's
human and economic resources, the Security Council shall be responsible for formulating, with the assistance of the Military Staff Committee
referred to in Article 47, plans to be submitted to the Members of the
United Nations for the establishment of a system for the regulation of
armaments.

Voting
Article 27[2]

1. Each member of the Security Council shall have one vote.

2. See note 1, above.

2. Decisions of the Security Council on procedural matters shall be made by an affirmative vote of nine members.

3. Decisions of the Security Council on all other matters shall be made by an affirmative vote of nine members including the concurring votes of the permanent members; provided that, in decisions under Chapter VI, and under paragraph 3 of Article 52, a party to a dispute shall abstain from voting.

Procedure
Article 28

1. The Security Council shall be so organized as to be able to function continuously. Each member of the Security Council shall for this purpose be represented at all times at the seat of the Organization.

2. The Security Council shall hold periodic meetings at which each of its members may, if it so desires, be represented by a member of the government or by some other specially designated representative.

3. The Security Council may hold meetings at such places other than the seat of the Organization as in its judgment will best facilitate its work.

Article 29

The Security Council may establish such subsidiary organs as it deems necessary for the performance of its functions.

Article 30

The Security Council shall adopt its own rules of procedure, including the method of selecting its President.

Article 31

Any Member of the United Nations which is not a member of the Security Council may participate, without vote, in the discussion of any question brought before the Security Council whenever the latter considers that the interests of that Member are specially affected.

Article 32

Any Member of the United Nations which is not a member of the Security Council or any state which is not a Member of the United

Nations, if it is a party to a dispute under consideration by the Security Council, shall be invited to participate, without vote, in the discussion relating to the dispute. The Security Council shall lay down such conditions as it deems just for the participation of a state which is not a Member of the United Nations.

CHAPTER VI
PACIFIC SETTLEMENT OF DISPUTES
Article 33

1. The parties to any dispute, the continuance of which is likely to endanger the maintenance of international peace and security, shall, first of all, seek a solution by negotiation, enquiry, mediation, conciliation, arbitration, judicial settlement, resort to regional agencies or arrangements, or other peaceful means of their own choice.

2. The Security Council shall, when it deems necessary, call upon the parties to settle their dispute by such means.

Article 34

The Security Council may investigate any dispute, or any situation which might lead to international friction or give rise to a dispute, in order to determine whether the continuance of the dispute or situation is likely to endanger the maintenance of international peace and security.

Article 35

1. Any Member of the United Nations may bring any dispute, or any situation of the nature referred to in Article 34, to the attention of the Security Council or of the General Assembly.

2. A state which is not a Member of the United Nations may bring to the attention of the Security Council or of the General Assembly any dispute to which it is a party if it accepts in advance, for the purposes of the dispute, the obligations of pacific settlement provided in the present Charter.

3. The proceedings of the General Assembly in respect of matters brought to its attention under this Article will be subject to the provisions of Articles 11 and 12.

Article 36

1. The Security Council may, at any stage of a dispute of the nature referred to in Article 33 or of a situation of like nature, recommend appropriate procedures or methods of adjustment.

2. The Security Council should take into consideration any procedures for the settlement of the dispute which have already been adopted by the parties.

3. In making recommendations under this Article the Security Council should also take into consideration that legal disputes should as a general rule be referred by the parties to the International Court of Justice in accordance with the provisions of the Statute of the Court.

Article 37

1. Should the parties to a dispute of the nature referred to in Article 33 fail to settle it by the means indicated in that Article, they shall refer it to the Security Council.

2. If the Security Council deems that the continuance of the dispute is in fact likely to endanger the maintenance of international peace and security, it shall decide whether to take action under Article 36 or to recommend such terms of settlement as it may consider appropriate.

Article 38

Without prejudice to the provisions of Articles 33 to 37, the Security Council may, if all the parties to any dispute so request, make recommendations to the parties with a view to a pacific settlement of the dispute.

CHAPTER VII
ACTION WITH RESPECT TO THREATS TO THE PEACE, BREACHES OF THE PEACE, AND ACTS OF AGGRESSION
Article 39

The Security Council shall determine the existence of any threat to the peace, breach of the peace, or act of aggression and shall make recommendations, or decide what measures shall be taken in accordance with Articles 41 and 42, to maintain or restore international peace and security.

Article 40

In order to prevent an aggravation of the situation, the Security Council may, before making the recommendations or deciding upon the measures provided for in Article 39, call upon the parties concerned to comply with such provisional measures as it deems necessary or desirable. Such provisional measures shall be without prejudice to the rights, claims, or position of the parties concerned. The Security Council shall duly take account of failure to comply with such provisional measures.

Article 41

The Security Council may decide what measures not involving the use of armed force are to be employed to give effect to its decisions, and it may call upon the Members of the United Nations to apply such measures. These may include complete or partial interruption of economic relations and of rail, sea, air, postal, telegraphic, radio, and other means of communication, and the severance of diplomatic relations.

Article 42

Should the Security Council consider that measures provided for in Article 41 would be inadequate or have proved to be inadequate, it may take such action by air, sea, or land forces as may be necessary to maintain or restore international peace and security. Such action may include demonstrations, blockade, and other operations by air, sea, or land forces of Members of the United Nations.

Article 43

1. All Members of the United Nations, in order to contribute to the maintenance of international peace and security, undertake to make available to the Security Council, on its call and in accordance with a special agreement or agreements, armed forces, assistance, and facilities, including rights of passage, necessary for the purpose of maintaining international peace and security.

2. Such agreement or agreements shall govern the numbers and types of forces, their degree of readiness and general location, and the nature of the facilities and assistance to be provided.

3. The agreement or agreements shall be negotiated as soon as possible on the initiative of the Security Council. They shall be concluded between the Security Council and Members or between the Security Council and groups of Members and shall be subject to ratification by the signatory states in accordance with their respective constitutional processes.

Article 44

When the Security Council has decided to use force it shall, before calling upon a Member not represented on it to provide armed forces in fulfilment of the obligations assumed under Article 43, invite that Member, if the Member so desires, to participate in the decisions of the Security Council concerning the employment of contingents of that Member's armed forces.

Article 45

In order to enable the United Nations to take urgent military measures, Members shall hold immediately available national air-force contingents for combined international enforcement action. The strength and degree of readiness of these contingents and plans for their combined action shall be determined within the limits laid down in the special agreement or agreements referred to in Article 43, by the Security Council with the assistance of the Military Staff Committee.

Article 46

Plans for the application of armed force shall be made by the Security Council with the assistance of the Military Staff Committee.

Article 47

1. There shall be established a Military Staff Committee to advise and assist the Security Council on all questions relating to the Security Council's military requirements for the maintenance of international peace and security, the employment and command of forces placed at its disposal, the regulation of armaments, and possible disarmament.

2. The Military Staff Committee shall consist of the Chiefs of Staff of the permanent members of the Security Council or their representatives. Any Member of the United Nations not permanently represented on the

Committee shall be invited by the Committee to be associated with it when the efficient discharge of the Committee's responsibilities requires the participation of that Member in its work.

3. The Military Staff Committee shall be responsible under the Security Council for the strategic direction of any armed forces placed at the disposal of the Security Council. Questions relating to the command of such forces shall be worked out subsequently.

4. The Military Staff Committee, with the authorization of the Security Council and after consultation with appropriate regional agencies, may establish regional sub-committees.

Article 48

1. The action required to carry out the decisions of the Security Council for the maintenance of international peace and security shall be taken by all the Members of the United Nations or by some of them, as the Security Council may determine.

2. Such decisions shall be carried out by the Members of the United Nations directly and through their action in the appropriate international agencies of which they are members.

Article 49

The Members of the United Nations shall join in affording mutual assistance in carrying out the measures decided upon by the Security Council.

Article 50

If preventive or enforcement measures against any state are taken by the Security Council, any other state, whether a Member of the United Nations or not, which finds itself confronted with special economic problems arising from the carrying out of those measures shall have the right to consult the Security Council with regard to a solution of those problems.

Article 51

Nothing in the present Charter shall impair the inherent right of individual or collective self-defence if an armed attack occurs against a Member of the United Nations, until the Security Council has taken measures necessary to maintain international peace and security.

Measures taken by Members in the exercise of this right of self-defence shall be immediately reported to the Security Council and shall not in any way affect the authority and responsibility of the Security Council under the present Charter to take at any time such action as it deems necessary in order to maintain or restore international peace and security.

CHAPTER VIII
REGIONAL ARRANGEMENTS
Article 52

1. Nothing in the present Charter precludes the existence of regional arrangements or agencies for dealing with such matters relating to the maintenance of international peace and security as are appropriate for regional action provided that such arrangements or agencies and their activities are consistent with the Purposes and Principles of the United Nations.

2. The Members of the United Nations entering into such arrangements or constituting such agencies shall make every effort to achieve pacific settlement of local disputes through such regional arrangements or by such regional agencies before referring them to the Security Council.

3. The Security Council shall encourage the development of pacific settlement of local disputes through such regional arrangements or by such regional agencies either on the initiative of the states concerned or by reference from the Security Council.

4. This Article in no way impairs the application of Articles 34 and 35.

Article 53

1. The Security Council shall, where appropriate, utilize such regional arrangements or agencies for enforcement action under its authority. But no enforcement action shall be taken under regional arrangements or by regional agencies without the authorization of the Security Council, with the exception of measures against any enemy state, as defined in paragraph 2 of this Article, provided for pursuant to Article 107 or in regional arrangements directed against renewal of aggressive policy on the part of any such state, until such time as the Organization may, on request of the Governments concerned, be

charged with the responsibility for preventing further aggression by such a state.

2. The term enemy state as used in paragraph 1 of this Article applies to any state which during the Second World War has been an enemy of any signatory of the present Charter.

Article 54

The Security Council shall at all times be kept fully informed of activities undertaken or in contemplation under regional arrangements or by regional agencies for the maintenance of international peace and security.

CHAPTER IX
INTERNATIONAL ECONOMIC AND SOCIAL CO-OPERATION
Article 55

With a view to the creation of conditions of stability and well-being which are necessary for peaceful and friendly relations among nations based on respect for the principle of equal rights and self-determination of peoples, the United Nations shall promote:

a. higher standards of living, full employment, and conditions of economic and social progress and development;

b. solutions of international economic, social, health, and related problems; and international cultural and educational cooperation; and

c. universal respect for, and observance of, human rights and fundamental freedoms for all without distinction as to race, sex, language, or religion.

Article 56

All Members pledge themselves to take joint and separate action in co-operation with the Organization for the achievement of the purposes set forth in Article 55.

Article 57

1. The various specialized agencies, established by intergovernmental agreement and having wide international responsibilities, as defined in their basic instruments, in economic, social, cultural, educational, health, and related fields, shall be brought into relation-

ship with the United Nations in accordance with the provisions of Article 63.

2. Such agencies thus brought into relationship with the United Nations are hereinafter referred to as specialized agencies.

Article 58

The Organization shall make recommendations for the co-ordination of the policies and activities of the specialized agencies.

Article 59

The Organization shall, where appropriate, initiate negotiations among the states concerned for the creation of any new specialized agencies required for the accomplishment of the purposes set forth in Article 55.

Article 60

Responsibility for the discharge of the functions of the Organization set forth in this Chapter shall be vested in the General Assembly and, under the authority of the General Assembly, in the Economic and Social Council, which shall have for this purpose the powers set forth in Chapter X.

CHAPTER X
THE ECONOMIC AND SOCIAL COUNCIL
Composition
Article 61[3]

1. The Economic and Social Council shall consist of fifty-four Members of the United Nations elected by the General Assembly.

2. Subject to the provisions of paragraph 3, *eighteen* members of the Economic and Social Council shall be elected each year for a term of three years. A retiring member shall be eligible for immediate re-election.

---

3. In 1965, the Economic and Social Council expanded its membership from eighteen to twenty-seven members; it expanded again to fifty-four members in 1973. The italicized text in Article 61 reflects amendment to the Charter that effected this change. The first amendment was passed by the General Assembly on December 17, 1963, and took effect on August 31, 1965. The second amendment was passed on December 20, 1971, and took effect on September 24, 1973.

3. At the first election *after the increase in the membership of the Economic and Social Council from twenty-seven to fifty-four members, in addition to the members elected in place of the nine members whose term of office expires at the end of that year, twenty-seven additional members shall be elected. Of these twenty-seven additional members, the term of office of nine members so elected shall expire at the end of one year, and of nine* other members at the end of two years, in accordance with arrangements made by the General Assembly.

4. Each member of the Economic and Social Council shall have one representative.

Functions and Powers
Article 62

1. The Economic and Social Council may make or initiate studies and reports with respect to international economic, social, cultural, educational, health, and related matters and may make recommendations with respect to any such matters to the General Assembly, to the Members of the United Nations, and to the specialized agencies concerned.

2. It may make recommendations for the purpose of promoting respect for, and observance of, human rights and fundamental freedoms for all.

3. It may prepare draft conventions for submission to the General Assembly, with respect to matters falling within its competence.

4. It may call, in accordance with the rules prescribed by the United Nations, international conferences on matters falling within its competence.

Article 63

1. The Economic and Social Council may enter into agreements with any of the agencies referred to in Article 57, defining the terms on which the agency concerned shall be brought into relationship with the United Nations. Such agreements shall be subject to approval by the General Assembly.

2. It may co-ordinate the activities of the specialized agencies through consultation with and recommendations to such agencies and through recommendations to the General Assembly and to the Members of the United Nations.

Article 64

1. The Economic and Social Council may take appropriate steps to obtain regular reports from the specialized agencies. It may make arrangements with the Members of the United Nations and with the specialized agencies to obtain reports on the steps taken to give effect to its own recommendations and to recommendations on matters falling within its competence made by the General Assembly.

2. It may communicate its observations on these reports to the General Assembly.

Article 65

The Economic and Social Council may furnish information to the Security Council and shall assist the Security Council upon its request.

Article 66

1. The Economic and Social Council shall perform such functions as fall within its competence in connection with the carrying out of the recommendations of the General Assembly.

2. It may, with the approval of the General Assembly, perform services at the request of Members of the United Nations and at the request of specialized agencies.

3. It shall perform such other functions as are specified elsewhere in the present Charter or as may be assigned to it by the General Assembly.

Voting
Article 67

1. Each member of the Economic and Social Council shall have one vote.

2. Decisions of the Economic and Social Council shall be made by a majority of the members present and voting.

Procedure
Article 68

The Economic and Social Council shall set up commissions in economic and social fields and for the promotion of human rights, and such other commissions as may be required for the performance of its functions.

Article 69

The Economic and Social Council shall invite any Member of the United Nations to participate, without vote, in its deliberations on any matter of particular concern to that Member.

Article 70

The Economic and Social Council may make arrangements for representatives of the specialized agencies to participate, without vote, in its deliberations and in those of the commissions established by it, and for its representatives to participate in the deliberations of the specialized agencies.

Article 71

The Economic and Social Council may make suitable arrangements for consultation with non-governmental organizations which are concerned with matters within its competence. Such arrangements may be made with international organizations and, where appropriate, with national organizations after consultation with the Member of the United Nations concerned.

Article 72

1. The Economic and Social Council shall adopt its own rules of procedure, including the method of selecting its President.

2. The Economic and Social Council shall meet as required in accordance with its rules, which shall include provision for the convening of meetings on the request of a majority of its members.

CHAPTER XI
DECLARATION REGARDING NON-SELF-GOVERNING TERRITORIES
Article 73

Members of the United Nations which have or assume responsibilities for the administration of territories whose peoples have not yet attained a full measure of self-government recognize the principle that the interests of the inhabitants of these territories are paramount, and accept as a sacred trust the obligation to promote to the utmost, within the system of international peace and security established by the present Charter, the well-being of the inhabitants of these territories, and, to this end:

a. to ensure, with due respect for the culture of the peoples concerned, their political, economic, social, and educational advancement, their just treatment, and their protection against abuses;

b. to develop self-government, to take due account of the political aspirations of the peoples, and to assist them in the progressive development of their free political institutions, according to the particular circumstances of each territory and its peoples and their varying stages of advancement;

c. to further international peace and security;

d. to promote constructive measures of development, to encourage research, and to co-operate with one another and, when and where appropriate, with specialized international bodies with a view to the practical achievement of the social, economic, and scientific purposes set forth in this Article; and

e. to transmit regularly to the Secretary-General for information purposes, subject to such limitation as security and constitutional considerations may require, statistical and other information of a technical nature relating to economic, social, and educational conditions in the territories for which they are respectively responsible other than those territories to which Chapters XII and XIII apply.

Article 74

Members of the United Nations also agree that their policy in respect of the territories to which this Chapter applies, no less than in respect of their metropolitan areas, must be based on the general principle of good-neighbourliness, due account being taken of the interests and well-being of the rest of the world, in social, economic, and commercial matters.

CHAPTER XII
INTERNATIONAL TRUSTEESHIP SYSTEM
Article 75

The United Nations shall establish under its authority an international trusteeship system for the administration and supervision of such territories as may be placed thereunder by subsequent individual agreements. These territories are hereinafter referred to as trust territories.

Article 76

The basic objectives of the trusteeship system, in accordance with the Purposes of the United Nations laid down in Article 1 of the present Charter, shall be:

a. to further international peace and security;

b. to promote the political, economic, social, and educational advancement of the inhabitants of the trust territories, and their progressive development towards self-government or independence as may be appropriate to the particular circumstances of each territory and its peoples and the freely expressed wishes of the peoples concerned, and as may be provided by the terms of each trusteeship agreement;

c. to encourage respect for human rights and for fundamental freedoms for all without distinction as to race, sex, language, or religion, and to encourage recognition of the interdependence of the peoples of the world; and

d. to ensure equal treatment in social, economic, and commercial matters for all Members of the United Nations and their nationals, and also equal treatment for the latter in the administration of justice, without prejudice to the attainment of the foregoing objectives and subject to the provisions of Article 80.

Article 77

1. The trusteeship system shall apply to such territories in the following categories as may be placed thereunder by means of trusteeship agreements:

a. territories now held under mandate;

b. territories which may be detached from enemy states as a result of the Second World War; and

c. territories voluntarily placed under the system by states responsible for their administration.

2. It will be a matter for subsequent agreement as to which territories in the foregoing categories will be brought under the trusteeship system and upon what terms.

Article 78

The trusteeship system shall not apply to territories which have become Members of the United Nations, relationship among which shall be based on respect for the principle of sovereign equality.

Article 79

The terms of trusteeship for each territory to be placed under the trusteeship system, including any alteration or amendment, shall be agreed upon by the states directly concerned, including the mandatory power in the case of territories held under mandate by a Member of the United Nations, and shall be approved as provided for in Articles 83 and 85.

Article 80

1. Except as may be agreed upon in individual trusteeship agreements, made under Articles 77, 79, and 81, placing each territory under the trusteeship system, and until such agreements have been concluded, nothing in this Chapter shall be construed in or of itself to alter in any manner the rights whatsoever of any states or any peoples or the terms of existing international instruments to which Members of the United Nations may respectively be parties.

2. Paragraph 1 of this Article shall not be interpreted as giving grounds for delay or postponement of the negotiation and conclusion of agreements for placing mandated and other territories under the trusteeship system as provided for in Article 77.

Article 81

The trusteeship agreement shall in each case include the terms under which the trust territory will be administered and designate the authority which will exercise the administration of the trust territory. Such authority, hereinafter called the administering authority, may be one or more states or the Organization itself.

Article 82

There may be designated, in any trusteeship agreement, a strategic area or areas which may include part or all of the trust territory to which the agreement applies, without prejudice to any special agreement or agreements made under Article 43.

Article 83

1. All functions of the United Nations relating to strategic areas, including the approval of the terms of the trusteeship agreements and of their alteration or amendment shall be exercised by the Security Council.

2. The basic objectives set forth in Article 76 shall be applicable to the people of each strategic area.

3. The Security Council shall, subject to the provisions of the trusteeship agreements and without prejudice to security considerations, avail itself of the assistance of the Trusteeship Council to perform those functions of the United Nations under the trusteeship system relating to political, economic, social, and educational matters in the strategic areas.

Article 84

It shall be the duty of the administering authority to ensure that the trust territory shall play its part in the maintenance of international peace and security. To this end the administering authority may make use of volunteer forces, facilities, and assistance from the trust territory in carrying out the obligations towards the Security Council undertaken in this regard by the administering authority, as well as for local defence and the maintenance of law and order within the trust territory.

Article 85

1. The functions of the United Nations with regard to trusteeship agreements for all areas not designated as strategic, including the approval of the terms of the trusteeship agreements and of their alteration or amendment, shall be exercised by the General Assembly.

2. The Trusteeship Council, operating under the authority of the General Assembly shall assist the General Assembly in carrying out these functions.

CHAPTER XIII
THE TRUSTEESHIP COUNCIL
Composition
Article 86

1. The Trusteeship Council shall consist of the following Members of the United Nations:

a. those Members administering trust territories;

b. such of those Members mentioned by name in Article 23 as are not administering trust territories; and

c. as many other Members elected for three-year terms by the General Assembly as may be necessary to ensure that the total number of members of the Trusteeship Council is equally divided between those Members of the United Nations which administer trust territories and those which do not.

2. Each member of the Trusteeship Council shall designate one specially qualified person to represent it therein.

Functions and Powers
Article 87

The General Assembly and, under its authority, the Trusteeship Council, in carrying out their functions, may:

a. consider reports submitted by the administering authority;

b. accept petitions and examine them in consultation with the administering authority;

c. provide for periodic visits to the respective trust territories at times agreed upon with the administering authority; and

d. take these and other actions in conformity with the terms of the trusteeship agreements.

Article 88

The Trusteeship Council shall formulate a questionnaire on the political, economic, social, and educational advancement of the inhabitants of each trust territory, and the administering authority for each trust territory within the competence of the General Assembly shall make an annual report to the General Assembly upon the basis of such questionnaire.

Voting
Article 89

1. Each member of the Trusteeship Council shall have one vote.

2. Decisions of the Trusteeship Council shall be made by a majority of the members present and voting.

Procedure
Article 90

1. The Trusteeship Council shall adopt its own rules of procedure, including the method of selecting its President.

2. The Trusteeship Council shall meet as required in accordance with its rules, which shall include provision for the convening of meetings on the request of a majority of its members.

Article 91

The Trusteeship Council shall, when appropriate, avail itself of the assistance of the Economic and Social Council and of the specialized agencies in regard to matters with which they are respectively concerned.

CHAPTER XIV
THE INTERNATIONAL COURT OF JUSTICE
Article 92

The International Court of Justice shall be the principal judicial organ of the United Nations. It shall function in accordance with the annexed Statute, which is based upon the Statute of the Permanent Court of International Justice and forms an integral part of the present Charter.

Article 93

1. All Members of the United Nations are *ipso facto* parties to the Statute of the International Court of Justice.

2. A state which is not a Member of the United Nations may become a party to the Statute of the International Court of Justice on conditions to be determined in each case by the General Assembly upon the recommendation of the Security Council.

Article 94

1. Each Member of the United Nations undertakes to comply with the decision of the International Court of Justice in any case to which it is a party.

2. If any party to a case fails to perform the obligations incumbent upon it under a judgment rendered by the Court, the other party may have recourse to the Security Council, which may, if it deems necessary,

make recommendations or decide upon measures to be taken to give effect to the judgment.

Article 95

Nothing in the present Charter shall prevent Members of the United Nations from entrusting the solution of their differences to other tribunals by virtue of agreements already in existence or which may be concluded in the future.

Article 96

1. The General Assembly or the Security Council may request the International Court of Justice to give an advisory opinion on any legal question.

2. Other organs of the United Nations and specialized agencies, which may at any time be so authorized by the General Assembly, may also request advisory opinions of the Court on legal questions arising within the scope of their activities.

CHAPTER XV
THE SECRETARIAT
Article 97

The Secretariat shall comprise a Secretary-General and such staff as the Organization may require. The Secretary-General shall be appointed by the General Assembly upon the recommendation of the Security Council. He shall be the chief administrative officer of the Organization.

Article 98

The Secretary-General shall act in that capacity in all meetings of the General Assembly, of the Security Council, of the Economic and Social Council, and of the Trusteeship Council, and shall perform such other functions as are entrusted to him by these organs. The Secretary-General shall make an annual report to the General Assembly on the work of the Organization.

Article 99

The Secretary-General may bring to the attention of the Security Council any matter which in his opinion may threaten the maintenance of international peace and security.

Article 100

1. In the performance of their duties the Secretary-General and the staff shall not seek or receive instructions from any government or from any other authority external to the Organization. They shall refrain from any action which might reflect on their position as international officials responsible only to the Organization.

2. Each Member of the United Nations undertakes to respect the exclusively international character of the responsibilities of the Secretary-General and the staff and not to seek to influence them in the discharge of their responsibilities.

Article 101

1. The staff shall be appointed by the Secretary-General under regulations established by the General Assembly.

2. Appropriate staffs shall be permanently assigned to the Economic and Social Council, the Trusteeship Council, and, as required, to other organs of the United Nations. These staffs shall form a part of the Secretariat.

3. The paramount consideration in the employment of the staff and in the determination of the conditions of service shall be the necessity of securing the highest standards of efficiency, competence, and integrity. Due regard shall be paid to the importance of recruiting the staff on as wide a geographical basis as possible.

CHAPTER XVI
MISCELLANEOUS PROVISIONS
Article 102

1. Every treaty and every international agreement entered into by any Member of the United Nations after the present Charter comes into force shall as soon as possible be registered with the Secretariat and published by it.

2. No party to any such treaty or international agreement which has not been registered in accordance with the provisions of paragraph 1 of this Article may invoke that treaty or agreement before any organ of the United Nations.

Article 103

In the event of a conflict between the obligations of the Members of the United Nations under the present Charter and their obligations under any other international agreement, their obligations under the present Charter shall prevail.

Article 104

The Organization shall enjoy in the territory of each of its Members such legal capacity as may be necessary for the exercise of its functions and the fulfilment of its purposes.

Article 105

1. The Organization shall enjoy in the territory of each of its Members such privileges and immunities as are necessary for the fulfilment of its purposes.

2. Representatives of the Members of the United Nations and officials of the Organization shall similarly enjoy such privileges and immunities as are necessary for the independent exercise of their functions in connection with the Organization.

3. The General Assembly may make recommendations with a view to determining the details of the application of paragraphs 1 and 2 of this Article or may propose conventions to the Members of the United Nations for this purpose.

CHAPTER XVII
TRANSITIONAL SECURITY ARRANGEMENTS
Article 106

Pending the coming into force of such special agreements referred to in Article 43 as in the opinion of the Security Council enable it to begin the exercise of its responsibilities under Article 42, the parties to the Four-Nation Declaration, signed at Moscow, 30 October 1943, and France, shall, in accordance with the provisions of paragraph 5 of that Declaration, consult with one another and as occasion requires with other Members of the United Nations with a view to such joint action on behalf of the Organization as may be necessary for the purpose of maintaining international peace and security.

Article 107

Nothing in the present Charter shall invalidate or preclude action, in relation to any state which during the Second World War has been an enemy of any signatory to the present Charter, taken or authorized as a result of that war by the Governments having responsibility for such action.

CHAPTER XVIII
AMENDMENTS
Article 108

Amendments to the present Charter shall come into force for all Members of the United Nations when they have been adopted by a vote of two thirds of the members of the General Assembly and ratified in accordance with their respective constitutional processes by two thirds of the Members of the United Nations, including all the permanent members of the Security Council.

Article 109[4]

1. A General Conference of the Members of the United Nations for the purpose of reviewing the present Charter may be held at a date and place to be fixed by a two-thirds vote of the members of the General Assembly and by a vote of any *nine* members of the Security Council. Each Member of the United Nations shall have one vote in the conference.

2. Any alteration of the present Charter recommended by a two-thirds vote of the conference shall take effect when ratified in accordance with their respective constitutional processes by two thirds of the Members of the United Nations including all the permanent members of the Security Council.

3. If such a conference has not been held before the tenth annual session of the General Assembly following the coming into force of the present Charter, the proposal to call such a conference shall be placed on the agenda of that session of the General Assembly, and the conference shall be held if so decided by a majority vote of the members of the General Assembly and by a vote of any seven members of the Security Council.

4. Article 109 was amended on December 20, 1965 (took effect on June 12, 1968), to increase the number of votes from Security Council members required to trigger a General Conference to review the Charter from seven to nine. The italicized text reflects this amendment.

CHAPTER XIX
RATIFICATION AND SIGNATURE
Article 110

1. The present Charter shall be ratified by the signatory states in accordance with their respective constitutional processes.

2. The ratifications shall be deposited with the Government of the United States of America, which shall notify all the signatory states of each deposit as well as the Secretary-General of the Organization when he has been appointed.

3. The present Charter shall come into force upon the deposit of ratifications by the Republic of China, France, the Union of Soviet Socialist Republics, the United Kingdom of Great Britain and Northern Ireland, and the United States of America, and by a majority of the other signatory states. A protocol of the ratifications deposited shall thereupon be drawn up by the Government of the United States of America which shall communicate copies thereof to all the signatory states.

4. The states signatory to the present Charter which ratify it after it has come into force will become original Members of the United Nations on the date of the deposit of their respective ratifications.

Article 111

The present Charter, of which the Chinese, French, Russian, English, and Spanish texts are equally authentic, shall remain deposited in the archives of the Government of the United States of America. Duly certified copies thereof shall be transmitted by that Government to the Governments of the other signatory states.

IN FAITH WHEREOF the representatives of the Governments of the United Nations have signed the present Charter.

DONE at the city of San Francisco the twenty-sixth day of June, one thousand nine hundred and forty-five.

STATUTE OF THE INTERNATIONAL
COURT OF JUSTICE

Article 1

The International Court of Justice established by the Charter of the United Nations as the principal judicial organ of the United Nations shall be constituted and shall function in accordance with the provisions of the present Statute.

CHAPTER I
ORGANIZATION OF THE COURT
Article 2

The Court shall be composed of a body of independent judges, elected regardless of their nationality from among persons of high moral character, who possess the qualifications required in their respective countries for appointment to the highest judicial offices, or are jurisconsults of recognized competence in international law.

Article 3

1. The Court shall consist of fifteen members, no two of whom may be nationals of the same state.

2. A person who for the purposes of membership in the Court could be regarded as a national of more than one state shall be deemed to be a

national of the one in which he ordinarily exercises civil and political rights.

Article 4

1. The members of the Court shall be elected by the General Assembly and by the Security Council from a list of persons nominated by the national groups in the Permanent Court of Arbitration, in accordance with the following provisions.

2. In the case of Members of the United Nations not represented in the Permanent Court of Arbitration, candidates shall be nominated by national groups appointed for this purpose by their governments under the same conditions as those prescribed for members of the Permanent Court of Arbitration by Article 44 of the Convention of The Hague of 1907 for the pacific settlement of international disputes.

3. The conditions under which a state which is a party to the present Statute but is not a Member of the United Nations may participate in electing the members of the Court shall, in the absence of a special agreement, be laid down by the General Assembly upon recommendation of the Security Council.

Article 5

1. At least three months before the date of the election, the Secretary-General of the United Nations shall address a written request to the members of the Permanent Court of Arbitration belonging to the states which are parties to the present Statute, and to the members of the national groups appointed under Article 4, paragraph 2, inviting them to undertake, within a given time, by national groups, the nomination of persons in a position to accept the duties of a member of the Court.

2. No group may nominate more than four persons, not more than two of whom shall be of their own nationality. In no case may the number of candidates nominated by a group be more than double the number of seats to be filled.

Article 6

Before making these nominations, each national group is recommended to consult its highest court of justice, its legal faculties and schools of law, and its national academies and national sections of international academies devoted to the study of law.

Article 7

1. The Secretary-General shall prepare a list in alphabetical order of all the persons thus nominated. Save as provided in Article 12, paragraph 2, these shall be the only persons eligible.

2. The Secretary-General shall submit this list to the General Assembly and to the Security Council.

Article 8

The General Assembly and the Security Council shall proceed independently of one another to elect the members of the Court.

Article 9

At every election, the electors shall bear in mind not only that the persons to be elected should individually possess the qualifications required, but also that in the body as a whole the representation of the main forms of civilization and of the principal legal systems of the world should be assured.

Article 10

1. Those candidates who obtain an absolute majority of votes in the General Assembly and in the Security Council shall be considered as elected.

2. Any vote of the Security Council, whether for the election of judges or for the appointment of members of the conference envisaged in Article 12, shall be taken without any distinction between permanent and non-permanent members of the Security Council.

3. In the event of more than one national of the same state obtaining an absolute majority of the votes both of the General Assembly and of the Security Council, the eldest of these only shall be considered as elected.

Article 11

If, after the first meeting held for the purpose of the election, one or more seats remain to be filled, a second and, if necessary, a third meeting shall take place.

Article 12

1. If, after the third meeting, one or more seats still remain unfilled, a joint conference consisting of six members, three appointed by the General Assembly and three by the Security Council, may be formed at any time at the request of either the General Assembly or the Security Council, for the purpose of choosing by the vote of an absolute majority one name for each seat still vacant, to submit to the General Assembly and the Security Council for their respective acceptance.

2. If the joint conference is unanimously agreed upon any person who fulfills the required conditions, he may be included in its list, even though he was not included in the list of nominations referred to in Article 7.

3. If the joint conference is satisfied that it will not be successful in procuring an election, those members of the Court who have already been elected shall, within a period to be fixed by the Security Council, proceed to fill the vacant seats by selection from among those candidates who have obtained votes either in the General Assembly or in the Security Council.

4. In the event of an equality of votes among the judges, the eldest judge shall have a casting vote.

Article 13

1. The members of the Court shall be elected for nine years and may be re-elected; provided, however, that of the judges elected at the first election, the terms of five judges shall expire at the end of three years and the terms of five more judges shall expire at the end of six years.

2. The judges whose terms are to expire at the end of the above-mentioned initial periods of three and six years shall be chosen by lot to be drawn by the Secretary-General immediately after the first election has been completed.

3. The members of the Court shall continue to discharge their duties until their places have been filled. Though replaced, they shall finish any cases which they may have begun.

4. In the case of the resignation of a member of the Court, the resignation shall be addressed to the President of the Court for transmission to the Secretary-General. This last notification makes the place vacant.

Article 14

Vacancies shall be filled by the same method as that laid down for the first election, subject to the following provision: the Secretary-General shall, within one month of the occurrence of the vacancy, proceed to issue the invitations provided for in Article 5, and the date of the election shall be fixed by the Security Council.

Article 15

A member of the Court elected to replace a member whose term of office has not expired shall hold office for the remainder of his predecessor's term.

Article 16

1. No member of the Court may exercise any political or administrative function, or engage in any other occupation of a professional nature.

2. Any doubt on this point shall be settled by the decision of the Court.

Article 17

1. No member of the Court may act as agent, counsel, or advocate in any case.

2. No member may participate in the decision of any case in which he has previously taken part as agent, counsel, or advocate for one of the parties, or as a member of a national or international court, or of a commission of enquiry, or in any other capacity.

3. Any doubt on this point shall be settled by the decision of the Court.

Article 18

1. No member of the Court can be dismissed unless, in the unanimous opinion of the other members, he has ceased to fulfill the required conditions.

2. Formal notification thereof shall be made to the Secretary-General by the Registrar.

3. This notification makes the place vacant.

Article 19

The members of the Court, when engaged on the business of the Court, shall enjoy diplomatic privileges and immunities.

Article 20

Every member of the Court shall, before taking up his duties, make a solemn declaration in open court that he will exercise his powers impartially and conscientiously.

Article 21

1. The Court shall elect its President and Vice-President for three years; they may be re-elected.

2. The Court shall appoint its Registrar and may provide for the appointment of such other officers as may be necessary.

Article 22

1. The seat of the Court shall be established at The Hague. This, however, shall not prevent the Court from sitting and exercising its functions elsewhere whenever the Court considers it desirable.

2. The President and the Registrar shall reside at the seat of the Court.

Article 23

1. The Court shall remain permanently in session, except during the judicial vacations, the dates and duration of which shall be fixed by the Court.

2. Members of the Court are entitled to periodic leave, the dates and duration of which shall be fixed by the Court, having in mind the distance between The Hague and the home of each judge.

3. Members of the Court shall be bound, unless they are on leave or prevented from attending by illness or other serious reasons duly explained to the President, to hold themselves permanently at the disposal of the Court.

Article 24

1. If, for some special reason, a member of the Court considers that he should not take part in the decision of a particular case, he shall so inform the President.

2. If the President considers that for some special reason one of the members of the Court should not sit in a particular case, he shall give him notice accordingly.

3. If in any such case the member of the Court and the President disagree, the matter shall be settled by the decision of the Court.

Article 25

1. The full Court shall sit except when it is expressly provided otherwise in the present Statute.

2. Subject to the condition that the number of judges available to constitute the Court is not thereby reduced below eleven, the Rules of the Court may provide for allowing one or more judges, according to circumstances and in rotation, to be dispensed from sitting.

3. A quorum of nine judges shall suffice to constitute the Court.

Article 26

1. The Court may from time to time form one or more chambers, composed of three or more judges as the Court may determine, for dealing with particular categories of cases; for example, labour cases and cases relating to transit and communications.

2. The Court may at any time form a chamber for dealing with a particular case. The number of judges to constitute such a chamber shall be determined by the Court with the approval of the parties.

3. Cases shall be heard and determined by the chambers provided for in this article if the parties so request.

Article 27

A judgment given by any of the chambers provided for in Articles 26 and 29 shall be considered as rendered by the Court.

Article 28

The chambers provided for in Articles 26 and 29 may, with the consent of the parties, sit and exercise their functions elsewhere than at The Hague.

Article 29

With a view to the speedy dispatch of business, the Court shall form annually a chamber composed of five judges which, at the request of the parties, may hear and determine cases by summary procedure. In addition, two judges shall be selected for the purpose of replacing judges who find it impossible to sit.

Article 30

1. The Court shall frame rules for carrying out its functions. In particular, it shall lay down rules of procedure.

2. The Rules of the Court may provide for assessors to sit with the Court or with any of its chambers, without the right to vote.

Article 31

1. Judges of the nationality of each of the parties shall retain their right to sit in the case before the Court.

2. If the Court includes upon the Bench a judge of the nationality of one of the parties, any other party may choose a person to sit as judge. Such person shall be chosen preferably from among those persons who have been nominated as candidates as provided in Articles 4 and 5.

3. If the Court includes upon the Bench no judge of the nationality of the parties, each of these parties may proceed to choose a judge as provided in paragraph 2 of this Article.

4. The provisions of this Article shall apply to the case of Articles 26 and 29. In such cases, the President shall request one or, if necessary, two of the members of the Court forming the chamber to give place to the members of the Court of the nationality of the parties concerned, and, failing such, or if they are unable to be present, to the judges specially chosen by the parties.

5. Should there be several parties in the same interest, they shall, for the purpose of the preceding provisions, be reckoned as one party only. Any doubt upon this point shall be settled by the decision of the Court.

6. Judges chosen as laid down in paragraphs 2, 3, and 4 of this Article shall fulfill the conditions required by Articles 2, 17 (paragraph 2), 20, and 24 of the present Statute. They shall take part in the decision on terms of complete equality with their colleagues.

Article 32

1. Each member of the Court shall receive an annual salary.

2. The President shall receive a special annual allowance.

3. The Vice-President shall receive a special allowance for every day on which he acts as President.

4. The judges chosen under Article 31, other than members of the Court, shall receive compensation for each day on which they exercise their functions.

5. These salaries, allowances, and compensation shall be fixed by the General Assembly. They may not be decreased during the term of office.

6. The salary of the Registrar shall be fixed by the General Assembly on the proposal of the Court.

7. Regulations made by the General Assembly shall fix the conditions under which retirement pensions may be given to members of the Court and to the Registrar, and the conditions under which members of the Court and the Registrar shall have their travelling expenses refunded.

8. The above salaries, allowances, and compensation shall be free of all taxation.

Article 33

The expenses of the Court shall be borne by the United Nations in such a manner as shall be decided by the General Assembly.

CHAPTER II
COMPETENCE OF THE COURT
Article 34

1. Only states may be parties in cases before the Court.

2. The Court, subject to and in conformity with its Rules, may request of public international organizations information relevant to cases before it, and shall receive such information presented by such organizations on their own initiative.

3. Whenever the construction of the constituent instrument of a public international organization or of an international convention adopted thereunder is in question in a case before the Court, the Registrar shall so notify the public international organization concerned and shall communicate to it copies of all the written proceedings.

Article 35

1. The Court shall be open to the states parties to the present Statute.

2. The conditions under which the Court shall be open to other states shall, subject to the special provisions contained in treaties in force, be laid down by the Security Council, but in no case shall such conditions place the parties in a position of inequality before the Court.

3. When a state which is not a Member of the United Nations is a party to a case, the Court shall fix the amount which that party is to contribute towards the expenses of the Court. This provision shall not apply if such state is bearing a share of the expenses of the Court.

Article 36

1. The jurisdiction of the Court comprises all cases which the parties refer to it and all matters specially provided for in the Charter of the United Nations or in treaties and conventions in force.

2. The states parties to the present Statute may at any time declare that they recognize as compulsory ipso facto and without special agreement, in relation to any other state accepting the same obligation, the jurisdiction of the Court in all legal disputes concerning:

a. the interpretation of a treaty;

b. any question of international law;

c. the existence of any fact which, if established, would constitute a breach of an international obligation;

d. the nature or extent of the reparation to be made for the breach of an international obligation.

3. The declarations referred to above may be made unconditionally or on condition of reciprocity on the part of several or certain states, or for a certain time.

4. Such declarations shall be deposited with the Secretary-General of the United Nations, who shall transmit copies thereof to the parties to the Statute and to the Registrar of the Court.

5. Declarations made under Article 36 of the Statute of the Permanent Court of International Justice and which are still in force shall be deemed, as between the parties to the present Statute, to be acceptances of the compulsory jurisdiction of the International Court of Justice for the period which they still have to run and in accordance with their terms.

6. In the event of a dispute as to whether the Court has jurisdiction, the matter shall be settled by the decision of the Court.

Article 37

Whenever a treaty or convention in force provides for reference of a matter to a tribunal to have been instituted by the League of Nations, or to the Permanent Court of International Justice, the matter shall, as between the parties to the present Statute, be referred to the International Court of Justice.

Article 38

1. The Court, whose function is to decide in accordance with international law such disputes as are submitted to it, shall apply:

a. international conventions, whether general or particular, establishing rules expressly recognized by the contesting states;

b. international custom, as evidence of a general practice accepted as law;

c. the general principles of law recognized by civilized nations;

d. subject to the provisions of Article 59, judicial decisions and the teachings of the most highly qualified publicists of the various nations, as subsidiary means for the determination of rules of law.

2. This provision shall not prejudice the power of the Court to decide a case *ex aequo et bono,* if the parties agree thereto.

CHAPTER III
PROCEDURE
Article 39

1. The official languages of the Court shall be French and English. If the parties agree that the case shall be conducted in French, the judgment shall be delivered in French. If the parties agree that the case shall be conducted in English, the judgment shall be delivered in English.

2. In the absence of an agreement as to which language shall be employed, each party may, in the pleadings, use the language which it prefers; the decision of the Court shall be given in French and English. In this case the Court shall at the same time determine which of the two texts shall be considered as authoritative.

3. The Court shall, at the request of any party, authorize a language other than French or English to be used by that party.

Article 40

1. Cases are brought before the Court, as the case may be, either by the notification of the special agreement or by a written application addressed to the Registrar. In either case the subject of the dispute and the parties shall be indicated.

2. The Registrar shall forthwith communicate the application to all concerned.

3. He shall also notify the Members of the United Nations through the Secretary-General, and also any other states entitled to appear before the Court.

Article 41

1. The Court shall have the power to indicate, if it considers that circumstances so require, any provisional measures which ought to be taken to preserve the respective rights of either party.

2. Pending the final decision, notice of the measures suggested shall forthwith be given to the parties and to the Security Council.

Article 42

1. The parties shall be represented by agents.

2. They may have the assistance of counsel or advocates before the Court.

3. The agents, counsel, and advocates of parties before the Court shall enjoy the privileges and immunities necessary to the independent exercise of their duties.

Article 43

1. The procedure shall consist of two parts: written and oral.

2. The written proceedings shall consist of the communication to the Court and to the parties of memorials, counter-memorials and, if necessary, replies; also all papers and documents in support.

3. These communications shall be made through the Registrar, in the order and within the time fixed by the Court.

4. A certified copy of every document produced by one party shall be communicated to the other party.

5. The oral proceedings shall consist of the hearing by the Court of witnesses, experts, agents, counsel, and advocates.

Article 44

1. For the service of all notices upon persons other than the agents, counsel, and advocates, the Court shall apply direct to the government of the state upon whose territory the notice has to be served.

2. The same provision shall apply whenever steps are to be taken to procure evidence on the spot.

Article 45

The hearing shall be under the control of the President or, if he is unable to preside, of the Vice-President; if neither is able to preside, the senior judge present shall preside.

Article 46

The hearing in Court shall be public, unless the Court shall decide otherwise, or unless the parties demand that the public be not admitted.

Article 47

1. Minutes shall be made at each hearing and signed by the Registrar and the President.

2. These minutes alone shall be authentic.

Article 48

The Court shall make orders for the conduct of the case, shall decide the form and time in which each party must conclude its arguments, and make all arrangements connected with the taking of evidence.

Article 49

The Court may, even before the hearing begins, call upon the agents to produce any document or to supply any explanations. Formal note shall be taken of any refusal.

Article 50

The Court may, at any time, entrust any individual, body, bureau, commission, or other organization that it may select, with the task of carrying out an enquiry or giving an expert opinion.

Article 51

During the hearing any relevant questions are to be put to the witnesses and experts under the conditions laid down by the Court in the rules of procedure referred to in Article 30.

Article 52

After the Court has received the proofs and evidence within the time specified for the purpose, it may refuse to accept any further oral or written evidence that one party may desire to present unless the other side consents.

Article 53

1. Whenever one of the parties does not appear before the Court, or fails to defend its case, the other party may call upon the Court to decide in favour of its claim.

2. The Court must, before doing so, satisfy itself, not only that it has jurisdiction in accordance with Articles 36 and 37, but also that the claim is well founded in fact and law.

Article 54

1. When, subject to the control of the Court, the agents, counsel, and advocates have completed their presentation of the case, the President shall declare the hearing closed.

2. The Court shall withdraw to consider the judgment.

3. The deliberations of the Court shall take place in private and remain secret.

Article 55

1. All questions shall be decided by a majority of the judges present.

2. In the event of an equality of votes, the President or the judge who acts in his place shall have a casting vote.

Article 56

1. The judgment shall state the reasons on which it is based.

2. It shall contain the names of the judges who have taken part in the decision.

Article 57

If the judgment does not represent in whole or in part the unanimous opinion of the judges, any judge shall be entitled to deliver a separate opinion.

Article 58

The judgment shall be signed by the President and by the Registrar. It shall be read in open court, due notice having been given to the agents.

Article 59

The decision of the Court has no binding force except between the parties and in respect of that particular case.

Article 60

The judgment is final and without appeal. In the event of dispute as to the meaning or scope of the judgment, the Court shall construe it upon the request of any party.

Article 61

1. An application for revision of a judgment may be made only when it is based upon the discovery of some fact of such a nature as to be a decisive factor, which fact was, when the judgment was given, unknown to the Court and also to the party claiming revision, always provided that such ignorance was not due to negligence.

2. The proceedings for revision shall be opened by a judgment of the Court expressly recording the existence of the new fact, recognizing that it has such a character as to lay the case open to revision, and declaring the application admissible on this ground.

3. The Court may require previous compliance with the terms of the judgment before it admits proceedings in revision.

4. The application for revision must be made at latest within six months of the discovery of the new fact.

5. No application for revision may be made after the lapse of ten years from the date of the judgment.

Article 62

1. Should a state consider that it has an interest of a legal nature which may be affected by the decision in the case, it may submit a request to the Court to be permitted to intervene.

2. It shall be for the Court to decide upon this request.

Article 63

1. Whenever the construction of a convention to which states other than those concerned in the case are parties is in question, the Registrar shall notify all such states forthwith.

2. Every state so notified has the right to intervene in the proceedings; but if it uses this right, the construction given by the judgment will be equally binding upon it.

Article 64

Unless otherwise decided by the Court, each party shall bear its own costs.

CHAPTER IV
ADVISORY OPINIONS
Article 65

1. The Court may give an advisory opinion on any legal question at the request of whatever body may be authorized by or in accordance with the Charter of the United Nations to make such a request.

2. Questions upon which the advisory opinion of the Court is asked shall be laid before the Court by means of a written request containing an exact statement of the question upon which an opinion is required, and accompanied by all documents likely to throw light upon the question.

Article 66

1. The Registrar shall forthwith give notice of the request for an advisory opinion to all states entitled to appear before the Court.

2. The Registrar shall also, by means of a special and direct communication, notify any state entitled to appear before the Court or international organization considered by the Court, or, should it not be sitting, by the President, as likely to be able to furnish information on the question, that the Court will be prepared to receive, within a time-limit

to be fixed by the President, written statements, or to hear, at a public sitting to be held for the purpose, oral statements relating to the question.

3. Should any such state entitled to appear before the Court have failed to receive the special communication referred to in paragraph 2 of this Article, such state may express a desire to submit a written statement or to be heard; and the Court will decide.

4. States and organizations having presented written or oral statements or both shall be permitted to comment on the statements made by other states or organizations in the form, to the extent, and within the time-limits which the Court, or, should it not be sitting, the President, shall decide in each particular case. Accordingly, the Registrar shall in due time communicate any such written statements to states and organizations having submitted similar statements.

Article 67

The Court shall deliver its advisory opinions in open court, notice having been given to the Secretary-General and to the representatives of Members of the United Nations, of other states and of international organizations immediately concerned.

Article 68

In the exercise of its advisory functions the Court shall further be guided by the provisions of the present Statute which apply in contentious cases to the extent to which it recognizes them to be applicable.

CHAPTER V
AMENDMENT
Article 69

Amendments to the present Statute shall be effected by the same procedure as is provided by the Charter of the United Nations for amendments to that Charter, subject however to any provisions which the General Assembly upon recommendation of the Security Council may adopt concerning the participation of states which are parties to the present Statute but are not Members of the United Nations.

Article 70

The Court shall have power to propose such amendments to the present Statute as it may deem necessary, through written communications to the Secretary-General, for consideration in conformity with the provisions of Article 69.

Part I

THE UNITED NATIONS CHARTER:
STRUCTURE, ORIGINS, AND INSTITUTIONAL CHANGE

Chapter 1

The UN Charter:
A Global Constitution?

Michael W. Doyle

How constitutional is the global order? The countries of the globe are increasingly interdependent, but do they together have a coherent legal order, assigning authority to decide rights and responsibilities? Few would choose the description "coherent" for the global order, if that connotes centralized. But even as a decentralized legal order, the global international system has no single constitution. The closest candidate to a global constitution is the UN Charter. Thus it is worth exploring how constitutional the Charter is in theory and practice. Sixty plus years into its evolution we can see two dominant features.

First, we can see that the Charter is not like a national federal constitution (e.g., the US Constitution), but neither is it an ordinary contract-like treaty. Its key traits in comparison to other constitutions are three: supranationality, inequality, and an "invitation to struggle" that leads, as in many constitutions, to an inevitable dialectic, including pushback from states when UN authority expands.

Second, unlike many domestic constitutions, the pushback more than holds its own. The UN, unlike either the EU or the US, has neither integrated parts nor centralized authority. Instead, to borrow the language of 1970s international integration, UN integration has "spilled around" more than "spilled over" into deeper cooperation.

To illustrate those points, I start with a comparison of the UN Charter to capital C domestic constitutions and to ordinary treaties. I then address with a broad brush the main features of the UN's supranationality and inequality. The Secretariat and its neutrality and independence are the next topics. I then consider two examples of tension between UN supranationality and sovereignty. I explore the trend toward "global legislation" associated with the Security Council's counterterrorist resolutions, 1373 and 1540. I then focus on the example of the Millennium Development Goals, the UN's recent attempt to remake itself as a development body. (Here I will offer an insider's reflections, drawing on my experience as Kofi Annan's special adviser from 2001 through 2003.) I conclude with a discussion of the wider constitutional significance and prospects of the UN in the light of the contrasting success of the history of US federalism and European integration.

GLOBAL CONSTITUTIONALISM

The answer to whether the UN Charter is a constitution depends on what we mean by a constitution and to what alternative we are contrasting a constitution. Consider these three.

First, if the relevant contrast is to the US Constitution—the constitution of a sovereign state—the answer is clearly, "no." The UN, as José Alvarez has argued, was not intended to create a world state. As the Charter's Preamble announces, it was created for ambitious but specific purposes: "to save succeeding generations from the scourge of war," "reaffirm faith in fundamental human rights," "establish conditions under which justice and respect for the obligations arising from treaties and other sources of international law can be maintained," and "promote social progress and better standards of life in larger freedom." The UN, moreover, is an organization based on the "sovereign equality of all its members" (Article 2.1), its membership being open to all "peace-loving states" (Article 4.1). This contrasts strikingly with the US Constitution's much more general, sovereign-creating purposes: "To form a more perfect union, establish justice, insure domestic tranquility, provide for the common defense, promote the general welfare and secure the blessings of liberty to ourselves and our posterity" (US Constitution, Preamble).[1]

Second, the UN Charter lacks at least two of the three key attributes that the Constitutional Court of South Africa identified as essential to a (their?) constitution. In *Pharmaceutical*, the court averred that a constitution is a unified system of law: "There is only one system of law. It is shaped by the

Constitution which is the supreme law, and all law, including the common law, derives its force from the Constitution and is subject to constitutional control."[2] The Charter lacks what Frank Michelman, in commenting on the South African case, has called the attributes of, first, "pervasive law" (i.e., "all law is subject") and, second, "basic law" (i.e., "derives its force").[3] The UN Charter, instead, reflects what Laurence Helfer calls the "disaggregated and decentralized" character of the international order.[4] Neither is all international law subject to the UN nor is the Charter the legal source of all international law. Much international law precedes the Charter and has been developed in parallel to it, including such fundamental elements of international law as the Genocide Convention, which requires its signatories (and as *jus cogens*, all states) to prevent, stop, and punish genocide seemingly irrespective of whether genocide is an "essentially" domestic matter under Article 2.7 and whether the Security Council has authority to act in matters beyond "international peace and security." The Charter does, however, have a degree of the third attribute of a constitution: supremacy.

Third, if we move to the other extreme and contrast the Charter to a standard contract-like treaty, the differences are also clear.[5] The UN Charter is a treaty, but a special treaty. Like a constitution it has supremacy (Article 103) even over treaties that would normally supersede it by "the last in time" rule (Vienna Convention, art. 30). This supremacy does not cover all international law (it is not pervasive or basic) but only the aspects of the Charter in which it imposes "obligations," most particularly, peace and security. Like the US Constitution (*Texas v. White*), moreover, the Charter is perpetual; it cannot be revoked by its constituents. Indeed, although states can be expelled, there is no provision for resignation. The League Covenant, in contrast, retains treaty-like provisions for revocation. Moreover, the Charter binds all states, whether members or not, in matters of peace and security (Article 39). Like a constitution, it is "indelible," in Thomas Franck's terminology. Unlike most treaties, no reservations can limit its effects on states that ratify it. And it is very hard to amend. Amendments require an international conference and a two-thirds affirmative vote of the entire membership, including all five permanent members of the Council (the "Permanent Five") (Article 109).[6]

Last and most important, it has institutional, for lack of a better word, "supranationality"[7] in the sense that it permits authoritative decisions without continuous consent. Like many constitutions, it both empowers and limits power. It does so by dividing powers between constituents and the constituted institution.[8] The Charter establishes a "horizontal" division of powers among the functional components of governance—the Council, General Assembly, Secretariat, International Court of Justice, and so on—which have quasi-executive, legislative, administrative, and judicial functions. The UN Secretariat is pledged to international independence in the performance of its duties (Article 100). Crucially, the UN makes or is authorized ("vertically") to make decisions without the continuous consent of its member states. Budgets can be adopted by a two-thirds vote, and the ICJ has held them as binding on all the members, including those who voted against the substantive measures that the budget funds (ICJ *Expenses Case*). Security Council decisions taken under Chapter VII in matters of international peace and security—those with at least nine out of fifteen votes, including no vetoes by the Permanent Five—are binding on all states (Articles 25 and 48). The Charter has also been interpreted flexibly to make "necessary and proper" functions viable. The requirement that Security Council votes on substantive matters pass with affirmative votes of the Permanent Five, for example, has been flexibly interpreted to mean no negative votes (vetoes), allowing permanent members to abstain without vetoing.[9]

This "supranationality" certainly exists on paper, but whether there is operational supranational constitutionalism and, if so, to what degree requires further analysis. To begin this analysis, we can scale supranationalism from:

1. First, nearly zero when, (1) *simple agency* is exercised on behalf of the member states (a principal gives directions, agent carries them out);
2. second, a *delegation* of specific functions to be (2a) *administered* independently (agent has discretion in how directives are implemented) or (2b) through delegation by *representation* of authority, when some are authorized to act for the whole (majority voting, delegation to committees);
3. or third, when there occurs a (3) *transfer of authority* to a central and independent institution (an agent, now a "trustee" is authorized to act in the interest of the principal or according to broad standards authorized by principal).[10] In UN practice all three can be found, and they mix together.

I now turn to how this operates in the UN system by focusing on the varying and unequal degrees of supranationality in the UN Charter, relations with the Secretariat, global "legislation" against terrorism, and the attempt to coordinate development embodied in the Millennium Development Goals (MDGs). In each case I will be looking at the rationale for the supranationality and the struggle that ensues between those authorized to act multi-laterally and the efforts of states to restrict the authority granted. The UN Charter, like so many constitutions before it, is an invitation to struggle.[11]

THE UN CHARTER: SUPRA OVER SOME AND LESS SO FOR OTHERS

Supranationality in the Charter affects the responsibilities of all member states, but some much more so than others, and in all cases states push back against attempts to assert international authority. All states are affected by the UN possession of a legal "personality," which is a minimal prerequisite of legal *delegated* agency (1). Legal personality permits it to undertake responsibilities and to act on behalf of the membership. It can bring a claim against a member without the consent of the member, and it can be sued by members without the consent of other members. In the *Reparations Case*, involving reparations for the assassination of a UN official, Count Bernadotte, the ICJ declared that the UN:

> is at present the supreme type of international organization and it could not carry out the intentions of its founders if it was devoid of international personality. It must be acknowledged that its Members, by entrusting certain functions to it, with the attendant duties and responsibilities, have clothed it with the competence to enable those functions to be effectively discharged.[12]

The management of UN finances illustrates a much more substantial facet of *delegated representational* supranationality (2b), one that bears on all members, albeit differently. In Articles 17 and 18 the Assembly is given the authority to "consider and approve" the budget, and the members undertake to bear those expenses "as apportioned by the General Assembly." The budget being an important matter, a two-thirds vote thus binds—in effect, taxes—the members to support the expenses of the organization. This differs notably from the League of Nations where unanimity ruled.[13] UN budget assessments, moreover, are enforced by the provision in Article 19 whereby any member will lose its vote in the Assembly if it is two years or more in arrears. This is a classic case of delegation tending toward full transfer of authority.

In December 1961, following the controversy over payment for the UN Emergency Force in the Sinai and the UN Operation in the Congo, and in particular the vehement rejections of financial responsibility by France and the USSR, the Assembly requested an advisory opinion from the ICJ on whether the expenses the organization had "incurred" were obligatory under Article

17. In its *Expenses Case* opinion of July 1962, the court's majority ruled expansively. Noting that even though some of the policy authorizations were made by the Assembly and not by the Council (which had "primary" responsibility for peace and security), the court found that the Council did not have exclusive responsibility for peace and security. Furthermore, the obligatory character of the expenses that verged toward a (3) *transfer of authority*, if properly approved by the Assembly, did not rest on the legitimacy of the underlying substantive purpose of the resolution.[14] This seemed to imply that the Assembly could legally tax where the UN could not otherwise legally oblige.[15]

But as interesting as the legal judgments were, political forces determined the outcome of the financing controversies. As early as 1946, money talked as the United States set limits on what it was prepared to pay (at 40 percent), whatever a *pro rata* estimate would indicate. When the USSR fell two years in arrears in 1964–65, the United States led a campaign to deprive the USSR of its Assembly vote.[16] When this failed, the United States announced that it would also assume a right to regard the budget as nonbinding (the "Goldberg Reservation"). The Assembly then moved to a procedure that recognized functional consensus (will the taxpayers pay?) as the basis for budgeting. In practice, this allowed the 8 countries that on average paid 75 percent of the budget to have a veto equivalent to the other 180-plus members. The United States, regarding the budget as advisory, regularly withheld assessments as leverage to promote institutional and other changes it sought to impose on the organization. Political pushback thus effectively amended the Charter in a pragmatic—but far from organizationally effective—direction as a wide range of states each adopted a bargaining veto vis-à-vis the biennial budget negotiations.

The most striking supranational—*representation and transfer of authority* (2b and 3)—features of the Charter system are of course the provisions of Chapter VII with regard to international peace and security. Here the UN is both supranational and discriminatory. In matters of international peace and security (Article 39) Council decisions bind all UN members (Articles 25 and 48) when they garner the requisite nine votes, including no vetoes by the Permanent Five. Nine members can govern the whole. But the Permanent Five—the United States, UK, France, Russia, and China—have the unequal right to remain unbound unless they concur or abstain. The working interpretation that abstentions by the Permanent Five do not count as vetoes reinforces their special status, allowing them the unique discretion not to veto without necessarily affirming and establishing informal precedents they might not want to recognize.[17]

In the *Lockerbie Case*, the ICJ majority held that Security Council resolution 748 trumped the provisions of the Montreal Convention, which allowed Libya at its discretion to either extradite or try suspected criminals (*aut dedere aut judicare*). In doing so it affirmed the supremacy of Council resolutions over conflicting international law.[18] Statements by the ICJ judges left open the possibility that Council resolutions might be held *ultra vires* by the ICJ if a relevant case were put before the court, but the overall weight of the opinion strongly reinforced the supranationality of the UN in peace and security vis-à-vis all member states, whether or not they had approved the particular Council decision.

This led some to question just how legitimate and representative the Council was when considered as a world governmental body.[19] But the more usual sovereign pushback was the refusal to negotiate agreements under Articles 43–47 to allocate forces under the direct command of the Council. The original Charter conception involved division-sized forces of aircraft, naval, and ground forces, all subject to the Council and commanded by the postwar equivalent of World War II's Allied joint command, a military staff committee appointed by the Council. Absent such "special agreements," states retained the right to refuse to deploy forces at the call of the Council, which was reduced to negotiating with potential troop contributors to form in Brian Urquhart's phrase, the UN equivalent of a "sheriff's posse" or simply delegating authority to "use all necessary means" to a coalition of willing states, absent Secretariat direction. In this way discretionary state sovereignty was reaffirmed in practice.

THE INTERNATIONAL CIVIL SERVANT AS "NEUTRAL MAN"

The issue of UN autonomy, and how much authority was or was not delegated by administration (2a), was nowhere better explored than in Secretary-General Dag Hammarskjöld's famous 1961 lecture "The International Civil Servant" (the "Oxford Lecture"). He began the lecture with a reference to and quotation from a recent interview with Chairman Nikita Khrushchev in which the Soviet leader stated, "While there are neutral countries, there are no neutral men."[20] The chairman had become concerned that the Secretary-General was harming, or at least not promoting, Soviet interests in the Middle East and Africa. This led him to propose a "troika" leadership for the UN— three co-secretaries-general, one appointed by Moscow, able to veto each other's actions. Then, he hoped, Soviet interests would be suitably protected from an interested, political administration.

The founders of the UN imbued the role of Secretary-General and the Secretariat more generally with various tensions. The essence of the role was to be administrative: a narrow sense of agency, not extending beyond administrative discretion. The Secretary-General was the "chief administrative officer of the Organization" (Article 97). He or she was to administer the various tasks assigned by the political principal organs (i.e., the Security Council, Assembly, Economic and Social Council, etc.) and direct the Secretariat. The founders at San Francisco debated whether to "elect" the Secretary-General but instead chose the word "appoint" to emphasize his administrative, nonpolitical character. Rejecting a three-year term as too short and subject to too much control, they favored a longer term to encourage independence from the Permanent Five whose approval would be needed for selection.[21] They embodied these principles in the requirement that the Secretariat be independent—of "an exclusively international character"—and that it would neither seek "instructions" from the members nor would the members seek to "influence" it (Article 100). The Secretariat, moreover, would be chosen for "efficiency, competence, and integrity" with due regard being paid to recruitment "on as wide a geographical basis as possible" (Article 101).

Responding to the pressure of sovereign pushback, the effective administrative independence of the Secretariat was curbed. It soon became the norm that Secretariat positions would be allocated by national quotas. At the higher reaches, leading member states would insist on holding specific posts and in some instances filling them with nationals whom they would specifically name.[22] This limited the administrative independence of the Secretariat. For the Secretary-General the most consequential effect was the inability to form a governmental cabinet of like-minded followers, such as a typical prime minister or president would do.[23] The Secretary-General was able to choose only his small executive office.

The Secretary-General had more success in transcending a purely administrative agency understanding of his role. Hammarskjöld, in the Oxford lecture, made a powerful case for neutrality as the ideal of the international civil servant. But he also noted that he could be neutral neither "as regards the Charter" nor "as regards facts."[24] Moreover, he was bound to become non-neutral, and inevitably political, when an organ of the UN assigned him responsibilities that conflicted with the interests of one or more member states.[25] In addition, he had one more key responsibility. Article 99 reads, "The Secretary-General may bring to the attention of the Security Council any matter which in his opinion may threaten the maintenance of international peace and security." This was an inherently political capacity and an important responsibility.

Though rarely invoked, Article 99 was the foundation for the ever-increasing political role of the Secretary-General as mediator and, to some, as the "world's chief diplomat." Apart from their role with the Council, secretaries-general saw themselves as representatives of the entire UN (the so-called Peking formula), particularly when the Council was locked in a confrontation with a state, as it was with China in the 1950s when Dag Hammarskjöld began a delicate series of negotiations to free captured US airmen.[26]

GLOBAL LEGISLATION AGAINST TERRORISM?

The single largest movement toward supranational transfer of authority (3) today appears to be the global war against terrorism led by the Security Council. To some, this looks like global supranational legislation imposed on states.[27] In resolution 1373 (2001), the Security Council, acting under Chapter VII, obliged states to prevent and suppress the financing of terrorist acts; criminalize the provision or collection of funds; freeze bank accounts of terrorists and their supporters; deny safe haven; prevent their movement; and cooperate in international investigations of terrorist acts. Security Council resolution 1540 was equally directive, requiring states to take measures to prevent non-state actors from acquiring weapons of mass destruction (nuclear, chemical, and biological). Both resolutions required states to participate in international monitoring and permitted the Security Council to name suspected individuals and entities for sanctions.[28]

The resolutions differ from the traditional powers of the Security Council as an executive agent that sanctions particular states or, more recently, individuals on the grounds of "threats to the peace, breaches of the peace or acts of aggression"—the Charter-mandated powers in Article 39, Chapter VII. Instead, the resolutions address states in general. Conventionally, in international law states are bound only by consent. Treaties require specific adherence (ratification) and international custom requires widespread practice motivated by a sense of lawfulness (*opinio juris*) and is not binding on states that persistently object. Permitting the Security Council to legislate also raises reasonable concerns about hegemonic international law because it steps on deeply embedded principles of sovereign equality, given the limited membership of the Security Council: 10 elected from 192, and 5 permanent with special veto privileges.[29]

All these concerns have merit. But national sovereignty is far from overturned. First, rather than reflecting the omnicompetent character of general legislation, the Security Council anti-terrorist resolutions (so far?) have stayed within the framework of international peace and security. Given the Security Council's recent focus on peacebuilding in the aftermath of civil wars, this limitation is by no means guaranteed to endure.[30] It simply has not been breached yet, and equivalently radical claims to Security Council authority, such as Responsibility to Protect, have been construed narrowly in practice, as they were during the Cyclone Kargis emergency in Myanmar.

Second, part of the significance of the anti-terrorist resolutions stems from their widespread acceptance in the aftermath of the 9/11 attacks on the US. Although a number of states expressed concerns about the possible precedents being set, within two years every state had submitted reports in compliance with Security Council resolution 1373.

Third, the resolutions rested on twelve previously negotiated conventions outlawing various aspects of specific terrorist activities (terrorism against airlines, against oil platforms, etc.). SCRs 1373 and 1540 could be seen as "gap filling" and substituting for the notorious inability of the international community to define terrorism per se.

Fourth, also important is that (unfortunately) many countries found the new sets of requirements to be excuses to step up measures to incarcerate and suppress domestic dissenters (now conveniently labeled as terrorists).[31] These states were hardly being imposed upon.

But most important, states have long—and now the EU has as well—made it clear that they do not regard international law or Security Council resolutions authorized under Chapter VII as superior to domestic civil liberties (in the EU) or national legislation (the US). In the US, federal legislation has the same status as treaties. It too is also "supreme." Among laws of equal status, the later-in-time rule applies (*Reid v. Covert*).[32] In Europe, as affirmed in the Kadi and al Barakat cases, the European Court of Justice (ECJ) ruled[33] that Security Council resolutions had to be compatible with basic EU constitutional law and preserve and protect basic rights to property, trial, and appeal in order to be enforced in Europe.[34] Other countries, including India, made similar statements when they commented on Security Council resolution 1540.[35]

THE MDGS: ROAD MAP TO CONFRONTATION

Supranationality also appears in "legislative" delegation to the Secretariat by the General Assembly. In the United Nations, as in most institutions, principals delegate to agents (e.g., member states to the Secretariat) because implementation is too detailed an activity to be managed by 193 states. The agents' job becomes problematic, controversial, and supranational when the program outlined by the principals is ambiguous or contested. Then the Secretariat is inherently engaged in political government. This is what happened when the "road map" to implement the Millennium Declaration was delegated to the Secretariat and administrative delegation (2a) seemed to trespass on transfer of authority (3).

At the UN Millennium Summit in September 2000, the members formally and unanimously dedicated themselves to a redefinition of goals and means. Since its inception the UN has been an organization by, for, and of states—and so it remained. But in 2000, under the leadership of Secretary-General Kofi Annan, it set out to acquire a parallel identity, a new model of itself. It was redefining the meaning of global good citizenship for our time by putting people rather than states at the center of its agenda. The Millennium Declaration set this agenda.[36]

At the Millennium Summit, world leaders agreed to a set of breathtakingly broad goals that are global, public commitments on behalf of "we the peoples" to promote seven agendas:

- peace, security, and disarmament
- development and poverty eradication
- protecting our common environment
- human rights, democracy, and good governance
- protecting the vulnerable
- special needs of Africa
- strengthening UN institutions

Promising an agenda for action—the international community's marching orders for the next fifteen years—the member states blithely transferred responsibility for designing a "road map" to implement these goals to the Secretary-General. "The Follow-up to the Outcome of the Millennium Summit" General Assembly resolution requested "the Secretary-General urgently to prepare a long-term 'road map' towards the implementation of the Millennium Declaration within the UN system and to submit it to the General

Assembly at its 56th session [nine months later]."[37] This report was to incorporate annual monitoring focusing on "results and benchmarks achieved," reflect the capacities of member states and the entire UN system, including the World Trade Organization and Bretton Woods institutions, and outline practical measures to meet the ambitious targets.

A small coordinating team in the Executive Office of the Secretary-General, the Strategic Planning Unit under the direction of Dr. Abiodun Williams, set about collecting from all the UN's agencies and programs information on what the UN system was already doing to promote these goals and what next steps seemed practicable to advance them. Once compressed and simplified, this encyclopedic list became the Road Map Report (A/56/326 of September 6, 2001). The striking part of the report was the treatment of the development goals, which came to be called the MDGs—the Millennium Development Goals.

Drawn from the development and environment chapters of the Millennium Declaration, the MDGs defined common aspirations in the worldwide effort to alleviate poverty and promote sustainable economic and social development. They pledged to "spare no effort to free our fellow men, women and children from the abject and dehumanizing condition of extreme poverty" and "to create an environment—at the national and global levels alike—which is conducive to development and the eradication of poverty." The eight MDGs that an interagency UN team crystallized from the two chapters of the Millennium Declaration were:[38]

1. Eradicate extreme poverty and hunger
   Target for 2015: Halve the proportion of people living on less than a dollar a day and those who suffer from hunger.
2. Achieve universal primary education
   Target for 2015: Ensure that all boys and girls complete primary school.
3. Promote gender equality and empower women
   Targets for 2005 and 2015: Eliminate gender disparities in primary and secondary education preferably by 2005 and at all levels by 2015.
4. Reduce child mortality
   Target for 2015: Reduce by two-thirds the mortality rate among children under five.
5. Improve maternal health
   Target for 2015: Reduce by three-quarters the ratio of women dying in childbirth.

6. Combat HIV/AIDS, malaria, and other diseases
Target for 2015: Halt and begin to reverse the spread of HIV/AIDS and the incidence of malaria and other major diseases.

7. Ensure environmental sustainability
Targets:
   • Integrate the principles of sustainable development into country policies and programs and reverse the loss of environmental resources.
   • By 2015, reduce by half the proportion of people without access to safe drinking water.
   • By 2020 achieve significant improvement in the lives of at least 100 million slum dwellers.

8. Develop a global partnership for development
Targets:
   • Develop further an open trading and financial system that includes a commitment to good governance, development, and poverty reduction—nationally and internationally.
   • Address the least developed countries' special needs and the special needs of landlocked and small island developing states.
   • Deal comprehensively with developing countries' debt problems.
   • Develop decent and productive work for youth.
   • In cooperation with pharmaceutical companies, provide access to affordable essential drugs in developing countries.
   • In cooperation with the private sector, make available the benefits of new technologies—especially information and communications technologies.

The MDGs soon became controversial and allegedly *ultra vires* bureaucratic impositions that went beyond what the member states had authorized as goals in the Millennium Declaration. The United States refused to acknowledge the MDGs as such, referring to them instead as the "internationally recognized development goals in the Millennium Declaration," making the UN's effort to brand and promote the goals difficult.[39] The crescendo of attack peaked with the rhetoric of Ambassador John Bolton, who used them as one leading reason to reject the outcome consensus on UN reform in the summer of 2005. Bolton portrayed the goals, targets, and indicators as a United Nations Development Program (UNDP) engineered coup, beyond what was agreed at the 2000 summit.[40] In fact, the Secretariat as a whole had been directed by a unanimous General Assembly resolution to prepare a "road map" on how to monitor and implement the goals that presupposed targets and indicators assigned to goals. Ranging far beyond UNDP, the World Bank, the IMF, and the UN system endorsed the goals, targets, and indicators prepared in response to the Assembly resolution. Bolton was at last overridden by President George W. Bush who accepted the MDGs by word and title in his September 2005 speech.

The goals, targets, and indicators of the MDGs in reality had three sources. The interagency team from the entire UN system that met over the spring and summer of 2001 drew first and most importantly on the Millennium Declaration. Contrary to the US critics, every goal had a textual source painstakingly provenanced in the declaration's text either in the development chapter or the environment chapter. Every significant commitment in the declaration's development chapter found a place in the MDGs as goal, target, or indicator. But the MDGs were not a verbatim copy of the declaration. The development chapter of the declaration, for example, had fourteen bulleted goals; the MDGs eight. The declaration could not be monitored without further specification. Some declaration goals were specific, time-bound, and targeted; others vague and aspirational. All the MDGs were made operational by being linked to best-then-available measurable indicators.

The second source was the preexisting development goals of the international community, most particularly the seven International Development Goals (IDGs). First developed in 1996 by the Organization for Economic Cooperation and Development (OECD), they won the endorsement of the World Bank, OECD, IMF, and UN Secretary-General Kofi Annan in a June 2000 report, *Better World for All: Progress Towards the International Development Goals* (BWfA Report). The IDGs included goals and targets to reduce extreme poverty and promote education and maternal health—all of which reappeared in the Millennium Declaration.

The BWfA Report soon became shrouded in controversy. Many developing states and many in the development NGO world rejected the seemingly one-sided program to monitor Third World progress without an equivalent measure of the contribution the wealthy countries were making to global progress. The developing world critics soon tagged the report with the title "Bretton Woods for All." Some countries (Catholic and Muslim and, after January 2001, the Bush administration) objected to the "reproductive health goal," which seemed to endorse birth control and possibly abortion services. Nonetheless, key development actors, including the Bretton Woods institutions and the influential UK development ministry (DFID, referred to in some UN circles as "the indispensable department"), had a stake in the viability of the IDGs and the principles of multidimensional, human-centered, output-oriented, and measurable development they embodied.

The UN system interagency team adopted the framework of the IDGs, replaced "reproductive health" from the IDGs[41] with "HIV/AIDS" from the Millennium Declaration, and added an "eighth goal"—a "global partnership for development" that assembled a variety of commitments in trade, finance, and development aid made by the wealthy countries and embodied in the Millennium Declaration. The result was the new eight, which in late June 2001 were called "the Millennium Development Goals."[42]

The third source was a determination to overcome generations of dispute among the Bretton Woods institutions, the UN Development Program, the UN Conference on Trade and Development, and other UN agencies. Each had grown into the habit of criticizing the others' reports and strategies, producing a cacophony on what development meant, how it should be measured, and whether progress was being made. The UN system interagency team assembled to road map the development section of the Millennium Declaration was a team of experts, particularly involving the heads of the statistical services within the respective organizations. Acutely aware that agreed indicators would shape development policy coordination and determine the high-priority statistics that national and international statistical agencies would collect, they took great care in choosing—within the usual confines of agency stakes and commitments—the best forty-eight indicators then available to measure eighteen targets that defined the eight goals.

In addition to rejecting the MDG framework in general, the Bush administration later objected that one of the forty-eight indicators to measure progress on the goals and targets mentions the international goal of seven-tenths of 1 percent of wealthy nations' GDPs for development assistance, even though the Bush administration itself affirmed this internationally agreed upon target at the Monterrey Conference in 2001. But the larger source of US concern was that the goals reflected a hardening of soft law. Unlike the other Millennium Goals in peace and security and humanitarian protection, the MDGs have moved from very soft law—an Assembly resolution—to hard international public policy endorsed officially by operative institutions such as the World Bank, the IMF, the World Health Organization, and others—bypassing an interstate treaty or agreement.

If we measure the hardness of law by how obligatory and either delegated or precise it is,[43] then the MDGs have indeed significantly hardened the issues they cover in the Millennium Declaration. The Millennium Declaration started out as a soft Assembly resolution: vague, hortatory, and undelegated in substance. When the member states delegated the formulation of a Road Map Report to the Secretariat they set in motion a hardening process that resulted in the MDGs. While all eight MDGs have textual support in the principles and authority provided by various parts of the declaration, they became precise targets and measurable indicators. More important, they became the template for development for the World Bank, IMF, and UN. They shape the Poverty Reduction Strategy Papers and the UN Development Assistance Frameworks that measure the progress of developing countries seeking development grants and loans from the WB, IMF, and UNDP. They increasingly influence bilateral donors. In effect, the MDGs are quasi-legislative in the developing world, a long step from the rhetoric they appeared to be in September 2000.

If the pushback from sovereign states was most striking in the US campaign to undermine the MDGs and in Ambassador Bolton's perfervid rhetoric, the more subtle and important pushback came from a much more important source. The goals were hortatory; the key source of implementation was national, not UN system. Whether the developing countries would actually adopt them in practice and whether the developed world would respond with a genuine partnership to create additional international opportunities for growth were the two decisive factors in what has become their mixed record of success.[44] This was soon reflected in the natural development of country-level MDGs that mixed existing development planning with the MDG framework. In some national development plans, the MDGs served as rhetorical window dressing; in others they played an operational role and became the operative framework for assessing the World Bank's Poverty Reduction Strategy Papers and UNDP's UN Development Assistance Framework.[45]

CONCLUSIONS: CENTRALIZATION, INTEGRATION, AND SPILL AROUND

Supranationality is one key element of a legal order that separates a constitution from an ordinary treaty. It opens the door to complex agency on behalf of the member states in which authoritative decisions are taken without continuous sovereign consent.

It is worth recalling, however, that in the UN constitutional order these decisions are inherently asymmetric, different for some states than for oth-

ers. This is clearly the case in Charter-based allocations of rights and responsibilities in peace and security, but it appears whenever the underlying
circumstances of state inequality cannot be rectified by the formal equality
of multilateral institutions.

Supranationality, as outlined at the beginning of the chapter, appears
in the manner in which seemingly pure administrative-delegated agency
becomes inherently political when it delegates executive powers (2a).
Secretary-General Dag Hammarskjöld famously anticipated this, and the
practice of secretaries-general in active mediation in international disputes
has confirmed it.

Supranationality also emerges in disputes over who controls the budget
and financing (2b). It shapes debates over who interprets the implementation of international treaties (the ICJ or the US Supreme Court) and in the
representation and transfer of authority (3) assertion of Security Council authority to legislate counterterrorist responsibilities to all states. It shows up
again in delegation of duties to the Secretariat (2a) when it leads to inadver-
tent transfers of authority (3) within the wider UN system, as illustrated by
the evolution of the Millennium Development Goals.

In the larger picture, we see that some constitutions centralize, integrate,
and acquire authority. They start out with sovereign capacities like the US (a
strong executive, a federal legislature with direct effect over citizens in the
component states) and grow dynamically by formal amendment and informal interpretation, as *McCulloch* (necessary and proper), the Civil War amendments, and the activist interpretation of the Commerce Clause federalized
both national authority and civil rights.[46]

Sometimes, in world politics, the constitutions of international organizations, starting out weak, deepen supranationality. They start with very weak
constitutions and yet grow dynamically as did the European Union, with the
leadership of the ECJ and the support of the pro-integrationist members. Spill-
over cooperation begat the need for more cooperation, which was met. A dialogue of exit and voice spiraled toward more integration, as curtailing selective
exit was matched by increased voice, and curtailing veto-prone voice by
majority voting was met by selective safeguard exit. Each step ratcheted up
central authority.[47] Where the stakes are high, where a small group of leading
states is closely connected and shares some basic goals, there supranational
and centralized solutions to cooperation problems sometimes grow.[48]

The evolution from GATT to WTO (from unanimity to authorize enforcement to unanimity to prevent the enforcement of a trade ruling) is a classic instance, even though the scope of WTO authority remains narrow and shallow. (WTO does not enforce trade law; it authorizes states to choose whether or not to enforce and thus sanctioned states to comply or simply bear the costs of breach.)[49]

The UN, on the other hand, did not, as did the US, begin with federal statal aspirations. It even lacked the community-building aspirations of some of the founders of the EU. But it did begin with significant supranational authority (Chapter VII). But unlike the other institutions, it changed but did not increase centralized supranational powers; instead of spilling over into deeper cooperation, it spilled around.[50] Every growth in central authority and independence met effective sovereign pushback. Integration did not spill over into more demands for greater integration and central authority, as increasing trade integration can encourage demands for greater currency and labor integration. Instead, it resulted in decentralization and disaggregation to protect national autonomy.

The political science principles of rational design suggest that the UN—unlike the EU and US—may have too many members, too little interdependence, and too much diversity to sustain an effective centralized supranational authority.[51] Its 193 members do not need to "hang together" (they do not, in Benjamin Franklin's immortal phrase, otherwise "hang separately"). And doing so is especially difficult, given diversity. Diversity is constitutionally guaranteed by the Charter in Article 2.4, guaranteeing territorial integrity and political independence, and 2.7, unless international peace and security is threatened. Contrarily, the US Constitution "Guarantee Clause" (IV:4) guarantees that all US states are similarly republican. Similarly, too, the EU guarantees that all candidate members are all democracies that meet the *acquis communautaire* standards. The UN Charter requires only that all states be "peace-loving" (Article 4.1)—and who isn't?

Where a constitution reflects a hegemonic constitutional moment, the constitutional order can either build or erode. The US supported early European integration, and the coalition of Germany and France pushed it forward. The UN Charter in 1945 reflected the predominance of the United States at the end of World War II. But the Cold War stymied institutional growth, and US hegemonic decline pushed evolution in the opposite direction.[52] When hegemony declines, supranationality generates sovereign pushback. Weak as it was and is, the UN "constitution" of 1945 still authorizes more than the members are now prepared to cede.

Ironically, the Charter is thus an especially precious institution, a reservoir of "political capital" for centralized legality- and legitimacy-granting purposes. Legal institutions in general can facilitate communication in the solving of coordination problems by providing pre-contracted pathways that make negotiations more efficient by establishing rules and common knowledge.[53] Supranationality leverages these factors by delegation to experts and by representation (which means that fewer parties need agree and the few can authorize the agreement of the whole). Legitimacy also supplements these sources of efficacious coordination by enhancing deference to decisions made within and by the institution.[54]

Thus the Charter is precious partly because of its supranational institutionalization of legitimacy, partly because it is so difficult to reform today, and especially because it incorporates in law more global governance than most states would otherwise agree to authorize. Today neither the US nor EU would rationally design a constitution as *weak* as the ones they were born with. And today, the world would not design something as *strong* as the UN Charter of 1945, one that cedes authority in international security to a Security Council of fifteen, even with a Permanent Five veto, or that grants budget authority—in legal effect, global taxation—decisions to a two-thirds vote of a General Assembly of all states without a veto. Practice is of course quite different from legal authorization, much more deferential to sovereignty concerns and much more subject to great power manipulation. But should a will for global governance develop, there already is an institutional way, outlined in the Charter.

Notes

This essay is part of a project organized by Ian Shapiro, and it draws on another paper, presented at a conference organized by Jeffrey Dunoff and Joel Trachtman and later published in their edited volume *Ruling the World: Constitutionalism, International Law and Global Governance* (London: Cambridge University Press, 2009). The other paper includes a section on UN peace operations, not included here, but lacks the discussion of counterterrorism. I am grateful for the comments of two anonymous reviewers and José Alvarez, Samantha Besson, Allen Buchanan, Jeffrey Dunoff, Ryan Goodman, Brian Graf, Dan Green, Stuart Kaufmann, Robert Keohane, Jack Levy, James Morrow, Steven Ratner, Eric Stein, and Joel Trachtman. I have benefited from the excellent research assistance and editorial suggestions of Geoffrey S. Carlson and David Hambrick of Columbia Law School, Abbas Ravjani of Yale Law School, and Svanhildur Thorvaldsdottir of the International Peace Institute, and from the assistance in preparing the text from Olena Jennings. A shorter version of this essay was delivered as the Harold Jacobson Lecture at the University of Michigan.

1. For this point, see José E. Alvarez, *International Organizations as Law-Makers* (New York: Oxford University Press, 2005), 67–68.

2. In re Pharmaceutical Mfrs. Ass'n of S.A. 2000 (3) BCLR 241 (CC) para. 44 (S. Afr.).

3. Frank Michelman, "What Do Constitutions Do That Statutes Don't (Legally Speaking)?" in Richard Bauman and Tzvi Kahana, eds., *The Least Examined Branch: The Role of Legislatures in the Constitutional State* (New York: Cambridge University Press, 2006).

4. Laurence R. Helfer, "Constitutional Analogies in the International Legal System," *Loyola of Los Angeles Law Review* 37 (2003): 207–8.

5. For a discussion of these differences, see Thomas Franck, "Is the UN Charter a Constitution?" in Jochen Frowein et al., eds., *Verhandeln für den frieden* (New York: Springer-Verlag, 2003), 95. And for an analysis of the various contract-like features of international law, see Robert Scott and Paul Stephan, *The Limits of Leviathan* (Cambridge University Press, 2006), especially chapters 5 and 6. For a wide-ranging survey of the debate on Charter constitutionalism, see Bardo Fassbender, "The United Nations Charter as Constitution of the International Community," *Columbia Journal of Transnational Law* 36 (1998): 529.

6. Interestingly, when James Madison considered what distinguished a "league or treaty" from a "constitution," he defined two traits: supremacy and non-breachability. That is, a constitution is superior even over later law and a breach by one state does not excuse compliance by others. Both these constitutional features are also found in Charter law. But Madison thought that they could be produced only by popular ratification rather than by treaty ratification, the Charter route. See James Madison, *Notes of Debates in the Federal Convention of 1787*, ed. E. Koch (New York, 1969), 352–53 and discussion in Murray Forsyth, *Unions of States* (Leicester: University of Leicester Press, 1981), 65.

7. I do not mean that the UN is sovereign over the member states; the UN is an organization of the member states. Thomas Franck calls this "institutional autochthony," stressing the independence (*competenz competenz*) of the institution. That is part of what I want to convey, but even more I want to highlight the ability of the institution and some members to bind all without explicit, case-by-case consent from each member.

8. States have reserved "essential" domestic jurisdiction to themselves and granted the UN international jurisdiction, in Article 2.6.

9. Oscar Schachter and Christopher C. Joyner, *United Nations Legal Order* (New York: Cambridge University Press/American Society of International Law, 1995), 170, note 4. ("Sometimes some Member States may start interpreting a particular provision in a certain way and after a while that interpretation becomes accepted by other Member States and by the organization itself. For instance, in connection with a resolution in the Spanish case, the Soviet Union's representative announced that in order not to veto an Australian resolution, he would abstain from vote. 1946 Security Council Official Records . . . 243 (39th mtg). Since then, despite occasional objections, it has been recognized in more than 100 cases that, despite the requirement in Article 27.3 that decisions of the Security Council on nonprocedural matters be made 'by an affirmative vote of seven members including the *concurring* votes of the permanent members' [emphasis added], a voluntary abstention of permanent members is not considered to be a veto.")

10. I build on but adapt for the UN a recent treatment of these issues by Dan Sarooshi, *International Organizations and Their Exercise of Sovereign Powers* (New York: Oxford University Press, 2005) and the analysis of accountability in Ruth Grant and Robert Keohane, "Accountability and Abuses of Power in World Politics," *American Political Science Review* 99 (2005): 1–15. I have benefited as well from José Alvarez's *International Organizations as Law-Makers* (New York: Oxford University Press, 2005).

11. There are, of course, a number of other ways to explore the constitutionality of the UN system, including, for example, comparing the UN to other regional and international organizations, analyzing the separation of powers among its principal organs, or exploring the role played by the International Court of Justice as a constitutional interpreter. Some of these examples, including exploring a constitu-

tional mind-set as Andreas Paulus does (building on the work of Marti Koskienniemi) or constitutional-ism as procedural standards, are taken up by other authors in the *Ruling the World* volume. The introduction by Dunoff and Trachtman is a particularly incisive survey of the issue.

12. Reparations for Injuries Suffered in the Service of the United Nations, Advisory Opinion, 1949 ICJ 174, Summary (Apr. 11).

13. Leland Goodrich and Edvard Hambro, *Charter of the United Nations: Commentary and Documents* (Boston: World Peace Foundation, 1949), 183–91.

14. See Certain Expenses of the United Nations (Article 17.2 of the Charter), Advisory Opinion, 1962 ICJ 151 (July 20).

15. See the interpretation by Stanley Hoffmann, "A World Divided and a World Court Confused: The World Court's Advisory Opinion on UN Financing," in Lawrence Scheinman and David Wilkinson, eds., *International Law and Political Crisis* (Boston: Little, Brown, 1968), 251.

16. Ruth Russell, "United Nations Financing and the Law of the Charter," *Columbia Journal of Transnational Law* 5 (1966): 68.

17. The late Oscar Schachter of Columbia Law School is widely credited for this creative, "constitutional" interpretation made when he was UN deputy legal adviser. For discussion, see Leo Gross, "Voting in the Security Council: Abstention from Voting and Absence from Meetings," *Yale Law Journal* 60 (1951): 209; and Myres S. McDougal and Richard N. Gardner, "The Veto and the Charter: An Interpretation for Survival," *Yale Law Journal* 60 (1951): 258–92.

18. Case Concerning Questions of Interpretation and Application of the 1971 Montreal Convention Arising from the Aerial Incident at Lockerbie (*Libya v. UK; Libya v. US*), Provisional Measures, 1992 ICJ 114 (Apr. 14). See also Michael Plachta, "The Lockerbie Case: The Role of the Security Council in Enforcing the Principles of *aut dedere aut judicare*," *European Journal of International Law* 12 (2001): 125.

19. See Derek Bowett, "The Impact of Security Council Decisions on Dispute Settlement Procedures," *European Journal of International Law* 5 (1994): 1; Michael Reisman, "Constitutional Crisis in the United Nations," *American Journal of International Law* 87 (1993): 83.

20. Dag Hammarskjöld, "The International Civil Servant in Law and Fact," Oxford Lecture (May 30, 1961), in Wilder Foote, ed., *Dag Hammarskjöld: Servant of Peace* (New York: Harper and Row, 1962), 329 (hereafter "International Civil Servant").

21. Report of Rapporteur of Committee I/2 on Chapter X (The Secretariat), 3–4, Doc. 1155 I/2/74(2), 7 U.N.C.I.O. Docs. 386 (San Francisco, 1945).

22. Secretary-General Annan waged a quiet campaign to persuade member states to present three nominees for "their" open posts. He did not always succeed. For a valuable survey of the role, see Simon Chesterman, ed., *Secretary or General: The UN Secretary-General in World Politics* (New York: Cambridge University Press, 2007).

23. Dag Hammarskjöld, "The Development of a Constitutional Framework for International Cooperation," in *Servant of Peace*, 259, note 19.

24. "International Civil Servant," 351–52, note 19.

25. "International Civil Servant," 344.

26. See Ian Johnstone, "The Role of the Secretary-General: The Power of Persuasion Based on Law," *Global Governance* 9 (2003): 441; Mark W. Zacher, "The Secretary-General and the United Nations' Function of Peaceful Settlement," *International Organization* 20 (1966): 724–49.

27. See Paul Szasz, "The Security Council Starts Legislating," *American Journal of International Law* 96 (2002).

28. For a thorough study of the legislative features, see Axel Marschik, "The Security Council as World Legislator? Theory, Practice, and Consequences of an Expanding World Power," Institute for International Law and Justice Working Paper 2005/18 (www.iilj.org). For an interpretation stressing the debate among legal scholars, see Ian Johnstone, *The Power of Deliberation* (New York: Oxford University Press, 2010), chapter 5. And for another valuable interpretation putting the debate in a

political, Schmittian context, see Jean Cohen, "Constitutionalization of International Law," *Constellations* 15 (2008).

29. José Alvarez, "Hegemonic International Law Revisited," *American Journal of International Law* (October 2003) 97: 4, pp. 873–88.

30. See Kristen Boon, "Coining a New Jurisdiction," *Vanderbilt Journal of Transnational Law* 41 (October 2008) for an account of jurisdictional expansion.

31. Kim Lane Scheppele, "The Migration of Anti-Constitutional Ideas: The Post-9/11 Globalization of Public Law and the International State of Emergency," in *The Migration of Constitutional Ideas*, ed. Sujit Choudhry (Cambridge: Cambridge University Press, 2006), 347–73.

32. 354 U.S. 1 (1957) ("This Court has . . . repeatedly taken the position that an Act of Congress, which must comply with the Constitution, is on a full parity with a treaty, and that when a statute which is subsequent in time is inconsistent with a treaty, the statute to the extent of conflict renders the treaty null. It would be completely anomalous to say that a treaty need not comply with the Constitution when such an agreement can be overridden by a statute that must conform to that instrument.") The question of whether the UN Charter constrained US law was also addressed by *Diggs v. Schultz* (470 F2d *Diggs v. Shultz*) in 1972.

33. Misa Zgonec-Rozej, "Kadi and Al Barakaat v. Council of the EU and EC Commission," *ASIL Insights* 12, no. 22 (October 28, 2008) http://www.asil.org/insights/volume/12/issue/22/kadi-al-barakaat-v-council-eu-ec-commission-european-court-justice. And also see http://courtofjustice.blogspot.com/2008/09/joined-cases-c-40205-p-and-c-41505-p-c-.html and http://eulaw.typepad.com/eulawblog/2008/09/terrorism-the-security-council-and-ec-law-journal.cfm.

34. By implication, the EU had become a "United States." It had moved from a treaty (subject to UN Charter, Article 103) to a constitution that within its borders was, like the US Constitution, superior to a treaty. The UN Charter, like other treaties, could only override "secondary" EU legislation (the legal equivalent of federal legislation and by the "later in time" rule).

35. Letter from PR India to SC, April 27, 2004, UN Doc. S/2004/329 of April 28, 2004, cited in Marschik, *Security Council*, 18.

36. United Nations Millennium Declaration, G.A. Res. 55/2, UN Doc. A/RES/55/2 (Sept. 8, 2000), available at http://www.un.org/millennium/declaration/ares552e.pdf.

37. G.A. Res. 55/162, paragraph 18, UN Doc. A/RES/55/162 (Dec. 18, 2000). Secretary-General Kofi Annan assigned me the task of putting together this report when I arrived at the UN as his special adviser in March 2001, three months after the General Assembly authorization.

38. The interagency team was remarkable for the quality of the cooperation it engendered. It included representatives from the OECD, UN DESA's Statistical Office, WB, IMF, UNICEF, UNFPA, other agencies, and the UNDP. Jan VanderMoortele, a development expert with UNDP, co-chaired meetings with these development and statistical experts. Much of the consensus the group achieved was the product of scientific experts, long frustrated by bureaucratic rivalry, persuading their principal agencies on the need for rational policy cooperation.

39. The actual source of US discontent seemed to me to be a policy disagreement. The Bush administration was launching the Millennium Challenge Account (MCA), which made governance reform (marketization, private enterprise, fiscal balance, open current accounts for international finance, democratization) the precondition for foreign aid. Once the political appointees in the administration had come into office in late 2001, they saw the MDGs as a reflection of the "old ideology" of northern responsibility for southern poverty and an ideological platform to make the shortfall in foreign aid the excuse for development failures. My response was that the MDGs were a "thermometer" designed to measure progress, not a strategy. There was no reason not to portray the MCA as the best (US) strategy for meeting the MDGs. This argument was welcomed in the US Treasury but not in the State Department.

40. John Bolton, *Surrender Is Not an Option* (New York: Simon and Schuster, 2007), 209–10.

41. Reproductive health was inserted into the MDGs—as a target in goal 5 (maternal health), not as a goal in itself—at the 2005 summit review conference for the MDGs. The US protested.

42. Much of my time in the spring and summer of 2001 was spent discussing and amending drafts of the emerging MDGs with various UN delegations including the G77 developing country caucus, the European Union caucus, and the US delegation in order to make sure that the necessary votes for approval would be forthcoming when the Road Map Report was presented to the General Assembly in the following September.

43. See Kenneth Abbott and Duncan Snidal, "Hard and Soft Law in International Governance," *International Organization* 54 (2000): 421.

44. See the annual MDG reports of Secretary-General, the latest being *The Millennium Development Goals Report 2008*, http://www.un.org/millenniumgoals/2008highlevel/pdf/newsroom/mdg%20reports/MDG_Report_2008_ENGLISH.pdf.

45. See, e.g., International Monetary Fund, PRSP Fact Sheet (Apr. 2008), http://www.imf.org/external/np/exr/facts/prsp.htm (last visited Nov. 25, 2008). ("PRSPs aim to provide the crucial link between national public actions, donor support, and the development outcomes needed to meet the United Nations' Millennium Development Goals [MDGs].")

46. Of course, other factors, including the weakness of national parties, also played a key role in determining the federal-state balance in the US, as noted in Jenna Bednar, William Eskridge, and John Ferejohn, "A Political Theory of Federalism," in John Ferejohn, Jack Rakove, and Jonathan Riley, eds., *Constitutional Culture and Democratic Rule* (Cambridge: Cambridge University Press, 2001), 223–67. For the evolving balance between centrifugal and centripetal tendencies, see Daniel Deudney, "Sovereignty, Arms Control, and the Balance of Power in the American States Union," *International Organization* 49 (Spring 1995): 191–228, and for a general discussion of federal constitutionalism as a process linking many different constitutional orders, from global to national, see Carl Friedrich, *Limited Government: A Comparison* (Englewood Cliffs, NJ: Prentice Hall, 1974) especially chapter 5 on "federal constitutionalism."

47. J. H. Weiler, "The Transformation of Europe," *The Constitution of Europe* (Cambridge: Cambridge University Press, 1999), 10–101, and Geoffrey Garrett et al., "The European Court of Justice, National Governments, and Legal Integration in Europe," *International Organization* 52 (1998).

48. See, for classic sources, Mancur Olson, *The Logic of Collective Action* (Cambridge: Harvard University Press, 1965), and Duncan Snidal, "The Limits of Hegemonic Stability Theory," *International Organization* 39 (1985): 579.

49. For discussion, see Warren Schwartz and Allan Sykes, "The Economic Structure of Renegotiation and Dispute Resolution in the World Trade Organization," *Journal of Legal Studies* 31 (2002): 179–204.

50. For the related literature on regional integration, see Joseph Nye, *Peace in Parts* (Boston: Little, Brown, 1977), William Wallace, *Regional Integration: The Western European Perspective* (Washington: Brookings, 1994), and Philippe Schmitter, "Central American Integration: Spill-Over, Spill-Around, or Encapsulation," *Journal of Common Market Studies* 9 (1): 1–48.

51. For a valuable development on the rational design of institutions that discusses these attributes, among others, to suggest how institutional designs can overcome coordination and cooperation challenges, see Barbara Koremenos, Charles Lipson, and Duncan Snidal, "The Rational Design of International Institutions," *International Organization* 55 (2001): 761–99.

52. For hegemonic cooperation, see Robert Keohane, *After Hegemony: Cooperation and Discord in the World Political Economy* (Princeton: Princeton University Press, 1984); John Ikenberry, *After Victory: Institutions, Strategic Restraint, and the Rebuilding of Order after Major Wars* (Princeton: Princeton University Press, 2001); and Fred Hirsch and Michael Doyle, "Politicization in the World Economy: Necessary Conditions for an International Economic Order," in Hirsch, Doyle, and Edward Morse, eds., *Alternatives to Monetary Disorder* (New York: Council on Foreign Relations/McGraw Hill, 1977), 9–64.

53. See Keohane (1984); Kenneth A. Oye, "Explaining Cooperation under Anarchy: Hypotheses and Strategies," *World Politics* 38 (1985): 1–24; and Cheryl Boudreau, Mathew D. McCubbins et al., "Making Talk Cheap (and Problems Easy): How Political and Legal Institutions Can Facilitate Consensus" (June 30, 2010) at SSRN http://ssrn.com/1555763.

54. But this does not make struggles over the operational meaning of legitimacy unimportant, as Ian Hurd explains in his account of the diplomatic wrangling over Libya sanctions, Ian Hurd, *After Anarchy: Legitimacy and Power in the United Nations Security Council* (Princeton: Princeton University Press, 2008), chapter 6.

Chapter 2

Lost in Transition?
The League of Nations and the United Nations

M. Patrick Cottrell

A t the final League of Nations Assembly in April 1946, Lord Robert Cecil proclaimed, "The League is dead; long live the United Nations!" This proclamation suggests a dynastic relationship between the two landmark institutions whereby part of the DNA of the League of Nations was passed on to its progeny. However, the connections between the United Nations and its institutional predecessor are largely downplayed in the modern international relations literature, in part because the League has been so widely discredited as a failure. But relegating the League of Nations to the proverbial dustbin of history would be a mistake, particularly in light of its potential to illuminate questions regarding the evolution of ideas and their implications for the United Nations and beyond.

The story of the League of Nations in the broader institutional landscape is more complex and contradictory than many give it credit for being. On one hand, the League experience caters to a realist narrative.[1] It was widely delegitimated in several core respects: its lack of great power support, its failure to stop aggression in the run-up to World War II, and the naïve utopianism that it symbolized. On the other hand, most of the founding ideas enshrined by the League provided the basis for its successor institution. The general lack of attention to institutional precursors and political context results in the tendency to view the League experience in a time-bound fashion. Yet many of

the ideas initially codified by the League—commitments to collective security, multilateralism, and self-determination—germinated during the interwar years and emerged even stronger in its successor.

This essay seeks to place the United Nations in a political developmental
context,[2] with a specific emphasis on the relationship with its League of Nations predecessor. In so doing, it advances two central arguments. First, the
United Nations did not emerge in a vacuum. The political debates that surrounded its negotiation and implementation took place on a historical continuum, tempered by past experiences. Second, for all of the criticism that
the League of Nations received, it paradoxically reinforced and even strengthened the consensus behind the idea of collective security. For this reason the
League, in ways that many overlook, continues to influence international
relations today. While many refer to the League of Nations as an "experiment," very few make the same reference to the UN. This may be in part
because the United Nations had the benefit of learning from the League
experience. As Woodrow Wilson himself remarked, "The League must
grow, it cannot be made."[3] Indeed, the League idea continues to grow today
in the modern United Nations.

ORIGINS OF A GRAND EXPERIMENT

The basic story of the League is well known.[4] The victors of World War I
founded the League of Nations in 1919 as the first international institution to
embody the collective security approach to the use of military power. Proponents envisioned it as the structure that could enable the "war to end all
wars" slogan to ring true. However, from its inception, the League of Nations experienced a string of severe setbacks that undermined its legitimacy
and ultimately resulted in its collapse. While there can be no doubt that the
League failed in many fundamental respects, it also left a lasting impact on
future events that transcends the conventional wisdom.

Weighing this impact first requires the recognition that the League experiment rested on ideas that had been percolating long before the Great War. The
notion of an international peace organization had floated in human con-
sciousness for centuries and with growing momentum during the previous
hundred years. The Concert of Europe that emerged from the last grand peace
in 1815, coupled with the incremental growth of international public unions
and peace movements that crested at The Hague conferences of the turn of the
century, helped warm the international community to multilateralism and
dispute resolution. Without these precursors, it is difficult to foresee how the

idea of a League of Nations could have occupied such a prominent and legiti-mate place in the negotiations of a postwar order. The League that emerged was more formal than the Concert, with explicit design features to promote the peaceful resolution of dispute, and it served as the touchstone organization for a web of affiliated multilateral agencies. Its creation was further legiti-mated by the utter devastation of the war, a sobering reminder of the impera-tive to seek an organization possible of securing a durable peace.

Somewhat paradoxically, the political context in which the lead negotiators operated also confounded efforts to create a workable organizational founda-tion upon which such a peace could rest. The League of Nations reflected a direct and pragmatic by-product of the political moment in time in which it was conceived, a bargain that embodied a significant degree of hypocrisy. The League's mandate system contradicted its claimed commitment to self-determination, as the framers of the Covenant were far more interested in Central and Eastern Europe than the rest of the world. The League made the commitment to collective security of its members, but because of prevailing political conditions, contained neither the procedural apparatus nor the sub-stantive commitment of the powerful to provide it. The League's intellectual architects embraced universal application of League principles yet afforded a special place for democracies and imposed a victor's peace on the losers of World War I, who would be an important piece of any postwar order. These themes would again loom large in the formation of a successor institution.

The League, in short, represented a landmark development in the course of human history by providing an institutional and cognitive blueprint for peace and security. But the resulting bargain, forged in a time of great upheaval and wariness, contained tensions from the outset that would fuel legitimacy con-tests and forever mar its existence. What is most notable, however, is not how these tensions led the façade of the League to crumble but rather how the League idea emerged from the disaster of the interwar years even stronger.

THE SHADOW OF THE LEAGUE AND THE MAKING OF THE UN

It is not novel to suggest that the League of Nations and United Nations have a common lineage.[5] But in the run-up to creating the United Nations, most sought to avoid such a comparison. Not only was this avoidance for psycho-logical reasons given the League's "aura of failure," but it was also because it struck a sensitive chord with the superpowers whose support was vital to any successor institution.[6] According to Inis Claude, the understatement of the League-UN bond represented a "a tactic to avoid offending the Russians, who had been alternately distrustful of, disillusioned with, and outraged by the old organization, and the Americans, who would have found it embarrassing to join an organization from which they had so long made it a cardinal point of national policy to abstain."[7]

It is partly the symbolism of the League as a deeply flawed institution and ultimately a disastrous failure, however, that made it such a crucial factor in creating the UN. According to one study of the Dumbarton Oaks Conference, where the United States, Russia, and Britain devised plans for the United Nations, "So fully was the League perceived to have failed that its main role in the planning for the conference—as, indeed, at the conference itself—was to serve as an example of what the new organization ought not to do."[8] Such a repudiation of the League makes it, on first glance, surprising that the failure did not derail efforts to reconstitute an international organization with universal aims to preserve world order.

Why did the great powers persevere?[9] First, they needed to establish an international order that dealt with postwar realities: a greater number of smaller states demanding equality and recognition, a global economy in tatters, and the desire for some mechanism to prevent yet another world war. Second, the League had such prominent defects that it was easy to think that they could be remedied. By serving as a foil in some key respects, the League experience informed some important changes in the negotiating process leading to its successor. Third, despite the obvious shortcomings of the League, it remained at the time a "continuing legal fact; several of its organs remained active during the war, and it thus offered a valuable element of continuity . . . officials were anxious to profit as much as possible from experience under the Covenant. The most careful study was therefore given to all aspects of the organization and activities of the League of Nations."[10] Where the League Covenant proved useful, sections were freely borrowed; flaws or gaps revealed by experience provided focal points for change.

This double-edged relationship begs the question: What would the United Nations have looked like if the League of Nations never existed? The framers of the UN drew at least three lessons from the League experience that would influence the negotiation and design of what continues to serve as the world's principal security institution.

Lesson #1: Construct the Political Moment before Being Held Hostage to It

One of the more remarkable features of the creation of the United Nations is that it was largely negotiated during the war. Like the League before it, the

UN emerged as part of a major structural shift in the international system and the political opportunity that accompanied it. However, for reasons suggested above, the League suffered from the outset because it reflected the prevailing historical and political constraints of the time in which it was negotiated. The experience of the peace treaty of Versailles highlighted the risks and dangers of waiting until the war was over to commence negotiations on a postwar order, when domestic political constraints and alliances might form to prevent agreement or water it down. The principal architects of the United Nations recognized these potential pitfalls and took steps early on to prevent the same fate for a successor institution.

In the first joint articulation of postwar aims from the United States and Britain, the fourth and fifth points of the Atlantic Charter, stated that they will "endeavor, with due respect for their existing obligations, to further the enjoyment by all States, great or small, victor or vanquished, of access, on equal terms, to the trade and to the raw materials of the world which are needed for their economic prosperity . . . and desire to bring about the fullest collaboration between all nations in the economic field with the object of securing, for all, improved labor standards, economic advancement and social security."[11] In January 1942, twenty-six governments, including China, Poland, and many Latin American states signed the "Declaration of the United Nations,"[12] elaborating further the basic principles and underscoring the imperative of continued cooperation of all major anti-Axis powers if there were to be an effective postwar security organization. The Moscow Conference of October 1943 produced a formal commitment, with Soviet support, to the idea of "establishing . . . a general international organization, based on the principle of sovereign equality of all peace loving states." The Allied powers reaffirmed this commitment four weeks later at the Tehran Conference. Thus by the time the principal framing states of the draft UN Charter convened in Dumbarton Oaks in 1944, much of the groundwork had already been laid.

From the Atlantic Charter to the finalized Charter that opened for signature in San Francisco in April 1945, the Allied powers made it a priority to negotiate a blueprint for the postwar order before an armistice was struck. By applying lessons from the League in the early negotiations of a United Nations, the framers secured a more credible commitment from the great powers early on and decoupled the organization from any peace settlement, thereby brightening the prospects for a sustained order.

Proceeding with negotiations for a United Nations during wartime also served an important domestic political purpose for the Allied powers, and the United States in particular. Whereas Wilson underestimated domestic political opposition and overestimated support for the League at home, FDR sought to preempt such a situation by locking in a framework for a postwar order before renewed isolationism and political obstructionism could take effect.[13] FDR was no stranger to the political controversy in the United States over the League of Nations. He witnessed firsthand the political downfall of Woodrow Wilson and gave hundreds of speeches offering a more prudent defense of the League as the Democratic vice presidential candidate in 1920, before losing the race and the League. The imperative of securing support within the US electorate for a policy conversion from isolationism to internationalism thus occupied FDR from the outset and colored US proposals for a United Nations, which served as touchstone documents in the negotiations at Dumbarton Oaks and in San Francisco.[14]

Thus, the League of Nations experience made at least two major differences before the United Nations even had a name. It prompted US and British officials to think about the postwar order even as it was very uncertain that they would be in a position to determine it. And it underpinned the determination of FDR and his team to cultivate the domestic political base predisposed to internationalism and supportive of a growing world role for the United States. Without the League experience and the legwork on the part of the Allies so early in the war that it prompted, it is likely the UN Charter negotiations would have been much more subject to influence from the prevailing political winds in the wake of FDR's death and as controversies over perceived Soviet expansionism in the postwar order gained steam.

Lesson #2: Reconcile Power with Principle

The lack of great power support to match the empty "war to end all wars" rhetoric throughout the early years of the League haunted the framers of the successor institution. The League's failure to prevent aggression that led to another world war inspired a commitment to prudence. Although negotiations continued to rest on the principle of peaceful dispute settlement and produced a pledge to settle differences without the use of force, the overarching questions facing the UN framers dealt fundamentally with the management of power. How could a new institution lock in the participation of the victorious military powers upon the disarmament of the Axis? How would the new institution work to prevent Axis powers from recovering powers of aggression and pave the way for their eventual membership? Should future aggression occur by any state, would the successor institution have sufficient capability to respond? The eventual answers to all three of these questions reflected an even stronger commitment to the idea of collective security.

Similar to the League, Article 1 of the UN Charter underscores the importance of "collective measures for prevention and removal of threats to the peace, and for suppression of acts of aggression" and seeks "peaceful means . . . for settlement of international disputes or situations that might lead to a breach of peace." But the process of constructing the UN Charter reflected a very different philosophical sentiment than the Kantian idealism so prevalent in the League discourse.[15] The sine qua non of the UN negotiations was to bind all the great powers to the new system. If the great powers and particularly the United States were invested members in the new UN, the overall imbalance of power that fueled World War II would be corrected. As US Secretary of State Cordell Hull wrote, "However difficult the road may be, there is no hope of turning victory into enduring peace unless the real interests of this country, the British Commonwealth, the Soviet Union, and China are harmonized and unless they agree and act together. This is the solid foundation upon which all future policy and international organization must be built."[16]

Accomplishing this goal meant first negotiating with Stalin and the Soviet Union. The Soviets, FDR believed, represented the pillar of collective security that Wilson had in mind little over two decades earlier. Yet getting Soviet buy-in would be no easy task. The Soviets bargained hard in pursuit of their interests in a postwar order, using the disproportionate Soviet suffering in World War II (a startling 27 million Soviet military and civilian deaths from war, disease, and war-induced famine compared to the 550,000 military deaths suffered by the United States by the end of the war) and agreement to creating the United Nations as leverage in negotiations to receive reparations for their sacrifice. In a draft cable to Churchill in September 1944, FDR wrote, "We are in agreement . . . as to the necessity of having the USSR as a fully accepted and equal member of any association of the great powers formed for the purposes of preventing international war. It should be possible to accomplish this by adjusting our differences through compromise by all parties concerned."[17]

Yoking power to the new global collective security organization also meant learning from the League's procedural shortcomings. Not only did the great powers need to be members of the institution, but they also needed an operational apparatus that was less prone to inaction. Any successor needed to replace the unanimity clause of the League, which required the aggressor to agree to action against itself, with a majority vote in the Security Council and providing measures for more military and economic teeth.[18] In these respects, the UN Charter incorporated the League proscription on the use of force for national objectives and requirements for dispute resolution, but it also empowered the new Security Council to decide whether the international peace was threatened, whether sanctions were to be imposed, and if so, the nature of the sanctions, including military force. Most important, such decisions would be binding upon all members of the United Nations, even those who voted against the measures.[19]

There was a catch to this bargain, of course. Each of the great powers—the United States, the Soviet Union, Britain, France, and China—would be granted permanent membership on the Security Council and veto power over any resolution. For some, this was a necessary bargain to make in order to sustain the UN. The British commentary on the Charter reflects this logic. "The successful working of the United Nations," it reads, "depends on the preservation of the unanimity of the Great Powers; not of course on the details of policy, but on its broad principles. If this unanimity is seriously undermined no provision of the Charter is likely to be of much avail."[20] Leland Goodrich made the further point in 1947 that much of the updated structure of the UN, the creation of a specialized Security Council with the P5 veto in particular, reflected knowledge of how the League operated informally. Thus, the Charter authors not only learned from observing the failures of the League but incorporated elements of League practice that were evolving in efforts by its leaders to get it to work despite existing structural problems.[21]

Smaller states contested the veto in San Francisco but were essentially presented with an ultimatum of no veto, no UN.[22] Proponents of the veto used the League Council to justify its existence. According to the statement made by the "Big Four" in support of the proposed Security Council, "As regards to the permanent members, there is no question under the Yalta formula of investing them with a new right, namely, the right of veto, a right which the permanent members of the League Council always had."[23] The goal was to make "the operation of the Council less subject to obstruction than was the case under the League of Nations rule of complete unanimity."[24] The justificatory discourse reassured other states that the proposed system reflected a spirit of cooperation with little distinction between the smaller and larger states, save the "responsibility" of the great powers to provide for international security.[25]

Consequently, in trying to avoid the fate of its League predecessor in a historically conditioned fashion, the UN collective security framework contained inherent tensions. It created essentially two classes of states: those that had complete sovereignty due to their veto powers and those that did not. The General Assembly represented a mouthpiece for world opinion, but it had no effective powers over the more oligarchic Security Council. Franklin Roosevelt recognized that this arrangement cut both ways, cautioning that a "policeman would not be . . . very effective . . . if, when he saw a felon break into a house, he had to . . . call a town meeting to issue a warrant before the felon could be arrested," while acknowledging that enforcement aims had to "depend on foundations that go deep into the soil of men's faith and men's hearts."[26]

Despite these tensions, it is difficult to envision the UN collective security apparatus being constructed as such without the League experience. The great powers and their domestic political constituencies would not have been as invested in the idea, and the lesser powers would have had a more difficult time agreeing to a veto. Amid a second world war, the League not only provided a focal point of negotiations, but it helped generate political will required to come to such a landmark agreement.

Lesson #3: Make the Successor More Universal, with a Greater Emphasis on Development and Human Rights

While the reinvigoration of the idea of collective security privileged the powerful, the reaffirmation of the ideas of multilateralism and self-determination in light of the League experience underscored the importance of creating a more universal institution. Consider first multilateralism.

In one respect, the League experience in the interwar years underscored the dangers of isolationism. The Great Depression and the connection between economic unrest and political extremism illustrated the ineluctable interdependence of modern nation-states, especially in the mind-set of FDR and the United States.[27] Isolationism did not represent the realistic option that it had two decades earlier, and the pursuit of multilateralism would play a major part in any postwar order. In another, less heralded, respect, the commitment to multilateralism might be most pronounced in areas where the legitimacy of the League did not come under major fire. Many of the more functional multilateral agencies that developed in conjunction with the League of Nations made significant advances in international cooperation during the interwar period.[28] It became clear that the multilateral project was not only worthwhile but should be expanded. The UN system that emerged from San Francisco in 1945 made at least three notable advances on the idea of multilateralism.

First, in the most pronounced evidence of a commitment to multilateralism, the United Nations quickly incorporated in near-identical form, and in some cases expanded, many of the League's foundations. For instance, the World Health Organization succeeded the League Health Organization; the United Nations Educational, Science, and Cultural Organization (UNESCO) took over from the Committee on Intellectual Cooperation; the International Court of Justice replaced the League's Permanent Court; and the Trusteeship Council inherited the responsibilities of the Mandates Commission.[29] Others have highlighted important yet overlooked linkages between the League and the creation of the IMF and the Bretton Woods system, in which "ideas shaped by painful experience in one institutional setting can be transmitted into another."[30] The commitment to multilateralism endured, and considering the vast expansion of governance arrangements in the wake of World War II, it emerged even stronger.

Second, the UN negotiations were relatively more inclusive than the League's. To be sure, the San Francisco Conference was not without political controversy, including disputes over whether states such as Argentina (formally neutral in the war but considered by some to be pro-Nazi) should be able to participate, ongoing concerns of Soviet "domination" of Poland and its implications for UN membership, and disagreements over principles that would guide the handling of dependent peoples.[31] Despite these controversies, each characteristic of the time period in which negotiations were conducted, the conference ultimately hosted delegations from over fifty countries and allowed them a greater role in orchestrating the broader UN system, particularly in the social, economic, and cultural areas. The pursuit of a more universal arrangement became a significant source of legitimacy for the emerging order, as the resulting organization could better provide a vehicle for expression of the opinion of humankind.

Third, the UN Charter capitalized on procedural advances in multilateral cooperation developed in the League context. One of the more innovative aspects of the League's operation was the establishment of its secretariat, organized along the lines of an international civil service, with members drawn from over thirty countries. The League's secretariat became viewed as an international authority for the quality of its officials and as a unique repository of information and experience relating to international organization and administration. Its secretary general could thus serve as a mouthpiece for much of the world. Moreover, the establishment of an annual League Assembly, at which small and medium powers could raise issues, give their views on world developments, and put pressure on the great powers, represented a major step forward. In these and other respects, the League's structure and methods were, to a considerable degree, adopted by the United Nations.[32]

The League experience in dealing with the principle of self-determination, though never formally enshrined in the Covenant, also figured prominently in the construction of its successor. The fundamental tension that existed in 1919 between promoting emerging norms in minority rights and self-determination and preserving state sovereignty, all the while maintaining a mandate system, colored the League experience throughout and remained a crucial issue at the dawn of the United Nations.[33] The League had particular difficulty "adjudicating, managing, and delimiting relations of sovereignty"[34] and struggled to find a way to neutralize the potential for nationalist conflict inherent in a system based on a principle of self-determination. As a result, "nearly as many people lived under foreign rule as during the days of the Austro-Hungarian Empire, except that now they were distributed across many more, much weaker, nation-states which, to undermine stability even further, were in conflict with one another."[35]

Nevertheless, the idea of self-determination also appeared to be reinforced and expanded in the formulation of its successor, despite the considerable trauma of the interwar years. Nationalism and independence movements in previously "dependent" areas would remain a major feature of the postwar international landscape. Ruth Russell, a participant in the negotiations of the UN Charter and author of perhaps the most detailed account of its creation, wrote, "American officials recognized that, valid or not, a widespread conviction existed among such peoples that independence would of itself bring about an era of welfare and prosperity. In this situation, the mandates system under the League of Nations, although providing a precedent for international action to assist dependent peoples, was felt to require considerable strengthening before it could serve the needs of the postwar world."[36]

Although there is certainly reason to doubt the actual willingness of the great powers to pursue lofty goals of self-determination worldwide, the universal language they wrote into the UN Charter would formalize these sentiments.[37] Whereas the Covenant only briefly made reference to self-determination in Article 10, references occur throughout the Charter, an indicator that the idea was more widely accepted and less politically sensitive than it was at the inception of the League.

There are a few reasons for this shift. Attitudes toward imperialism evolved from 1919 to 1945. According to Mazower, the League order was predicated on "a basically imperial conception of world governance in which leadership would be provided by mature statecraft of great powers, with newcomers brought in when deemed 'civilized.' "[38] The League remained Eurocentric, undergirded by a mandate system and protective of less developed peoples rather than welcoming them as equals.[39] Neither the United States nor the Soviets saw need for a mandate system that preserved a hierarchy that no longer reflected the balance of power, nor did the greater numbers of smaller countries that populated the San Francisco Conference in 1945. Consequently, the new United Nations Charter renamed mandates as "trusteeships," gave the General Assembly more supervisory power over these trusteeships than had existed in its predecessor, and strengthened the petitions process, including a provision for on-site visits by the Trusteeship Council.[40]

The events of the interwar years and World War II also prompted a new, more vigorous approach to human rights. This shift was reflected in a "rapid retreat from international action within a framework of group rights or its minority protection, and a replacement by a framework of universal human rights instead."[41] The more pronounced dedication to rights was interwoven in the Charter and included references to racial equality that were notably absent from the League discourse.

Although strengthened commitments to self-determination and equal rights might have facilitated the decolonization process, they did not relieve all of the preexisting tensions of the interwar years. Sovereignty remained a bedrock principle of the UN system, but could the United Nations simultaneously promote universal rights of individuals while preserving the sovereignty of existing states? In promoting the principle of self-determination, how would the UN define its involvement in conflicts where borders were contested or unclear as the decolonization process took hold? And with democratic principles embedded in the principled discourse of rights and self-determination, could the United Nations promote democracy in an order underpinned by sovereign equality? Nevertheless, it is again difficult to imagine this momentum toward universalism, manifested in terms of multilateralism and self-determination, without the League experience to build on.

CONCLUSION

The League of Nations gave way to the United Nations, but the slate was not wiped clean in the transition. The League experience, despite its operational failure as an experiment in collective security, had a much more formative impact on the United Nations than many recognize. Historian Charles Webster, who was also closely involved with the UN negotiations as practitioner, wrote that although "we pretended we had a tabula rasa and were receiving direct inspiration," the new organization "bore a most embarrassing resemblance to its predecessor. Again and again, without any direct reference to what had transpired during twenty years at Geneva, we arrived, surprisingly, at results that might seem to have been modeled on the earlier organization."[42]

Webster indicates a more subconscious, yet complementary, stream of cognitive influence—one that can be traced to the enduring power of the ideas that underpinned the creation of the League in the first place. Whereas the League and the UN differed in their means of implementing collective security, they were unified in their devotion to the idea. Even such prominent critics of the League as E. H. Carr did not contest the idea of collective security per se, but rather the means by which it could be achieved.[43] The new United Nations sought above all else to resolve the tension between great power interests and Wilsonian ideals. Had it not been for ideas first packaged together and formalized on a grand scale in the League, the UN would likely "have been—at best—a short-lived alliance of the victorious Great Powers."[44]

The United Nations itself thus needs to be viewed as part of a temporal evolutionary process. The UN drew lessons from the League experience in a contingent fashion, as the League had drawn lessons from institutional developments that preceded it. In some respects, such as on collective security matters, the League served as a foil. In others, such as the continued development of the economic and social agencies appended to the League (and henceforth the UN), it served as an inspiration. The United States, too, used its own League experience as a key reference point in the imperative of locking in domestic support for an internationalist postwar order early and shoring up an international coalition for a successor to the League so early in the war.

Of course, the League and the UN also have considerable differences in both their creation and their features, in part because they are by-products of the political context in which they were conceived. The League Covenant was drawn up after World War I ended; the United Nations was devised while war was ongoing. The Covenant was negotiated in conjunction with the Treaty of Versailles, but the UN was drafted at a conference especially convened for that purpose. The League lacked great power support and had weak enforcement apparatus; the great powers comprised the backbone of the UN Security Council, which could respond to aggression with force if it so chose. The League emphasized minority rights; the UN stressed universal rights. Yet most of these differences are contingent in that they simultaneously reflect the exigencies of a certain time period and a conscious effort to learn from the recent past.

But the influence of the League does not stop with its institutional successor. Both the League and the United Nations were experiments that seek ways to realize the promise of the same fundamental ideas. Indeed, multilateralism, self-determination, and collective security continue to construct debates over the preferred means to provide for international peace and security to this day. Might time and circumstance one day lead the international community toward another (perhaps post-Westphalian) institutional experiment? "Treating traditional sovereignty as a cornerstone for the United Nations," UN Intellectual History Project co-founder Thomas Weiss declares, "is a fundamental structural weakness in urgent need of replacement."[45] If such a day comes, the United Nations experience will almost certainly play a central role in the transition.

Notes

The author wishes to thank Eleanor "Nelly" Evans and Megan Schwab for valuable research assistance related to this chapter.

1. See, for instance, F. H. Northedge, *The League of Nations: Its Life and Times, 1920–1946* (Leicester: Holmes and Meier, 1986) and John Mearsheimer, "The False Promise of International Institutions," *International Security* 19 (1994): 5.

2. Political developmental analyses often employ a historical institutionalist approach, which is distinguished by its emphasis on temporality and the structural context of institutions. From this perspective, history is not simply a chain of independent events but rather a continuous stream in which timing and sequence matter a great deal. For an overview, see, e.g., Kathleen Thelen, "How Institutions Evolve: Insights from Comparative-Historical Analysis," in James Mahoney and Dietrich Rueschemeyer, eds., *Comparative Historical Analysis in the Social Sciences* (New York: Cambridge University Press, 2002). For an international relations perspective, see Orfeo Fioretos, "Historical Institutionalism in International Relations," *International Organization* 65 (2011).

3. Quoted in Thomas J. Knock, *To End All Wars* (New York: Oxford University Press, 1992), 41. On Wilson's role in the League formation, see Knock, *End All Wars*, and John Milton Cooper, *Breaking the Heart of the World* (New York: Cambridge University Press, 2001).

4. For classic accounts of the League of Nations history, see F. P. Walters, *A History of the League of Nations* (1952) and Northedge, *Life and Times.*

5. See, for instance, Leland Goodrich, "From League of Nations to United Nations," *International Organization* 1 (1947): 3–21; and Gerhard Niemayer, "The Balance Sheet of the League Experiment," *International Organization* 6 (1952): 537–58. For a more recent account, see Mark Mazower, *No Enchanted Palace: The End of Empire and the Ideological Origins of the United Nations* (Princeton: Princeton University Press, 2009). For a cautionary analysis about mapping the League experience onto the modern UN, see Alexandru Grigorescu, "Mapping the UN–League of Nations Analogy: Are There Still Lessons to Be Learned from the League?" *Global Governance* 11 (2005): 25–42.

6. Ruth B. Russell, *A History of the United Nations Charter: The Role of the United States, 1940–1945* (Washington: Brookings Institution, 1958), 208.

7. Inis L. Claude, *Swords into Plowshares; the Problems and Progress of International Organization* (New York: Random House, 1971), 66. See also J. D. Armstrong, Lorna Lloyd, and John Redmond, *From Versailles to Maastricht: International Organization in the Twentieth Century* (New York: St. Martin's Press, 1996).

8. Robert Hilderbrand, *Dumbarton Oaks: The Origins of the United Nations and the Search for Postwar Security* (Chapel Hill: University of North Carolina Press, 1990). Quoted in John Ruggie, "Third Try at World Order? America and Multilateralism after the Cold War," *Political Science Quarterly* 109 (1994): 558.

9. See Armstrong, *Versailles to Maastricht*, and Claude, *Swords into Plowshares.*

10. Russell, *Role of the United States*, 208.

11. Atlantic Charter found at http://avalon.law.yale.edu/wwii/atlantic.asp.

12. According to L. Emmerji, Richard Jolly, and Thomas Weiss, *Ahead of the Curve? UN Ideas and Global Challenges* (Bloomington: Indiana University Press, 2001), the very name United Nations reportedly was a suggestion that Roosevelt proposed while Churchill was in the bathtub.

13. For general accounts of the origins of the UN with a focus on FDR, see, e.g., Townsend Hoopes and Douglas Brinkley, *FDR and the Creation of the U.N.* (1997), and Stephen C. Schlesinger, *Act of Creation* (Boulder: Westview Press, 2003). See also Russell, *Role of the United States*; Hilderbrand, *Dumbarton Oaks*; and Lawrence Finkelstein, "From Seeds to System: the UN Charter," *UN Chronicle* (March 2005).

14. Russell, *Role of the United States*, chapter IX.

15. Armstrong, *Versailles to Maastricht*, chapter 3.

16. Memoirs of Cordell Hull quoted in Claude, *Swords into Plowshares*, 75.

17. Fdr-69: Draft Cable, FDR to Churchill Re: Soviet Participation in the United Nations Organization, September 27, 1944. FDR Presidential Library, Hyde Park, NY, important documents collection.

18. See, for example, documents from FDR's "safe" file at http://docs.fdrlibrary.marist.edu/psf/box5/a69d02.html.

19. Ramesh C. Thakur, *The United Nations, Peace and Security: From Collective Security to the Responsibility to Protect* (Cambridge: Cambridge University Press, 2006), 29.

20. Quote in Armstrong, *Versailles to Maastricht*, 64.

21. I am grateful to one of the anonymous reviewers for raising this point. See Goodrich, *From League of Nations to United Nations*, especially 10–16.

22. Armstrong, *Versailles to Maastricht*, 64.

23. UNCIO 1945, 11, p. 713, quoted in Ian Hurd, *After Anarchy: Legitimacy and Power at the United Nations* (Princeton: Princeton University Press, 2007), 100. The "Big Four" refers to the United States, the Soviet Union, Britain, and China. France, which was not a sponsor but a permanent member in the Security Council plan, supported the statement.

24. Ibid.

25. Hurd, *After Anarchy*, 101.

26. Quoted in H. M. Jaeger, "'World Opinion' and the Founding of the UN: Governmentalizing International Politics," *European Journal of International Relations* 14 (2008): 600–601.

27. See John Ikenberry, *After Victory: Institutions, Strategic Restraint, and the Rebuilding of Order after Major Wars* (Princeton: Princeton University Press, 2001), chapter 6, and Paul Kennedy, *Parliament of Man* (2006), 30, among others.

28. For example, the Permanent Court of International Justice, established under Article 14 of the League Covenant (though not formally part of the League), started work in 1922 and was kept busy from the outset. Between 1922 and 1940 the PCIJ dealt with twenty-nine contentious cases between states and delivered twenty-seven advisory opinions, showing that a standing international court had at least some role to play in international politics. See http://www.icj-cij.org/court/index.php?p1=1&p2=1.

29. Susan Pedersen, "Back to the League of Nations," *American Historical Review* 112 (2007).

30. Louis Pauly, "The League of Nations and the Foreshadowing of the IMF," *Essays in International Finance, International Finance Section Princeton University*, no. 201 (1996).

31. I am grateful to an anonymous reviewer for the suggestion to include references to these controversies, which reflect the changing politics of the time. For additional detail see, for example, Schlesinger, *Act of Creation*.

32. Some also point to similarities with the European Economic Community. See Ruth Henig, *The League of Nations: The Makers of the Modern World* (New York: Haus Publishing, 2010).

33. Mazower, *No Enchanted Palace*.

34. Pederson, *Back to the League*, 1099.

35. Henry Kissinger, *Diplomacy* (New York: Simon and Schuster, 1994), 241.

36. Russell, *Role of the United States*, 211.

37. Article 1 declares that the UN seeks "to develop friendly relations among nations based on respect for principle of equal rights and self-determination of peoples." Article 2 states that the "organization is based on the principle of sovereign equality of all its Members" and that "nothing . . . shall authorize the UN to intervene in matters which are essentially within the domestic jurisdiction of any state."

38. Mazower, *No Enchanted Palace*, 194–95.

39. Ibid.

40. Armstrong, *Versailles to Maastricht*, Claude, *Swords into Plowshares*, and Mazower, *No Enchanted Palace*. See UN Charter, Chapters XII and XIII.

41. Ian Clark, *Legitimacy in International Society* (New York: Oxford University Press, 2005), 137.

42. Charles Webster, quote in Armstrong, *Versailles to Maastricht*, 62.

43. Martha Finnemore and Kathryn Sikkink, "International Norm Dynamics and Political Change," *International Organization* 52 (Autumn 1998): 889.

44. Jean Siotis, "The Institutions of the League of Nations," in *The League of Nations in Retrospect: Proceedings of the Symposium Organized by the United Nations Library and the Graduate Institute of International Studies Geneva* (New York: W. de Gruyter, 1983), 30.

45. Thomas G. Weiss, *What's Wrong with the United Nations and How to Fix It* (New York: Polity Press, 2009), 32.

Chapter 3

Has the UN Lived Up to Its Charter?

Stephen Schlesinger

Global security was the central issue that brought fifty nations together in San Francisco to draft the UN Charter in the spring of 1945. After suffering two catastrophic world wars within just twenty or so years, the three leaders of the anti-Nazi alliance—Franklin Roosevelt, Winston Churchill, and Josef Stalin—all agreed, along with the heads of some forty-seven other nations, to form a body that would bring an end to global violence and protect all states from future aggression. The organization would be designed as a universal one to assure common security around the globe. The single-minded focus of the meeting in California would center on collective security— indeed, every other issue at the conference was treated with considerably less urgency. Finally, such was the emphasis on preventing the outbreak of war that the original three sponsors of the gathering insisted that all governments, no matter what their ideological stripes—dictatorships, theocracies, Communist states, and republics—be admitted to the organization to assure the peace.

The conference opened as the war was ending, arousing exceptional worldwide interest. Delegates gathered in San Francisco began work on the most important organ to be established at the 1945 UN conference—the Security Council. The Council, as the only body within the UN that dealt with conflict issues and whose decisions were binding on all member states, triggered the most intense controversy at the meeting. A dispute ensued over the fact that the drafters of the UN Charter designated only five members of the Council—the United States, the USSR, China, France, and Great Britain—as permanent members of the body with veto powers. The rest of the states on the Council were relegated to serving two-year rotating terms without the right of veto. The argument for the exclusive role of these five prominent nations was that as the most powerful countries in the world in 1945 (despite wartime ruination in France and China), they were the countries most likely to contribute troops and resources to UN enforcement actions and thus should be able to decide on which missions they were willing to risk the lives of their soldiers.

Fierce opposition to this arrangement erupted at the conference from smaller states. But the US and Soviet Union soon convinced the lesser nations of the need for this agreement, not necessarily by reasoned argument— though Washington did strenuously point out that the US Senate would not enact the UN pact without the veto—but by the blunt threat of otherwise abandoning the conference altogether. The least influential countries, in time, retreated from their position, realizing that without the most powerful states as members of the UN, the organization would be ineffective; with them inside, there was at least a chance that these formidable nations might be subject to world pressure or, at a minimum, moral condemnation. The debate over the veto, though, never ended. Over the past seven decades, the smaller nations have launched periodic efforts to expand the number of veto states or to abolish the veto outright, emphasizing that the Security Council as created in 1945 no longer represents the power realities of our contemporary era. None so far have succeeded.

The permanent powers, meantime, had disputes of their own over the veto. The Russians privately demanded that the veto be made absolute, so that any of the five countries could bring a halt to discussion of critical matters in the Security Council. The three Western nations and China resisted this position, arguing that there should be free and unhindered talks about any crisis; they were additionally fearful that if such talks were not allowed in the Council, the smaller states might reject the notion of a global security body and quit the conference. The Western position eventually prevailed when Roosevelt's successor, Harry Truman, personally intervened with Stalin to convince him to abandon his campaign for the absolute veto.

Soon after the conference ended, however, the Cold War intervened. The Security Council fell victim to the poisonous ideological distrust between the US and the Soviet Union. Over the next forty-five years, Moscow or Washington, in turn, using either vetoes or intimidation, blocked the other from taking Council action and—except on a few occasions—the body remained on the sidelines. This stalemate, in effect, ended the promise of cooperation among the wartime victors that Roosevelt and Truman—and the drafters of the Charter—had depended on.

At first, though, the five veto nations attempted to demonstrate a capacity to respond creatively to crises, primarily by drawing on the UN's mandate to keep the peace. They soon championed the practice of "peacekeeping"—an operational concept never mentioned in the original UN Charter. In 1948, for example, the Security Council placed UN peacekeeping troops in Jerusalem to reinforce a cease-fire between Israel and its adversaries, and, in that same year, it assigned UN observers to patrol the 38th parallel dividing the two antagonistic states, North and South Korea. But, as the strains between Washington and Moscow grew, the Security Council dallied on undertaking any enforcement actions. One exception came in 1950, with the USSR boycotting the Council, when the UN authorized the dispatch of coalition forces to repel an attack on South Korea by North Korea.

The UN's most prominent role during the Cold War, was seeking to halt warfare—or at least keep it in abeyance. In 1956, during the Suez Crisis, after fighting occurred between Egypt and Israel, the UN deployed peacekeeping troops to enforce a cease-fire between the two countries; still later on, it took similar measures to enforce cease-fires in Cyprus in 1964, the Dominican Republic in 1965, and Lebanon in 1978, among other states. After the end of the Cold War, the UN increased these missions. In the first five years of the twenty-first century, the number of UN peacekeepers grew by nearly 500 percent. Overall in the UN's history, there have been over sixty peacekeeping operations.

Following the San Francisco meeting, the UN adopted other practices to circumvent the stalemates of the Cold War years. As it had done with peacekeeping, the UN embraced multiple innovative measures never enumerated in the UN's founding document. These included, for example, policing missions, preventative diplomacy, sanctions, conflict resolution, troubleshooting, fact-finding, arbitration, conciliation, mediation, sanctions, weapons interdictions, drug controls, disarmament, observer missions, and arms inspections. This array of UN operational modes were reminders that the organization's Charter was a flexible enough instrument to be able to adapt to changing circumstances and respond to fresh threats to peace.

But when the USSR imploded in 1990 the Security Council finally came back fully into play, fulfilling the original promise of the founders to collectively deter aggression. At that time, the Council authorized a UN force to expel Saddam Hussein's Iraqi troops that had invaded Kuwait. Thereafter the Council began to reclaim a vital presence on the world scene. It imposed sanctions on states like Iran and North Korea over nuclear armaments. It brought peace to places like Guatemala, El Salvador, Mozambique, Angola, Namibia, East Timor, and Kosovo. However, it did not always stop strife—for example, in areas of combat like Rwanda and Srebrenica and Sri Lanka. Nor did it always prevent unilateral military interventions by its permanent member states, most notably, in failing to halt the American invasion of Iraq in 2003. Still, throughout its entire history, the organization could claim to have successfully tamped down multiple conflicts around the planet, any of which might have spun out of control and led to a third world war. For that alone, the founding fathers indisputably won vindication for their global venture.

Today the challenge before the United Nations remains the control of weapons of mass destruction in the hands of non-state actors and terrorists. This especially chilling matter for the contemporary era—where lethal and uncontrolled adversaries have the potential to use nuclear, chemical, or biological bombs to destroy entire civilizations—was not foreseen in San Francisco. To thwart such attacks, the UN has, over time, acted to strengthen a cluster of treaties like the Nuclear Non-Proliferation Treaty, the Test-Ban Treaty, the Chemical Weapons Convention, and related pacts, as well as to upgrade its own measures tracking the operations of extremists. In the principal UN agency dealing with nuclear matters, the International Atomic Energy Agency, efforts have been under way to better thwart the nuclear schemes of rogue states. The UN, in this way, has remained faithful to the warrant of the 1945 founders to seek to reduce murderous conflict around the planet.

In particular, with its ability to offer warring parties a neutral forum or special emissaries to help settle differences, the UN through the offices of the Secretary-General or the Security Council or the General Assembly has assisted many times in bringing about pacific outcomes in disputed situations, especially in helping to avoid potential confrontations between nuclear-armed powers. Indeed, the UN's greatest, if most unheralded, contribution may be its role in helping diminish the overall incidence of violence around the world—an explicit injunction of the UN's architects.

One report by the University of British Columbia and published in 2005 showed that political violence, except for international terrorism, declined worldwide after the early 1990s.[1] By 2003, it found there were 40 percent fewer conflicts than in 1992. The number of genocides and other mass slaughter of civilians also declined by 80 percent. Not all of this was solely attributable to the UN, but the organization's presence, with its diplomatic outreach and security apparatus and its challenges to member nations to live up to the Charter, went some ways toward encouraging the reduction of confrontation around the globe. The UN's original planners might today argue that war prevention is indeed being carried out in the ways they had envisaged.

But not all of the goals advanced at San Francisco garnered immediate broad agreement. As in the veto disputes, for example, the framers of the UN Charter did not find consensus on whether regional organizations should be part of the UN's overall structure. This dispute caused one of the most heated debates at the San Francisco conclave. The Latin American bloc, which had formed a body of its own before the meeting, insisted that the UN must recognize its new organization as a sub-unit of the Charter before it would take part in the proceedings. The Latins threatened to abandon the UN conference if they did not get their way. The US, which had sought to centralize all power in the UN itself and regarded the concept of regional organizations as potentially weakening the UN's authority, opposed the Latin demand.

Eventually Washington backed down from its stance, fearful that the Latin American nations might desert the conference. The US and the Latin states in due course adopted Article 51, which permits the formation of regional bodies within the UN system. In the years since its enactment, this provision has led to the establishment of such pacts as NATO, SEATO, and the Warsaw Pact. In practice, however, regional organizations proved to be weak and unreliable entities—with the exception of NATO—though recently others like the African Union and the Arab League have started to come more into their own. Now, given the more frequent latter-day empowerment of regional bodies, the UN has, on occasion, been able to shift its responsibilities for troops and civilian supervision to these local alliances, saving the world body considerable expense for deployment and other financial burdens.

Another area of deep disagreement in San Francisco came over decolonization. The issue surfaced initially on how to deal with the lands left stateless from World War II, as well as how to handle the territories controlled by the old League of Nations. The arguments revolved around three categories of possessions—the League's holdings, conquered wartime territories, and parcels voluntarily offered up by states to the UN. To resolve these questions, the UN drafters created the Trusteeship Council. The colonial powers, especially the British, the French, and the Dutch, among others, fought hard to retain their prewar possessions. The US insisted on holding onto the Pacific islands it had seized from the Japanese. Acrimonious discussions among the permanent member states ensued. On many occasions, these disputes grew so overwrought that they threatened to break up the conference.

A compromise was eventually reached. Lands voluntarily turned over to the UN were exempted from dispute. In deference to colonial overlords, however, the UN drafters allowed those states to retain their territories, have the word "independence" dropped from the trusteeship section, and limit the "dependent peoples" to at best a restricted "self-government." The US, though, quietly inserted the word "independence" in other parts of the Charter, desirous of moving the agenda for decolonization forward. The resulting formula, while offering a mixed resolution, soon led to many changes in the world map. Indeed, within thirty years or so dozens of new sovereign states came into existence. Not all were the direct consequence of the UN's handiwork, but all came in under the UN's umbrella, more than doubling the roster of UN members and reshaping the geography of the globe. Washington, for its own fortunes, retained the strategic islands from Japan while not being made subject to further UN scrutiny.

Meantime, a further row arose in San Francisco over the jurisdictional reach of the newly established International Court of Justice. Under the UN Charter, every member state was an ipso facto party to the court. But a debate ensued over whether the court would have compulsory jurisdiction or voluntary jurisdiction over disputes among member states. The US opposed the "compulsory" option on the grounds that such a UN treaty could never pass the US Senate. Many smaller nations wanted obligatory jurisdiction, though, to protect themselves against stronger states. Eventually the US won the argument. This meant that the court's jurisdiction to issue binding judgments was limited to instances in which countries themselves consented to the court's authority. Still, the court's very existence assured that certain norms and rulings might become part of the political and juridical practices of various countries.

There were arguments, too, in San Francisco over the powers of the Secretary-General. The conference gave mixed and somewhat ambiguous responsibilities to the Secretary-General. Under Article 99, it made the UN chieftain the "chief administrative officer" of the UN and permitted him to "bring to the attention of the Security Council any matter which in his opinion may threaten the maintenance of peace and security." This provision led to much controversy. Some critics said it did not amount to anything of importance. However, subsequent Secretary-Generals, especially Dag Hammarskjöld and others, used the language to enhance their authority and their ability to maneuver freely in various crisis situations.

In addition, the General Assembly and the Security Council, on occasion, entrusted certain special duties to the Secretary-General, adding further to his potential outreach. Still Secretary-Generals remained subject to Charter limitations—primarily to the fact that the five permanent member states held ultimate power over their office. The UN's overseer also owed allegiance to all 193 statutory member states of the organization. As a final limitation, the organization never gave the Secretary-General the normal governance prerequisites of taxing power, a sitting army, legislative prowess, or broad powers of command. At his best, he was a moral leader; for most of his time, a consensus figure; sometimes, an incidental observer.

Nonetheless, over the next sixty-five years, each Secretary-General gradually expanded the parameters of his office. The first Secretary-General, Trygve Lie, using the language of Article 99, pressed the Council in 1946 to demand that Russian troops leave Iran. The Soviets objected to his intervention, but Lie won the argument, legitimizing the right of the UN head to lay out crucial issues for the Council's agenda. Lie's successor, Dag Hammarskjöld, displayed other remarkable improvisational talents that enlarged the office's range even more. At several junctures he acted independently, on the basis of General Assembly resolutions, for example, to free American airmen captured by the Chinese and later to assemble a UN peacekeeping operation during the Suez Crisis.

Subsequent UN heads, like U Thant and Kurt Waldheim, were less agile. But as the Cold War period eased, Javier Pérez de Cuéllar, then Secretary-General, was able to bring an end to the bloody Iran-Iraq war by challenging the Council to reach "a meeting of the minds" over the conflict. By 1990, with the fall of the Berlin Wall, the role of the Secretary-General grew more expansive. The Security Council acted in unison for the first time in forty-five years, as noted, to oust Iraqi invaders from Kuwait.

In the 1990s, Secretary-General Boutros-Boutros Ghali, launched numerous new peacekeeping and enforcement missions. But in doing so, he moved too fast and was often criticized for his high-handed manner. In particular, he was unable to convince the Security Council to stop genocidal wars in Rwanda in 1994 and Srebrenica in 1995. Only with Kofi Annan's assumption of the office in the mid-1990s did the UN begin to regain a balance, purpose, and standing. Annan embraced new initiatives, such as humanitarian intervention, the Millennium Development Goals, a global business compact, and a major reform movement in 2005 that helped to substantially reorganize the UN. Annan himself, however, was damaged by a number of UN financial scandals. But the historical record has shown that, over six decades, the seven Secretary-Generals have generally elevated rather than diminished the authority of their office.

In San Francisco the creators of the UN ardently sought, in addition, to establish common standards of decent human behavior by which all societies could be measured, especially in the field of civil rights. The UN Charter hence embraced the notions of fundamental civil rights, justice, international law, social progress, self-determination, lack of discrimination, and "larger freedom" for all. Toward that end, the UN set up the Economic and Social Council (ECOSOC), which in 1946 established the UN Commission on Human Rights that, for two decades, followed a policy of promoting human rights and helping write human rights treaties. In 1948, the UN adopted the Universal Declaration of Human Rights. All these noble initiatives however were stymied by the Cold War.

Then, in 1967, the UN began to single out and name human rights violators. By 1993, it had established the Office of the UN High Commissioner for Human Rights. In 2006, the UN finally did away with what many critics saw as an erratic and flawed UN Commission on Human Rights and replaced it with a smaller but still evolving Human Rights Council. The earlier body had selected its members in secret negotiations in behind-the-scenes meetings; the new one makes selections through openly competitive elections. The newer council also has the authority to examine human rights abuses in all states, not just some. Finally the new council meets year-round, not just for six weeks as the commission had.

During these years, the UN also set up war crimes tribunals. In the final quarter of the twentieth century, it helped establish the International Tribunals for Yugoslavia and Rwanda, the Special Court for Sierra Leone, the Special Tribunals for Cambodia and Lebanon, and the Ad-Hoc Court for East

Timor. In addition, the General Assembly, more controversially, helped to create in 1998 via the Rome Statute, the International Criminal Court (ICC), designed to prosecute leaders of regimes who, among other crimes, committed atrocities against their own citizens. As of 2012, 121 states had become members, 32 others had signed the ICC treaty but had not yet ratified it, and 40 had neither signed nor ratified the pact. The original sponsors of the UN Charter, including China, Russia, and the United States, did not enlist in the ICC—a reminder that great powers often sidestep entities that restrict their authority. Even without their involvement in the court, however, these states held, through the Security Council, considerable sway over the body. The Council, for example, can refer cases outside ICC jurisdiction to the court, and it can also defer cases for a year or, if they want, indefinitely from being heard by the court.

The UN's focus on human rights, though, has shown persuasive results. In 1950, Freedom House found that 33 percent of the world's population lived under free or partly free rule; by the year 2000, that figure had jumped to 64 percent.[2] One should not necessarily substantiate a correlation between the existence of the UN and the spread of greater democratic governance, but one could, nonetheless, plausibly argue that new countries wishing to join the most exclusive association of nations on earth (over 140 additional ones following the UN's birth) have to pay closer attention to the ideals embodied in the UN Charter in order to be accepted as members.

A further mission of the UN's authors at San Francisco was the development of international law. The calamities of two world wars had left the global legal system in tatters. It was a larger hope of the designers of the Charter that the UN could help reestablish legality around the planet. The founders, for example, quickly reconstituted a world court (the International Court of Justice) on the ruins of the League of Nation's Permanent Court of International Justice. The UN also took upon itself, under Article 103 of the Charter, to champion the further advancement of world law by sponsoring, over the decades, some 300 global pacts dealing with issues ranging from airline safety, maritime procedures, slavery, global crime, drug contraband, sexual trafficking, communications policy to the control of nuclear weapons (the Non-Proliferation Treaty and the comprehensive Test-Ban Treaty) and the regulation of small arms traffic.

The UN's ability to expand the global legal system was helped by its capacity to bring together states around specific concerns. The General Assembly would typically take an issue, convene a conference around it, induce participating states to agree on a law or set of laws to deal with the problem, and then issue a set of principles or a range of legal instruments for ratification by the legislatures or parliaments of member states. Once the state-based bodies pronounced favorably on the new laws, they were enshrined as international law. The legal record of the last six decades shows that the UN has, indeed, fulfilled one of the most important goals of its framers.

The UN has also played an enormous role as a norm entrepreneur. Acting as the guardian of the principles embodied in the Charter, the UN has sought adherence to its universal precepts in various ways by all states. For example, the UN Charter has set our standards in building a more cohesive international community and ensuring the orderly development of global human life. This is particularly true in instances where the UN has helped support sovereignty, self-determination, and territorial integrity in, for example, overseeing the decolonization process and also in helping failed states to recover and rebuild their societies. In other cases, the UN has promulgated norms on the use of force and developmental aims for all its member nations.

Because it has been viewed as a universal organization, the UN has been able to legitimate moral codes for all countries, most pertinently via the 1948 Universal Declaration of Human Rights. The UN, recognized worldwide as an arbiter of disputes and a regulator of state behavior, has, in a way, become the overall spokesman for community interests against rogue states or self-seeking individuals. Its relative autonomy has, in fact, allowed it to push forward societal ideals, statistical frameworks, and political mores. Still, as the UN is based on the old Westphalia system of nation-states, it is not necessarily able to apply its rule-making to non-state actors or even sometimes to the inner workings of the UN itself.

A further imperative at San Francisco was to prevent future economic collapse from undermining countries. The UN originators, extremely conscious of the devastating impact that the worldwide depression of the 1930s had had on societies around the globe, sought to prevent financial breakdowns from leading to impoverishment, failed states, terrorism, and war. For this reason, they created the Economic and Social Council (ECOSOC) to head off economic calamity. To signify its importance in the organization, the founders accorded this council the same standing as the Security Council. Although ECOSOC did not prove to be a success in the way the drafters originally envisaged, it helped launch a series of other UN initiatives, including a revived International Labor Organization in 1946 (which took over from the League of Nations' body set up in 1919); the establishment of the United Nations Development Program (UNDP) in 1965, with its extensive aid programs and its influential human development reports in the 1990s; the founding of the World Trade Organization, which replaced the General Agreement on Tariffs and Trade (GATT); the UN's Habitat agency dealing with urbanization; Kofi Annan's Global Compact between business and the UN; the Millennium Development Goals of 2000; and the Peace-building Commission and the Democracy Fund of 2005 to stabilize failing states.

Here, again, the delegates in San Francisco would have applauded the efforts by the organization to assure overall sustainable development. But in truth the UN still plays a minor role in nurturing economic growth around the globe. More and more, the leading industrial states have turned to the World Bank, the International Monetary Fund, and regional banks, as well as ad hoc organizations like the G-8 and now the G-20, to coordinate economic recovery and prosperity. For the most part, ECOSOC, the UNDP, Habitat, and the Millennium Development Goals remain on the sidelines.

Finally, the founders set out to deal with natural disasters, health crises, and environmental degradation. In face of starvation, displaced persons, over-population and food scarcity, tsunamis, cyclones, floods, earthquakes, and other natural disasters, as well as man-made debacles like war, the UN set up the Food and Agricultural Organization (FAO) in 1945, UNHCR (the UN High Commissioner for Refugees) in 1950, and the World Food Programme in 1962. In face of pandemics and chronic illness like malaria, the World Health Organization came into being in 1948 and has, among other things, eliminated smallpox, is on the verge of wiping out polio, and is now fighting to overcome AIDs.

In the face of environmental calamities of various sorts, the UN established the World Meteorological Organization in 1950 to observe and report on weather and climate conditions. In 1972 the UN convened the Stockholm Conference, which helped create the UN Environment Programme that, in turn, spawned environmental bodies in many member states, including in the US. Currently the UN is involved in a worldwide campaign against global warming. Much of this work is embryonic and modest in comparison to the size of the problems, but many of these endeavors are helping to establish important new modes of oversight and control.

Lately the UN has undertaken significant internal reforms in its management system—something that the founding fathers never foresaw as a paramount issue. These changes have come about mainly as a result of long-held concerns about nepotism in UN hiring, inflated UN budgets, perceived conflicts of interest in UN contracting, and scandals like the Oil-for-Food imbroglio during the Annan years. The UN has tightened ethics regulations, laid down clearer guidelines on hiring and firing, streamlined rules on contracting, minimized gender discrimination, limited job tenure, and strengthened employment reviews. These measures have helped to stem some of the abuses at the UN, but much remains to be done.

One major provision in the UN Charter, which has changed over the years from the framers' original intention, is the matter of national sovereignty. Under Articles 2.1 and 2.7, every nation was given dominion over its own internal affairs. But Article 2.7 also noted that only matters "essentially" within a state's domestic jurisdiction would be protected from outside meddling. What was "essential" is the question—and, in any case, a member state always had to be bound by its collective obligations under the Charter. Nonetheless most states regarded the idea of sovereignty as a sacrosanct one.

The diminishment of state sovereignty, though, has proceeded apace. In 1967, the Commission on Human Rights was granted authority to probe into the human rights violations of member nations and issue critical reports on such abuses. Then the UN began to take responsibility to intervene to end civil wars in various countries, though such interventions usually came at the request of warring forces. In 1999, Secretary-General Kofi Annan delivered a speech to the General Assembly calling for direct UN humanitarian intervention without a prior invitation in countries that were committing genocide against their own citizens.

All of this led, in due course, to the formulation of the "responsibility to protect" provision as part of the UN reforms of 2005. The notion behind "responsibility to protect" is that there is no longer any such thing as absolute sovereignty and that a nation has a right to sovereignty only if it upholds its responsibility to look after the well-being of its peoples. If it does not, if it commits serious crimes against its populace, then the international community has a responsibility to intervene. This terminology has given the Security Council a clearer legal basis on which to act. So far the UN has employed this new provision on only a few occasions, but its role may be growing in the Security Council.

The founders might have found changes on sovereignty as troubling, though, as it was considered a central building block of the organization—notably, that the organization would always be based on the nation-state system and that a country's internal affairs were off-limits to the assembly.

Among the veto countries there still remains strong sentiment for this view—especially in China and in most instances, Russia—though less so in France, Great Britain, and the United States. Many smaller nations within the UN, though, have argued adamantly against tampering with the sovereignty provisions, fearful that doing so would give larger nations a greater latitude to intervene in their internal affairs.

Still, in many ways the UN remains a flawed body. The failure of the Security Council and General Assembly to intervene to stop genocide in places like Rwanda, Srebrenica, Darfur, and the Congo; their inability to prevent all instances of aggression around the planet; their weaknesses in limiting the spread of nuclear weapons; their difficulties with improving the environment and solving poverty—their powerlessness, in short, to create a normal world—are profoundly disquieting.

A larger issue, too, may be the fact that whatever endeavors the UN has undertaken, whether it be in disaster relief, medical assistance, environmental protection, human rights, development aid, drug smuggling, or sexual trafficking, the organization lacks the depth of resources and authority to make a significant dent in the problems. The UN remains vitally dependent on the cooperation of its member states for whatever operations it undertakes. All the signatories to the UN treaty, especially the five permanent members, have only volitional obligations in these matters. This might possibly change if the UN membership agreed to hold a new Charter convention to restructure the body and take the momentous step of creating a world government. But this is exceedingly unlikely.

The built-in limitations of the UN body hamper its ability to live up to the Charter. Overall, the structure of the UN has remained unchanged since 1945. The Security Council has expanded from eleven members to fifteen members, but only five countries continue to be permanent members with veto power. The UN has a vestigial military staff committee but no troops or rapid response forces. The institution retains its Trusteeship Council, though the era of decolonization has long since ended. It still relies on voluntary contributions for financial support. The body is not a democracy; there are no elected delegates. It remains a collection of states, some free and some not. It is not a global legislature, though the organization has a growing array of civic bodies and nongovernmental organizations attached to it (under Article 71 of the Charter) and works loosely with parliamentary bodies.

At the start of the second decade of the twenty-first century, nonetheless the UN appears to be operating at a higher capacity than ever before. It has become the background "noise" of contemporary political life—hovering around us, though not always openly. The UN's survival and growth, with all of its infirmities, remains a testament to the shrewdness of its founders in formulating a Charter based on a unique mix of realism and idealism. Although the nation-state system continues to undergird the organization and power realities (however out-of-date) control the Security Council, the UN's capacity to serve as the venue for all nations and to reinvent itself as fresh crises demand—intervening when necessary but most importantly lowering the incidence of violence, promoting peaceful settlements as well as diplomatic compromises, and providing nonmilitary outlets for anger—is impressive. Manifold uncertainties remain in the years ahead. Still, the organization's durability is remarkable.

Notes

1. "Human Security Report, 2005: War and Peace in the Twenty-First Century," Human Security Centre, University of British Columbia (New York: Oxford University Press 2005).

2. "Freedom in the World 2011" report, Freedom House, 1301 Connecticut Avenue NW, Floor 6, Washington, DC, 20036.

Chapter 4

Change and the United Nations Charter

Edward C. Luck

The United Nations has had a complicated, even uneasy, relationship with change. At times and on some subjects, it has been a prime promoter of change. At other times and on other matters, it has clung to the status quo with remarkable tenacity. Much of the micro explanation, of course, lies with the political winds of the moment. But what of the macro picture: what were the larger strategic assumptions and intentions that framed the establishment of the United Nations system more than six decades ago? What did the founders have in mind and how were their intentions expressed in the Charter they so carefully crafted and debated? In a dynamic world, was the United Nations to be a place to resist change, to accommodate change, to steer change, or to promote change? Was it to preserve or upend the values, rules, institutions, and power relationships of the existing international order? Is the United Nations a fundamentally conservative or progressive organization? Depending on where and when one looks, each of these propositions could conceivably be answered in the affirmative.

To address these questions, this essay opens with a consideration of the historical, strategic, and political forces that led to the crafting of both the conservative and progressive elements of the Charter. It focuses on the perspectives and interests of the founding members, particularly the "Big Three" powers—the United States, the Soviet Union, and the United Kingdom—

whose deliberations largely framed the Charter. It views the principles, purposes, and provisions of the Charter first from a conservative and second from a progressive perspective. The essay then turns to a consideration of how practice has evolved since 1945 and whether the initial expectations about the organization's relationship to change have been sustained.

THE CONSERVATIVE CHARTER

During World War II, most of the planning for postwar organization centered in Washington, DC, London, and Moscow, in order of effort and intensity. As the capitals of the Big Three allies opposed to the Axis powers, this was to be expected. Throughout the war, the United States was the driving force behind the planning process. This paramount position was accepted, even welcomed, by the others both because of America's emerging military and economic primacy and because its absence from the League of Nations was widely regarded as the most fatal of the flaws of that first experiment in world organization. Planners and, more important, political leaders in the three capitals, for all their ideological differences, could readily agree on two cardinal objectives. One, the new organization had to be perceived to be a major departure from the League: strong where the League was weak, with real enforcement powers, and with the sustained commitment of the United States.[1] Two, the new body, especially in its policing and enforcement powers, would depend heavily on the continuing collaboration of the Big Three allies. They would have the primary responsibility to ensure that the Axis powers or others could not threaten the "peace-loving" members of the United Nations, as well as the chief authority to decide when and how collective enforcement action would be taken.

In an attempt to lock in the collective responsibility of the leading wartime allies for securing the postwar peace, the Charter contained some innovative provisions. The Big Three—plus China and France—were granted permanent membership in the Security Council. Despite considerable grumbling on the part of a handful of delegations at the founding conference in San Francisco in spring 1945, it was agreed that there would have to be unanimity among the five permanent members of the Security Council to authorize enforcement action. To some, the selection of those five countries to be permanent members—something decided by the Big Three during their wartime deliberations—must have appeared somewhat arbitrary. France and much of China were occupied by Axis forces during the early stages of the postwar planning process. Although President Franklin Roose-

velt was an early and insistent advocate of including China in his Four Police-
men strategy, British officials considered China to be at best an "imagined"
power.[2] For its part, London was keen to see France restored to its former
status so that it could again serve as a continental buffer against potential
German or Soviet aggression. Moscow had deep doubts about both countries, due in part to their war record and in part to their westward political
leanings. Indeed, the Dumbarton Oaks preparatory conferences had to be
organized in two parts, with the Anglo-American allies meeting first with
the Soviet delegates and then later with the Chinese. Despite objections even
within his own delegation, Roosevelt championed Brazil as a sixth permanent member as late as the Dumbarton Oaks meetings. Not surprisingly,
none of the other participating capitals shared his enthusiasm.

The unanimity rule and the permanent status for the five powers were
certainly conservative provisions, as they sought to institutionalize the status
quo by attempting to perpetuate the predominant positions of the expected
chief victors of the ongoing world war. With unvarnished realism, the leading military powers sought to convince their less potent allies that the key to
international peace and security lay in the maintenance of their dominant
strategic positions. Sovereign equality was adopted as a cardinal principle of
the new organization (Article 2.1), but it was defined as meaning that member states should have equal status under international law, not within every
organ of the new world organization.[3] It is noteworthy, in that regard, that
the principle is not mentioned elsewhere in the Charter. It is not even cited
in Article 18.1 as the rationale for the one-nation, one-vote rule in the General Assembly, where decisions on political matters would not be binding.
The United Nations was not to be "democratic," a word never used in the
Charter. This core inequality was accepted by the larger membership for
compelling reasons of national interest, not because they relished the prospect of second-class status in the postwar architecture.

At the time it was widely believed that the unanimity rule would help to
preserve collaborative relationships among the big powers by guaranteeing
that the Security Council's historically unique enforcement powers could
not be used against any one of the five without its consent. Not only had the
United States failed to join the League, as noted above, but the Soviet Union,
which refused to join the "robber's league" until 1934, was expelled after
five years for its invasion of Finland.[4] The prevailing assumption was not
that the interests and values of the Big Three had permanently converged
and that the new organization would be a league of the like-minded, but

that the veto power would be needed precisely because serious differences of view were likely to arise in the postwar period without the Axis threat to compel comity among the unlikely allies. Though British Prime Minister Sir Winston Churchill was perhaps the most candid about his qualms about postwar dealings with the Soviet Union, he was hardly alone in his concerns. In May 1945, before the Charter had been signed, Acting US Secretary of State Joseph Grew wrote in a private memorandum that the veto would leave the world body "powerless to act against the one certain future enemy, Soviet Russia."[5]

The Soviet delegates tended to be the most outspoken about the necessity of the unanimity rule, more than once threatening to abandon the negotiations without it.[6] They understood that Moscow would be outnumbered in the postwar General Assembly as well as in the Security Council and would have to rely on the veto rather than numbers to protect its interests from time to time. Marshal Stalin cautioned his American colleagues at one of the wartime conferences "against what he termed a tendency on the part of small nations to create and exploit differences among the great powers in order to gain the backing of one or more of them for their own ends." In his words, "a nation need not be innocent just because it is small."[7]

Their American counterparts, with an eye on gaining Senate consent to ratification, were equally insistent, though sometimes it was convenient to let the Russians take the blame in public. In a private meeting with congressional leaders in May 1944, Secretary of State Cordell Hull assured them that "our Government would not remain there a day without retaining its veto power."[8] In one of the more dramatic moments at the San Francisco Conference, Senator Tom Connally, a member of the US delegation and chairman of the Senate Foreign Relations Committee, reports that he admonished other delegations:

You may go home from San Francisco—if you wish . . . and report that you have defeated the veto. . . . But you can also say, *"We tore up the Charter."* At that point, I sweepingly ripped the Charter draft in my hands to shreds and flung the scraps upon the table.[9]

President Franklin Roosevelt insisted that the founding conference be held before the war ended and the postwar squabbling began. As he put it in his State of the Union address in January 1945, "The nearer we come to vanquishing our enemies the more we inevitably become conscious of differences among the victors."[10]

The victors could readily agree, however, on a third conservative provision: keeping tight control over the process to amend the Charter by requiring unanimity among the five permanent members.[11] Should the wartime conferences prove to be the high point of their collaboration, then at least the Charter provisions they produced would survive their postwar disputes. This would provide assurance, as well, of the permanence of their permanent status in the Council whatever their individual postwar fortunes. As expected, there was much criticism of this proposed provision at the founding conference in San Francisco. So the United States proposed an idea that had been discussed only superficially at Dumbarton Oaks: that a general review conference could be held by the tenth annual session of the General Assembly. Though the conference would be governed by majority vote, any proposed amendment to the Charter would still have to clear the Article 108 hurdle for amendments, i.e., ratification by two-thirds of the member states, including all five permanent members.[12] Given Cold War politics, the review conference was never held, and resentment about the permanent members having veto power over eliminating the veto power can still be heard in reform debates in the General Assembly. Change can—and does—come to the organization, but structural or constitutional change still requires unanimity among the privileged five.[13] In terms of internal change, the United Nations has learned to excel at adaptation even as more fundamental reform of institutional prerogatives and structures has moved slowly, if at all.[14]

THE PROGRESSIVE CHARTER

More often than not, the more progressive dimensions of the Charter came either from the US delegation, from the representatives of smaller countries, or, particularly on human rights issues, from the scores of nongovernmental representatives—consultants and observers—that the Roosevelt and Truman administrations invited to San Francisco.[15] The US delegation was the only one to bring plans for postwar human rights instruments to Dumbarton Oaks.[16] Often these initiatives were supported by the Chinese and/or British delegations. Soviet diplomats tended to be skeptical of many of these ideas but usually saw them as of secondary importance, as they kept their eyes trained on the big-ticket geopolitical and security matters. It would be an overstatement to assert that the progressive provisions of the Charter snuck into the document by the back door or by stealth, but they certainly were not the issues that gained the most public, media, and high-level political attention. As will be argued later in this essay, the relatively humble origins of these "soft" provisions belie the influence they have had over time not only on the work and reputation of the United Nations but also on the character and practice of world affairs.

The progressive spirit behind much of the Charter emerges first in its Preamble. Mark Mazower urges a cautious interpretation of its rhetorical promise:

> When we remember that it was Jan Smuts, the South African premier and architect of White settler nationalism, who did more than anyone to argue for, and help draft, the UN's stirring preamble, it is surely necessary to be cautious about making our own hopes and dreams too dependent on the stories we tell about the past.[17]

Fair enough, and one should not overlook the fact that Stalin, not known for his respect for human rights, signed on to the Charter. This was neither the first nor the last time that high-minded discussions of human rights attracted substantial doses of cynicism as well as idealism. According to Mazower, though Smuts had little involvement in preparations for San Francisco, once there he "had the satisfaction of seeing his text adopted unanimously, with a few modifications, as the preamble to the UN Charter itself."[18] This account neglects the fact that Smuts' draft was "considerably altered" at a meeting of Commonwealth countries prior to San Francisco.[19] The most memorable words in the Preamble came from the American delegation, not from Smuts. His opening lines—"The High Contracting Parties, determined to prevent a recurrence of the fratricidal strife which twice in our generation has brought untold sorrow and loss upon mankind"—were replaced with "We the peoples of the United Nations, determined to save succeeding generations from the scourge of war, which twice in our time has brought untold sorrow to mankind."[20] Several other changes were made to his text, including the addition of a new third line on establishing "conditions under which justice and respect for the obligations arising from treaties and other sources of international law can be maintained," which had been sought by Latin American delegations.[21]

In most respects the Charter remained a highly state-oriented document, but to refer to "we the peoples" as the ultimate source of its authority was a remarkable departure from standard diplomatic practice. The phrase came from Virginia Gildersleeve, dean of Barnard College and the only woman on the US delegation. A political activist and feminist, she focused in San Francisco on promoting human rights and human welfare issues in the Charter text, including a provision for a commission on human rights (Article 68). She was assigned to the committee responsible for establishing the Economic and Social Council—the other council—the one she claimed would be "in charge of doing things rather than preventing things from being done."[22] By background and political orientation, she far better represented the human rights advocates—many of them from civil society—at San Francisco than did aging Field Marshal Smuts. Indeed, at a critical juncture, she quietly informed key nongovernmental representatives that they should urgently press for a more far-reaching human rights stance by the US delegation on which she served.[23] She also teamed with women on the Chinese delegation to lobby for mention in the Charter of the need to oppose gender discrimination.[24]

The bandwagon for including human rights provisions in the Charter started long before Smuts jumped aboard. Less than a month after the United States entered the war, the January 1, 1942, declaration by the twenty-six United Nations—the anti-Axis alliance—stated, "Complete victory over their enemies is essential to defend life, liberty, independence and religious freedom, and to preserve human rights and justice in their own lands as well as in other lands." In 1942, as part of early planning for postwar organization, State Department officials proposed that an international bill of rights be part of the postwar architecture.[25] Despite some worries about congressional reaction, it was the US delegation that first proposed human rights language at Dumbarton Oaks. Initially both the Soviet and British sides resisted, but eventually language was worked out that all could live with. To this news, President Roosevelt expressed his pleasure and surprise that the Soviet delegation had accepted this "extremely vital" provision.[26]

Whoever deserves the credit, the Charter repeatedly (seven times in all) refers to human rights goals, and this was three years before the Universal Declaration on Human Rights was successfully negotiated. The Preamble reaffirms "faith in fundamental human rights, in the dignity and worth of the human person, in the equal rights of men and women and of nations large and small." Its third purpose (Article 1.3) includes the words "promoting and encouraging respect for human rights and for fundamental freedoms for all without distinction as to race, sex, language, or religion." The General Assembly is to "initiate studies and make recommendations" on "assisting in the realization of human rights and fundamental freedoms for all without distinction as to race, sex, language, or religion" (Article 13.1b).

According to Article 55c, "The United Nations shall promote . . . universal respect for, and observance of, human rights and fundamental freedoms for all without distinction as to race, sex, language, or religion." Under Article 62.2, the Economic and Social Council "may make recommendations for the purpose of promoting respect for, and observance of, human rights and fundamental freedoms for all." It is to "set up" a commission "for the promotion of human rights," as stipulated by Article 68. Once again, the new international trusteeship system is "to encourage respect for human rights and for fundamental freedoms for all without distinction as to race, sex, language, or religion" under Article 76c.

Certainly the prime concern of the founders was the maintenance of international peace and security, most notably to prevent further aggression by the "enemy states." Some of the framers of the Charter, however, recognized that the sources of conflict often lay below the interstate level and that the treatment of populations and their economic welfare would matter in any sustainable equation for world peace. Rosemary Righter, a journalist and crafter of tough-minded editorials about the world body for the London *Times*, expressed this new orientation well. In her view, the United Nations, much more than the League, "sought not only to ensure stability . . . but to systematize the promotion of change. The Charter was consciously innovative, and nowhere more so than in its explicit concern with the rights of individuals to humane and equal treatment under the law."[27]

Those objecting to such a progressive interpretation of the Charter, whether scholars or representatives of states jealous of their sovereignty, have taken refuge in the strong words of Article 2.7, which presents the last of the seven principles underlying the Charter. They regularly cite its opening words: "Nothing contained in the present Charter shall authorize the United Nations to intervene in matters which are essentially within the domestic jurisdiction of any state or shall require the Members to submit such matters to settlement under the present Charter." Clear enough, but the paragraph concludes with an important qualifier: "but this principle shall not prejudice the application of enforcement measures under Chapter VII." Rarely cited, this clause leaves it to a political body, the Security Council, to determine under Article 39 whether "any threat to the peace" exists. In San Francisco, this article was sufficiently ambiguous to offer some reassurance to Soviet delegates wary of Western-inspired violations of their country's sovereignty and to feed the expectations of those delegations, like New Zealand, that looked for an international response to atrocities committed against national minorities, as in Nazi Germany.[28]

There is substantial evidence, moreover, that the drafters in San Francisco did not want Article 2.7 to be interpreted as a blanket protection for national leaders determined to run roughshod over the rights of their populations. The drafting committee, in explaining the wording of Article 2.7, declared that if fundamental freedoms and rights are "grievously outraged so as to create conditions which threaten peace or to obstruct the application of the provisions of the Charter, then they cease to be the sole concern of each State."[29] Even today, this would be a strong statement of the limits of sovereignty, one that would make some member states more than a little uncomfortable. That it was made by the drafting committee at the UN's founding conference before the end of World War II is eloquent evidence that some of the delegates, at least, were remarkably far-sighted.

The New Zealand delegation reports that its concerns over whether Article 2.7 could inhibit the authority of the United Nations to respond to atrocity crimes were eased by the knowledge that it would not prevent the Security Council from taking enforcement action in such cases.[30] Under Article 34, moreover, "the Security Council may investigate any dispute, or any situation which might lead to international friction or give rise to a dispute, in order to determine whether the continuance of the dispute or situation is likely to endanger the maintenance of international peace and security." Part of Chapter VI on the pacific settlement of disputes, Article 34's references to "disputes" and "situations" undoubtedly encompassed economic and trade issues, as well as social and human rights matters. A number of delegations at San Francisco emphasized the economic and social roots of conflict. Reflecting these concerns, Article 65 states that "the Economic and Social Council may furnish information to the Security Council upon its request."

In the early planning for the United Nations, the Big Three were not equally enthusiastic about including economic and social matters on its agenda. Despite Marxist teachings about the economic and class determinants of war, the Soviet representatives at Dumbarton Oaks were initially unreceptive to entreaties from their American and British colleagues about the advantages of having the new body address the economic and social factors that could foster instability or conflict on the one hand or sustain peace and security on the other. As early as December 1943, Secretary of State Cordell Hull outlined a plan for a postwar world organization that would serve "first, to establish and maintain peace and security, by force if necessary; and second, to foster cooperative effort among the nations for the progressive improvement of the general welfare."[31] To American eyes, the professionalism and expertise accumulated by its secretariat and affiliated agencies, prominently including the International Labor Organization, constituted one of the League's premier strengths. Indeed, though the United States never joined the League, it participated actively in many of its technical, social, and economic activities. As Leland Goodrich put it in 1947, "It has generally been observed that the most permanently worthwhile activities of the League of Nations were in the field of international economic and social cooperation."[32]

The functionalist theories of David Mitrany, which called for collaboration among countries on functional activities as the first step toward building the habit and practice of international organization, had many adherents, especially among Western postwar planners, in those years.[33] According to his theory, over time collaboration on functional matters would lay a foundation for cooperation on political matters, but in the early stages care should be taken to avoid the politicization of uncontroversial functional work that benefits all. As Leland Goodrich put it, "Whereas the League technical organizations dealing with health, economic and financial cooperation were developed within the framework of the League and operated under the general direction and control of the principal League organs, the approach of the United Nations has been a different one." By establishing relatively autonomous organizations to meet "special needs," the United Nations system could address a wider range of actions than "a League system operating more completely under the influence of political considerations," in his view. The drawback of such a functional approach, he concluded—apparently as obvious in 1947 as in the years since—was the difficulty of sustaining "effective coordination."[34]

To the Soviet delegation at Dumbarton Oaks, however, the League's economic and social work had been a distraction from its core business of ensuring international peace and security. Ambassador Andrei Gromyko, who headed the delegation, claimed that 77 percent of the issues addressed by the League had not been directly related to the maintenance of peace and security.[35] What was needed, in the Soviet view, was a world organization devoted solely to security, while cooperation on economic and social challenges could be taken up by a separate body. The Americans countered with a proposal for an Economic and Social Council, not unlike the recommendation by the 1939 Bruce Report for the League to establish a Central Committee for Economic and Social Questions.[36] According to this line of thought, a fundamental problem with the League's structure was that its Council and Assembly had overlapping responsibilities for the whole spectrum of League activities, ranging from security to economic to social matters. By creating a second council for the new organization, the Americans argued, the Security Council could focus on its core security responsibilities. The Chinese concurred. Eventually the Soviets relented on the general point, which apparently was not for them a deal-breaker.

At San Francisco, the Anglo-American emphasis on economic and social issues found broad support among the other delegations, as the resulting Charter gave economic and social advancement a prominent place among its purposes, just as it had for human rights. From Leland Goodrich's perspective, "Perhaps the most important advance of the Charter over the Covenant of the League is to be found in its provisions defining the objectives, policies, machinery and procedure of international economic and social cooperation."[37] These provisions, again and again, reflected a positive, forward-looking agenda. "We the peoples," proclaimed the Preamble, are "determined . . . to promote social progress and better standards of life in greater freedom" and "for these ends . . . to employ international machinery for the promotion and social advancement of all peoples." From a realist's perspective, this may be the "soft" side of the United Nations, but it was also intended to be an active, positive, and progressive dimension of its work as well.

Throughout the Charter, action words, such as "promote," "advance," and "strengthen," were used in connection with economic, social, and human rights goals and activities. Among the new organization's purposes, according to Article 1.3, was "to achieve international co-operation in solving international problems of an economic, social, cultural or humanitarian character." The reference to cultural issues offered at least a pale reflection of Chinese concerns about intercultural dialogue and equality among the races, not just the states.[38] The last purpose—"to be a centre for harmonizing the actions of nations in the attainment of these common ends" (Article 1.4)—captured the world body's comparative advantage as a forum or political arena through which disparate member states could seek to identify common ground, to articulate normative standards, and to develop practical strategies and policies for advancing their collective interests.[39] It would, in other words, serve as a catalyst or facilitator for change.

THE CHARTER IN PRACTICE

The best constitutions, of course, work as well in practice as they do in theory. This is not the place to make a careful weighing of practice over the past decades or to assess the extent to which it has fulfilled the promise of the Charter (which is less a constitution than an agreed framework for guiding the interactions of sovereign states). But some conclusions can be drawn about how the attitudes toward change manifested in Dumbarton Oaks and San Francisco have held up through the years. The discussion above suggests that the founders were relatively conservative and cautious when crafting the Charter's peace and security provisions and bolder and more progressive when they turned to its provisions on economic, social, and human rights matters. Two big caveats are in order, however. The enforcement provisions of Chapter VII were unprecedented in the history of international organization. They reflected a coincidence of circumstances that could not have been replicated at any point since 1945. Those provisions certainly constituted a bold step, but one tied to a decidedly conservative purpose: to perpetuate the wartime alliance indefinitely, with decisions to take enforcement action requiring unanimity among five of the allies. The fine words in the Charter about change in the economic, social, and human rights realms, moreover, are not binding, unlike many of the decisions of the Security Council. They express intentions and expectations; no doubt some member states took them to be little more than exhortations.

Three change-related questions are in order here. One, did the United Nations turn out to be more than the "League of the Satisfied" that the *New Republic* warned against when preliminary ideas for the League of Nations were floated in 1915? Two, have the provisions of the Charter been sufficiently flexible to permit the organization to adapt to changing times and to retain its relevance as issues and players shifted? Three, through the course of more than six decades of change, has the organization been able to remain faithful to its founding purposes and principles, so eloquently expressed in Articles 1 and 2?

League of the Satisfied?

Both the League of Nations and the United Nations began as the inspirations of the victors of a world war. They sought, naturally, to create international institutions that would help to sustain their hard-won positions at the top of the international pecking order, i.e., to protect the status quo. Reflecting the concerns of liberal internationalists that early ideas for the League leaned too far in this direction, the editors of the New Republic, including Walter Lippmann, asked whether less satisfied powers, like Germany, might protest that "you bar the future, and you call it peace." In trying to prevent war, they cautioned, such schemes "take a static view of the world. They come quite naturally from citizens of satisfied powers, weary of the burden of defending what they have got. They ignore the fact that life is change."[40] In calling for term limits on Article 10 of the League Covenant, which was no more than a weak echo of a collective security pledge, Elihu Root suggested that any such "attempt to preserve for all time unchanged the distribution of power and territory . . . would not only be futile; it would be mischievous. Change and growth are the law of life, and no generation can impose its will in regard to the growth of nations and the distribution of power, upon succeeding generations."[41] Writing almost a century later, Mark Mazower contends that "what emerged at San Francisco was the League reborn, only now modified and adjusted—thanks to the Big Three conversations at Dumbarton Oaks—to the frank realities of a new configuration of great power politics."[42]

The founders of the United Nations, however, had learned some valuable lessons from the failures of its predecessor. As noted above, a perennial weakness of the League was that it never had all of the world's major powers in its ranks. In addition to going to some lengths to secure American participation, including having the founding conference and its headquarters on its territory, the framers of the UN Charter made no provision for members to leave the organization. Despite the Charter's inclusion of several "enemies" clauses, Article 4.1 provided a route for former Axis powers to join the world body, provided that they had become "peace-loving," accepted "the obligations contained in the present Charter," and were judged to be able and willing to carry them out. Politically, it required a recommendation by the Security Council, including unanimity among the five permanent members, plus a two-thirds vote in the General Assembly. For the first two decades, these membership decisions often proved contentious, given the divisive politics of the Cold War. Yet over time the former "enemies" became some of the best friends and strongest supporters of the world body.

For all of the grand rhetoric at San Francisco, the Charter does not identify universality as a goal for the new organization. Some of the allies would no doubt have been more comfortable with that objective than would have others of them. Yet that has been the inexorable, if uneven, path it has followed. Twenty-six countries signed the Declaration of United Nations in early 1942. Fifty-one attended the founding conference in San Francisco three years later, and 193 are now members. Most of the members that came aboard in the 1950s and 1960s, of course, were former colonies. Not surprisingly, decolonization was much more prominent in Washington's view of United Nations' priorities than in London's (or later in Paris's).[43] The Chinese delegations to Dumbarton Oaks and San Francisco were quite passionate about the need to take a progressive stance on decolonization. Facilitating the decolonization process became one of the organization's early success stories, as the more heralded peace and security roles were often stymied by the lack of unanimity in the Security Council.

In the process, the world body began to look less and less like a "League of the Satisfied." The General Assembly came to be just what its name implies—a forum for all the world's voices (at least those representing states) to be heard. The two countries most responsible for inspiring and crafting the world body—the United States and the United Kingdom—increasingly found themselves on the defensive in the house they had done so much to build. To Winston Churchill, this was not what he had in mind. Complaining of a General Assembly "swollen by the addition of new nations," he contended in 1957 that "the shape of the United Nations has changed greatly from its original form and from the intentions of its architects. . . . It is anomalous that the vote or prejudice of any small country should affect events involving populations many times exceeding their numbers."[44] Perhaps by happenstance more than by design, a rough balance had developed between a relatively conservative Council and a relatively progressive Assembly. Change had come to the world and to the United Nations, and both endured.

Changing Times

As noted above, the "soft" side of the United Nations has proven to be remarkably resilient. In some ways, the fact that the Charter's references to economic and social progress and to promoting human rights were so vague and general—if enthusiastic—that they allowed interested member states, the international secretariat, and civil society partners to craft institutions, methods, and procedures capable both of responding to immediate challenges and of being modified as conditions and needs changed. The relevant provisions of the Charter provided a framework for action, not a rigid or detailed template. The emphasis on functionalism did permit most of the UN system's vast array of agencies, funds, and programs to weather the dysfunctional politics of the Cold War with relatively little damage to their core missions. Those with voluntary funding—i.e., most of the development, humanitarian, and technical entities in the system—have not had to depend on highly political decisions about funding from the General Assembly. None of these assets could guarantee effective performance on the ground, sound management, or systemwide policy coherence, but they did ensure that the system would be relatively agile and responsive to changing times.

Indeed, among the areas in which the world body has left its mark, some of the most prominent were not mentioned in the Charter, such as development, environment, population, election monitoring, peacekeeping, peacebuilding, human protection, nuclear energy, and counterterrorism. Like a stream, the organization's energies have tended to flow around political bottlenecks to areas of lesser resistance and greater demand. That would be expected in such a highly political environment, where the member states ultimately determine the organization's course. Each issue, however, has had its own constituencies and stakeholders, cutting across civil society, the Secretariat, and groups of member states, including importantly those governments and parliaments that have provided the requisite financial and material support. The more successful mandate holders have generally been those who have managed these relationships most ably within the very wide playing field defined by the Charter.

But what of the Security Council, the last bastion of the founding powers? Would it prove to be sufficiently flexible to adapt and remain relevant to changing times and challenges? Or was adaptation to be left to these "softer" issues? Here one should make distinctions among what the Council does (its agenda and scope of interest), how it does it (its tools and working methods), and its composition (who decides what it should do and how its tools should be utilized). On the first two scales, the Security Council has proven to be one of the United Nations' more innovative and flexible organs.[45] Its longevity and its ability to survive the deep divides among its permanent members during the Cold War years are remarkable by any standard. The United Nations' founding conference took place before the first atomic explosion, yet the Council's mandate and methodologies did not have to be substantially altered to cope with the new realities. The hundreds of Soviet and later American vetoes that were cast during the Cold War certainly frustrated many specific initiatives, but they did not lead any of the permanent members to abandon the body or their continuing conversation about how to maintain international peace and security, as had happened to the League.

With the invention of peacekeeping in the Suez Crisis, the world body found what would become its distinctive icon, the blue helmets, as well as an instrument that could be applied in a range of modes and circumstances. With the end of the Cold War, the Council rediscovered Chapter VII, including the utility of economic and diplomatic sanctions, travel bans, and arms embargoes as means of influencing both governments and armed groups. Between sanctions committees, thematic working groups, and, post-9/11, counterterrorism committees, the Council developed a thick layer of subsidiary bodies that multiplied its workload and reach. Like the General Assembly, the Council found that the Charter provisions permitting it to create its own subsidiary machinery as needed were an open door to innovation and adaptation to changing circumstances. Since the mid-1990s, a series of changes in Council procedures has begun to address persistent questions about its transparency and accountability. The Council, in short, has been the most flexible UN body when it comes to adjusting its working methods over time.

With its core permanent membership providing continuity and, occasionally, enforcement muscle, and its annual influx of non-permanent members bringing fresh perspectives and greater political acceptability, the Council is widely viewed as the most effective and efficient organ in the UN system. After so many years, however, the continuity in permanent membership is coming to be increasingly viewed as an anomaly, a reminder of the world order of earlier times. Emerging powers, such as Brazil, India, and South Africa, as well as former enemies Germany and Japan, are demanding a place at the horseshoe table. Yet a widely acceptable formula for accomplishing the structural reform of the Council without hindering its effectiveness remains elusive. Meanwhile, questions about its political legitimacy and the degree of compliance with its decisions are being posed with greater frequency and passion. The once-compelling logic that made the inequitable compromises of Dumbarton Oaks widely acceptable is losing its grip on the larger UN membership, as well as on "we the peoples." Change will have to accelerate or the reputation, and ultimately the effectiveness, of the Council will come increasingly into question.

Founding Purposes and Principles

In a few years, the Charter will be seventy. It has reached that relative longevity, in part, because it combined two visions. The first vision was of a conservative approach to sustaining the relationships among the leading victors of the last world war and to forging some rudimentary and admittedly uneven sense of a common responsibility for the maintenance of international peace and security. The second vision was of a more progressive approach to advancing human rights and human welfare, through both normative developments and operational programs. As we have seen, the first vision was shared quite uniformly among the big powers and accepted with some grumbling by the rest of the member states. The second vision was widely accepted by the broader membership but held with varying degrees of enthusiasm by the big powers.

The ideological divides of the Cold War era made both the codification and the implementation of human rights and humanitarian norms a prolonged struggle. For those four decades, it was commonplace to think of the progressive and normative vision as "soft" and impractical, as the weak and hortatory side of the Charter. The conservative, security-oriented side of the Charter sustained the United Nations through those dark years, it seemed. Yet, it could be argued that the normative side of the Charter helped both to inspire civic activism in the Soviet Union and Eastern Europe and to provide standards for global and regional pressures for reform and change in the Soviet system. In the two decades plus since the end of the Cold War, there appears to have been an unconscious but inexorable movement toward rebalancing our understanding of how the parts of the Charter relate to each other and were meant to form an integrated whole. History has demonstrated the value of both its conservative and progressive dimensions, even as it suggests that a point has been reached when some of its conservative provisions, particularly concerning the composition and functioning of the Security Council, need a fresh look.

In giving the February 2011 Cyril Foster Lecture at Oxford, Secretary-General Ban Ki-moon spoke of some of the ways in which the United Nations has served as the agent, as well as the object, of change. He focused on the rise of human protection norms, particularly the Responsibility to Protect, and linked them to the Charter's founding conception of sovereignty and the balance between rights and responsibilities envisioned in Article 2.7. Though aspects of these normative developments may seem new or even radical to some, to this author they provide a lens through which to get a fuller and richer understanding of what many of the UN's architects had in mind so many years ago. In 1945 they declared that change is good. In that regard, nothing has changed. The progressive agenda for international organization remains a work in progress.

Notes

1. As Professor Leland M. Goodrich, who served as secretary to the committee at the founding conference in San Francisco devoted to the pacific settlement of disputes, put it: "Within the counsels of the United Nations, there was an apparent readiness to write the old League off as a failure, and to regard the new organization as something unique, representing a fresh approach to the world problems of peace and security. Quite clearly there was a hesitancy in many quarters to call attention to the continuity of the old League and the new United Nations for fear of arousing latent hostilities or creating doubts which might seriously jeopardize the birth and early success of the new organization." "From League of Nations to United Nations," *International Organization* 1 (February 1947): 3.

2. David L. Bosco, *Five to Rule Them All: The Security Council and the Making of the Modern World* (Oxford: Oxford University Press, 2009), 25.

3. Ruth B. Russell, *A History of the United Nations Charter: The Role of the United States, 1940–1945* (Washington, DC: Brookings Institution, 1958), 672.

4. Bosco, *Five to Rule Them All*, 18.

5. Robert C. Hilderbrand, *Dumbarton Oaks: The Origins of the United Nations and the Search for Postwar Security* (Chapel Hill: University of North Carolina Press, 1990), 254.

6. For a more detailed analysis of the positions of the Big Three regarding the establishment of the Security Council, see Edward C. Luck, "A Council for All Seasons: The Creation of the Security Council and Its Relevance Today," in Vaughan Lowe, Adam Roberts, Jennifer Welsh, and Dominik Zaum, eds., *The United Nations Security Council and War: The Evolution of Thought and Practice since 1945* (Oxford: Oxford University Press, 2008), 61–85.

7. James F. Byrnes, *Speaking Frankly* (New York: Harper and Brothers, 1947), 64–65.

8. Townsend Hoopes and Douglas Brinkley, *FDR and the Creation of the U.N.* (New Haven: Yale University Press, 1997), 126. For a more extensive discussion of US domestic political factors related to the veto provision, see Edward C. Luck, *Mixed Messages: American Politics and International Organization, 1919–1999* (Washington, DC: Brookings Institution Press for the Century Foundation, 1999), 153–62.

9. Tom Connally, *My Name Is Tom Connally* (New York: T. Y. Crowell, 1954), 282–83.

10. Quoted in Luck, "Council for All Seasons," 78–79.

11. For the deliberations on the amendment process at Dumbarton Oaks, see Russell, *History of the United Nations Charter*, 426–27.

12. The discussions in San Francisco of this proposal, which became Article 109 of the Charter, are chronicled in Russell, ibid., 742–49.

13. According to Article 27, the approval of all nonprocedural matters before the Council requires unanimity among the five permanent members. The same applies to the admission, suspension, or expulsion of members (Articles 4, 5, and 6), the appointment of the Secretary-General (Article 97), and the authorization of enforcement action by regional arrangements or agencies (Article 53.1). By practice, through what is sometimes called the "cascade effect," the permanent members are normally included on most committees of the General Assembly and other principal organs.

14. Edward C. Luck, *Reforming the United Nations: Lessons from a History in Progress* (New Haven: Academic Council on the United Nations System, Yale University, 2003).

15. Stephen C. Schlesinger, *Act of Creation: The Founding of the United Nations* (Boulder: Westview Press, 2003), 122–26. For their role on human rights, see William Korey, *NGOs and the Universal Declaration of Human Rights: "A Curious Grapevine"* (New York: Palgrave, 2001), 29–50.

16. Russell, *History of the United Nations Charter*, 423.

17. Mark Mazower, *No Enchanted Palace: The End of Empire and the Ideological Origins of the United Nations* (Princeton: Princeton University Press, 2009), 9.

18. Ibid., 61.

19. Russell, *History of the United Nations Charter*, 912.

20. Ibid., 913.

21. Ibid., 765–67 and 913–18.

22. Rosalind Rosenberg, "Virginia Gildersleeve: Opening the Gates," Living Legacies, Great Moments and Leading Figures in the History of Columbia University, *Columbia University Alumni Magazine*, Summer 2001, p. 7. More broadly, see Virginia C. Gildersleeve, *Many a Good Crusade: Memoirs of Virginia Gildersleeve* (New York: Macmillan, 1954).

23. Korey, *NGOs and the Universal Declaration*, 36–39.

24. Russell, *History of the United Nations Charter*, 793.

25. Ibid., 323–25.

26. Hilderbrand, *Dumbarton Oaks*, 91–93.

27. Rosemary Righter, *Utopia Lost: The United Nations and World Order* (New York: Twentieth Century Fund Press, 1995), 25.

28. Luck, "Council for All Seasons,"67. Also see New Zealand Delegation to the United Nations Conference on International Organization, San Francisco, *Report on the Conference* (Wellington: Department of External Affairs, 1945), 28. In remarkably prescient ways, the struggle that small delegation had with the dilemmas of humanitarianism in a world of sovereign states anticipated the current debates about the Responsibility to Protect.

29. United Nations Secretary-General Ban Ki-moon, Cyril Foster Lecture at Oxford University, "Human Protection and the Twenty-First Century United Nations," SG/SM/13385, February 2, 2011.

30. New Zealand Report, 28.

31. Hoopes and Brinkley, *FDR and the Creation of the U.N.*, 111.

32. Goodrich, "From League of Nations to United Nations," 19.

33. David Mitrany, "The Functional Approach to International Organization," *International Affairs* 24 (July 1948): 350–63, and *The Progress of International Government* (New Haven: Yale University Press, 1933).

34. Goodrich, "From League of Nations to United Nations,"20.

35. Hilderbrand, *Dumbarton Oaks*, 87–88.

36. Russell, *History of the United Nations Charter*, 303–6.

37. Goodrich, "From League of Nations to United Nations," 19.

38. Hilderbrand, *Dumbarton Oaks*, 240. The Chinese delegation at Dumbarton Oaks also stressed the further codification of international law. Russell, *History of the United Nations Charter*, 430–31.

39. Grayson Kirk contended in 1946 that this was true for the security side of the organization as well. "Structurally, the new organization was to be little more than a mechanism through which the existing sovereign states would try to coordinate their policies with respect to matters vital to world peace." This comment was made in the context of his discussion of Article 43, which laid out a system of standby forces, since none of the major powers were about to irrevocably commit their forces to a standing international military force. In essence, he suggests that the Security Council was to form the basis for a concert of great powers to address the major security challenges of the day. That, in itself, was no small accomplishment. Grayson Kirk, "The Enforcement of Security," *Yale Law Journal* 55, no. 5 (August 1946): 1083.

40. Editorial, "A League of Peace," *New Republic*, March 20, 1915. Quoted in Luck, *Mixed Messages*, 142 and 167.

41. Ibid., 167.

42. Mazower, *No Enchanted Palace*, 194.

43. For a discussion of self-determination and trusteeship in US policies and in those of its principal allies, see Stewart Patrick, *Best Laid Plans: The Origins of American Multilateralism and the Dawn of the Cold War* (Lanham, MD: Rowman and Littlefield, 2009), 173–211.

44. Winston Churchill, Address to the American Bar Association, July 31, 1957, reprinted in the *American Bar Association Journal* 43 (October 1957): 915.

45. Edward C. Luck, *The UN Security Council: Practice and Promise* (London: Routledge, 2006).

Part II

EARLY IMPACT AND STATE FORMATION

Chapter 5

The United Nations and the Emergence of Independent India

Srinath Raghavan

The relationship between independent India and the United Nations is usually viewed through the prism of the Kashmir dispute. This is not surprising, for Kashmir was one of the earliest international disputes that came up for consideration by the Security Council. Resolutions adopted by the Security Council remain unfulfilled, and the dispute rages on more than six decades after it was first brought to the UN. The chronic character of the problem apart, there is another reason why Kashmir tends to dominate discussions of India and the UN. Independent India's ostensible refusal to abide by the Security Council resolutions on Kashmir is seen as unmasking the reality behind the internationalist rhetoric and posturing of its first and longest-serving prime minister, Jawaharlal Nehru.

Even the more sympathetic treatments of Nehruvian internationalism have had to confront this issue. In his important account of the ideological origins of the UN, Mark Mazower has underlined Nehru's pioneering role in undermining the status-quo bias inherent in the organization and in transforming it into an anticolonial forum. Mazower argues that with the attainment of independence, India quickly lost its radical edge and turned into a defender of the status quo.[1] This explanation seems unsatisfactory. After all, India continued to play an important role in UN involvement across the globe. In a recent assessment, Manu Bhagavan has argued that "Indian policy towards the UN was on two tracks, one of idealism and the other of realpolitik. India appealed to the former especially when others were called to task, but resorted to the latter when India's own positions or resources were called into question."[2] This explanatory framework is certainly more useful than the arguments that underscore the thorough-going hypocrisy of independent India's attitude toward the UN. And yet it begs the question of how the Indian leadership came to assume that such a patently inconsistent approach would promote either its interests or its ideals.

This essay suggests that independent India's approach to the UN was more nuanced and shaded than existing accounts would have us believe. Nehru certainly thought that the UN could pave the way for a new form of internationalism in the postwar world. But he also recognized that it afforded a concrete opportunity for an emerging India to brand its image on the international stage and thus pursue its interests with legitimacy.

Nehru's approach to the UN reflected his awareness of the multidimensional character of power. The use of military and economic power certainly enables a state to constrain the options of its adversaries. But power is also exercised when a state devotes its efforts to creating or reinforcing political norms and practices that influence and shape other states' behaviour.[3] This process of setting and cementing norms requires a keen and acute sense of the sources of legitimacy in international politics and a willingness to work with and strengthen international institutions. This awareness, I should like to suggest, lies at the core of postcolonial India's early stance toward the UN. To flesh out this argument, I shall focus on the periods immediately preceding and following India's independence in August 1947.

BRITAIN, THE UN, AND INDIAN INDEPENDENCE

The Atlantic Charter signed by Franklin Roosevelt and Winston Churchill in July 1941 underlay the subsequent creation of the United Nations. Twenty-six states signed on to the declaration to uphold the Charter and unite against the Axis powers. Britain's stance on the Atlantic Charter brought to the fore its views on the compatibility of the principles of the charter with those of the British Empire and also the differences between Britain and the US. The Charter stated that America and Britain "respect the right of all peoples to choose the form of government under which they live; and they wish to see sovereign rights and self-government restored to those who have been forcibly deprived of them." The ambiguities inherent in the Charter surfaced soon afterwards. Churchill clarified that this principle applied only to

European states and not to entities constituting the British Empire. Roosevelt disagreed and insisted that it held for all peoples, but eventually he gave up.[4]

Indian nationalists were, of course, quick to seize on Britain's unwillingness to adopt a consistent stance. Mohandas K. Gandhi was characteristically witty and incisive in his observations on the Charter: "What is the Atlantic Charter? It went down the ocean as soon as it was born! I do not understand it. Mr. Amery [British secretary of state for India] denies that India is fit for democracy, while Mr. Churchill states the Charter could not apply to India. Force of circumstances will falsify their declarations."[5] Gandhi was prescient, but not adequately so. Faced with the prospect of a Japanese invasion of India, Churchill reluctantly agreed to parley with the Indian nationalists in early 1942. His offer to Indian leaders of a share in the executive responsibility for the defense of India but without commensurate transfer of real power fell far short of the Indian leadership's expectations. Thereafter, the outbreak of the popular anti-British "Quit India" movement led to the internment of the Indian National Congress's leadership for the duration of the war.

When the San Francisco Conference was convened in early 1945, the British government nominated three eminent non-nationalists to represent India at the conference. In a statement to the press prior to the conference, Gandhi reiterated his view that the "exploitation and domination of one nation over another can have no place in a world striving to put an end to all wars." Complete independence for India was an essential first step toward peace. This would demonstrate to all colonized peoples that their "freedom is very near and that in no case will they henceforth be exploited." Gandhi demanded that "the camouflage of Indian representation through Indians nominated by British imperialism should be dropped. Such representation would be worse than no representation. Either India at San Francisco is represented by an elected representative or not represented at all."[6] During the conference itself, the question of India's independence served as a platform that brought together diverse groups and personalities that pressed the new organization to grant independence to India and justice and equality for all colonial subjects.[7]

Five weeks after the end of the war in Europe, leaders of the Indian National Congress were released from prison. Soon after, negotiations for the future of India commenced between the British, the Muslim League, and the Congress. In the opening round of negotiations, the leader of the Muslim League, M. A. Jinnah sought to drive home two points. First, the Hindus and Muslims were two nations entitled to parity in any scheme of transfer of power. Second, Jinnah should be the "sole spokesman" for the Muslims of India. Following the failure of the first round of talks, the viceroy of India, Archibald Wavell, announced elections for a central legislature that would work toward a constitutional structure for a free India. The Muslim League presented the elections to the Muslim electorate as virtually a referendum on Pakistan. The gambit paid off. The Muslim League's electoral performance gave substantial weight both to its political position and to the demand for Pakistan.

By the time the elections were held, a Labour government led by Clement Attlee had come to power in Britain. Leaders of the Labour Party were sympathetic to Indian demands for self-rule. But their willingness to relinquish the Raj did not imply that Britain was ready to accept an emasculated role in world affairs. Indeed, the British had no desire either to wind up their empire or to forsake the panoply of a major power.[8] Following World War II, they wished to rid themselves of the incubus of governing India and to refashion the imperial system for the exigencies of the postwar international order. As far as South Asia was concerned, Whitehall's policies were mainly shaped by strategic considerations. The large standing army; the vast reservoir of potential military manpower; the rich natural resources and the industrial potential; India's importance in securing sea lines of communication in the Indian Ocean and in defending the Middle East and the Far East: all of these mandated both preserving Indian unity and ensuring India's continued presence in the Commonwealth.[9]

In pursuit of these aims, a cabinet mission of three senior members of the Labour government was sent to India in late March 1946. The mission was tasked to create a constitutional package for a united India and to plan for the transfer of power. The Cabinet Mission spent three months in India, holding a number of meetings with the leaders of the Congress and the Muslim League. Neither party was able to advance suggestions that met with the other side's approval. Eventually, the mission advanced its own plan for a united India. Both the Congress and Muslim League accepted the plan with serious reservations—concerns that rendered the plan unworkable, provided impetus to communal violence, and eventually cleared the way for the partition of India.

The inability and unwillingness of the Congress and Muslim League to work together, and the deteriorating situation on the ground, led the British government to consider the possibility of handing the India problem over to the UN. Although the option was discarded quite quickly, these deliberations cast interesting light on Britain's views about the new international body and its old empire.

The question of UN involvement in India came up for discussion at a cabinet meeting on June 5, 1946—just when the official charter of the UN was being ratified. Since the situation in India could degenerate into an all-out civil war that might conceivably affect international peace, the cabinet decided to examine the option at some length. The secretary of state for foreign affairs, Ernest Bevin, initiated consultations with senior India hands in the bureaucracy and circulated a detailed memorandum outlining the options and likely outcomes.

Bevin observed that the assistance of the UN was not required for "suggestions and recommendations for settlement of an internal dispute in India." Rather, the UN could provide "practical assistance in the way of forces to maintain order and maintain communications." In consequence, the Security Council would be a more appropriate forum than the General Assembly to consider the issue. The Assembly would meet only once a year and would, in any case, have to refer any question of taking military action to the Security Council. The greater concern was to ensure that the terms of discussion could be controlled by the British government. As Bevin observed: "The majority view of the General Assembly is essentially that of small States, and its sympathy would no doubt lie with what was conceived to be the desires of the Indian people. It would be likely to be critical of the position of His Majesty's Government."[10]

There were two possibilities of reference to the Security Council. First, the government of India could itself draw attention to the matter under Article 35 (Chapter VI) of the UN Charter as a "situation which might lead to international friction." The Council would then proceed to examine how to deal with the situation. By exercising this option, Bevin emphasized, Britain "would in fact have abandoned its sovereign authority over India and would have invited the United Nations Organisation to assume that responsibility." The political consequences of such an action would be "incalculable from every point of view." The Soviet Union would use its veto to prevent any action favorable to British interests. In the event that the Council was ready to authorize military action to restore order in India, the Soviet Union might be the only country both willing and able to supply the necessary forces. This option, Bevin concluded, would be tantamount to "handing over the Empire of India to the Soviet Union."

The second possibility envisioned by Bevin was that any other member of the UN might bring the situation in India to the Security Council's notice.

If the issue was brought to the table under Article 35, Britain could invoke Article 2.7 of the Charter, which forbade UN intervention in matters under the "domestic jurisdiction" of a state. If the question was raised under Chapter VII, Britain could argue that the situation in India did not constitute a threat to international peace and security. In any event, Britain retained the right to veto any action proposed by the Security Council.

Bevin's deeper concern was that a reference to the UN would weaken Britain's international position by suggesting a "decline in British power and resolution." This would have an impact on all aspects of the British imperial system.[11] The Americans had been urging the British "not to abandon essential strategic positions in India and even to combine with them in an approach to the Government of India to be allowed to participate in the use and upkeep of some of these positions." The American concern was about the Soviet Union, and any policy that offered Moscow an opportunity to meddle in India would not go down well with Washington. Indeed, "An open abandonment by us of our positions in India without safeguards [being sought by the Cabinet Mission] might well embarrass them [the US] to the point where they would feel unable to give us any public support in the matter." By contrast, if Britain refrained from approaching the UN, it could count on American support. Furthermore, a reference to the UN might signal that Britain was abandoning the Muslims of India and so enflame Arab opinion, which was already testy owing to the Palestine issue. Finally, a move toward the UN would "adversely affect our prestige throughout the Far East and correspondingly diminish our influence and authority." This, after all, was an area where Japanese conquests during the war had already dented British standing.[12]

The British cabinet accepted Bevin's view that their imperial interests would best be served by refraining from any moves toward involving the UN in the consideration of India's future. Interestingly, the Indian leadership then preparing to take charge of the transition government looked at the UN in rather different light.

EMERGING INDIA IN THE UN

As vice president (de facto prime minister) of the interim government constituted in September 1946, Jawaharlal Nehru paid attention to the UN from the outset. Nehru's views on the UN were quite pragmatic. The structure of the UN, he recognized, accorded a privileged position to the great powers, which went against the idea of a democratic assembly. He believed that the power of veto was "obviously undesirable," but it stemmed from the "recognition of real facts prevailing in the world today." The major powers had "a special position in the world today and if they fall out there is trouble which the smaller powers cannot check." Much like Jan Christian Smuts, the other towering figure in the British imperial system and the UN, Nehru believed that the veto was an essential concession for the viability of the UN. "Any secession by any of the major powers would obviously have far-reaching consequences." It was important, he believed, to ensure "the continuance of the U.N.O. as some kind of forum where the Great Powers as well as small can function together."[13]

At the same time, Nehru thought that the UN afforded an opportunity for India both to position itself as a major actor and to transform key aspects of the existing international system. In Nehru's conception, these two efforts were braided together. For it was by pushing for a new normative agenda that India would strengthen its international position and acquire legitimacy to help pursue its interests. "Whatever the present position of India might be," observed Nehru, "she is potentially a Great Power." In the years ahead, India would "play a very great part in security problems of Asia and the Indian Ocean, more especially of the Middle East and South-East Asia." But Asia was very poorly represented in the Security Council. In consequence, he held that India should be elected a non-permanent member of the Security Council. "India is the centre of security in Asia . . . [and] must have a central place in any council considering these matters." Nehru felt that India should put forward its case for election: "Even if we fail in getting elected, the very fact that we have put out a strong case will influence world opinion and raise India in the eyes of the world." Indeed, it was not wise to accept a "secondary position right from the beginning."[14] More broadly, Nehru held that "there was no reason why Europe or the Americas should be considered the pivots of the modern world and Asia should be ignored." Asia was going to emerge as a centre of gravity of international politics: "The sooner this is recognised and given effect to the better."[15]

The major issue where Nehru wished India to frame a new agenda was on the matter of the colonized territories. Nehru was well aware that the UN Charter was biased in favor of preserving the position of the major imperial powers. He was equally attuned to the intellectual links between the prevailing idea of internationalism and the theorists and advocates of the British Commonwealth.[16] Writing from prison during the war years, Nehru had criticized the widely propagated idea that "internationalism would triumph if we [India] agreed to remain as junior partners in British Empire or Commonwealth . . . this particular type of so-called internationalism is only an extension of a narrow British nationalism."[17] India would have to take the lead in fashioning a new internationalism. Nehru believed that many of the colonized countries of Asia and Africa looked to India for support and leadership in their attempts to obtain political and economic freedom. India, he believed, should help them

> both because it is the correct approach and also in the narrow interests of India herself. It is admitted now that any world structure should have a certain uniformity and cohesion. It is becoming progressively impossible for different principles to be applied to different areas or countries, specially those under some kind of colonial domination. The United Nations Charter itself recognizes some of these principles.[18]

Two issues gave Nehru the opportunity to try and change some rules of the game. The first was the introduction by South Africa of the Asiatic Land Tenure and Indian Representation Act, which came to be known as the "Ghetto Act."[19] The act effectively segregated the Indian community in South Africa by regulating the acquisition and occupation of real estate by Asians in the provinces of Natal and Transvaal. Further, it conferred limited franchise on Indians and discriminated against South African nationals of Asian or "colored" origin. The viceroy of India had already been alerted to the matter, but Nehru pushed it vigorously once he entered office. A strong Indian delegation led by Nehru's sister, Vijayalakshmi Pandit, was sent to the General Assembly to decry the Ghetto Act.

Smuts was surprised by this move. He had been among the champions of Article 2.7 of the Charter, which proscribed interference in matters falling under a state's "domestic jurisdiction." When the issue came up for discussion, the US, Britain, South Africa, and other Commonwealth states wanted to refer the matter to the International Court of Justice to pronounce on India's claim that the treatment of Indians in South Africa was incompatible with the latter's obligations under the UN Charter.

Nehru, however, held that this move was "a dilatory one and should certainly be opposed."[20] The Indian delegation accordingly insisted that the matter was a political, not legal, one—a stance that resonated with several members of the Assembly. When India's motion was put to vote, it was upheld by a comfortable majority. Nehru was understandably delighted with the outcome. The General Assembly had "not only vindicated India's honour but has shown itself a guardian of human rights. This is full of hope for the future of the United Nations Organization."[21] And of course, the outcome bolstered India's own standing. India's performance also pointed the way for a more activist role by the General Assembly: on Palestine, on Franco's Spain, and on several trusteeship disputes. Nehru himself came round to the view that it was preferable "to rely on [the] General rather than on [the] Security Council which was dominated by a few Powers."[22]

The second issue in which India played an important role concerned the future status of South-West Africa. South Africa under Smuts sought to annex this erstwhile League of Nations "mandate." The question came up in the very first meeting of the UN General Assembly in London. The South African representative made it clear that his government would seek not to convert the administration of South-West Africa into a UN trusteeship but rather to annex it outright. Although the move was disliked by the US, Smuts managed to obtain the backing of the British government. Significant opposition, however, came from within Africa itself. The leader of Bechuanaland, Tsekhedi Khama, stood up to Smuts, fearing that his own land would be up for annexation after South-West Africa. Although the British initially sought to muffle Khama's voice, the latter managed to lobby and obtain the support of several members of the UN.

India was forthcoming in its support for the cause. As Nehru noted, India had "no particular interest in South-West Africa but she must support the interests of Africans." Nevertheless, "on principle we must oppose any such annexation of mandated or any other territory anywhere." India should instead demand UN trusteeship based on the principle that "sovereignty ultimately resides in the people concerned and their wishes and interests are paramount."[23] These efforts paid off. When the issue came up for discussion in the General Assembly some months later, the British chose to back down when faced with the widespread opposition to annexation. A watered-down South African motion was rejected by a large majority, and South Africa was asked to come up with trusteeship arrangements instead.[24]

Manu Bhagavan has argued that Nehru's early approach to the UN reflected his desire to create a new form of supranationalism—a world of "post-sovereign nation states" governed by "the meta-sovereign institution of the UN." Nehru's aims, in this reading, presaged the debates on sovereignty of the post–Cold War period. Bhagavan attempts to underline this point by considering India's role in the Commission on Human Rights, which resulted in the Universal Declaration of Human Rights.[25] To be sure,

Nehru did talk about "One World" and related ideas. But his own position on the balance between rights of states and human rights was more carefully considered.

Bhagavan rightly points out that the Indian representative at the Commission on Human Rights, Hansa Mehta, advanced a draft that stated: "The Security Council of the United Nations shall be seized of all alleged violation of human rights, investigate them and enforce redress within the framework of the United Nations." But, and by contrast, Nehru's instructions to the Indian delegation had been more circumspect. India should make it evident that it stood for "equality of opportunity for all peoples and races . . . [and that] there should be no discrimination on grounds of race, religion . . . on grounds of sex." The only thing that he wished to ensure was that "all non-nationals should be treated alike. Certain fundamental or human rights must be guaranteed to the non-nationals."[26] Beyond this, however, Nehru was clear that the rights of nationals of a state must "necessarily differ from those of non-nationals."[27] Indeed, when Mehta advanced her draft, Nehru's discomfort was obvious. "It was not our intention," he wrote, "that any formal resolution be submitted on behalf of India." Further discussion on the draft, he suggested, should be deferred.[28]

Nehru's conception of human rights, then, was certainly progressive, but the claim that he sought to erode the sovereignty of the state seems an overstatement. Indeed, this went against the grain of another core principle of his foreign policy, nonalignment. For at the core of the idea of nonalignment was the preservation of autonomy of the state in international politics. Subsequently, Nehru would also champion the so-called five principles of peaceful coexistence: one of the principles being noninterference in internal affairs of another country. This struggle for an appropriate balance between sovereign interests of the state and internationalism came out most clearly in the early crises faced by independent India.

THE UN AND INDEPENDENT INDIA

Independent India confronted its first international crisis when the princely state of Junagadh proclaimed its decision to join the newly created Pakistan. Situated in the Kathiawar region of western India, Junagadh was ruled by a Muslim nawab but its population consisted of a majority of Hindus. Junagadh shared no land frontiers with Pakistan, and its outlet to the sea was a few hundred kilometers from the Pakistani port of Karachi. Notwithstanding India's protests, Pakistan accepted Junagadh's accession in mid-September 1947.

India responded to Junagadh's accession to Pakistan by imposing a blockade of essential supplies and by deploying forces round Junagadh. Prime Minister Nehru, however, was anxious to avoid the possibility of a war with Pakistan and resisted pressure from his colleagues to take more forceful steps. Nehru suggested adopting a coercive strategy of graduated military pressure and offering a referendum or plebiscite to determine the wishes of Junagadh's populace on accession to India or Pakistan. In considering these alternatives, Nehru was aware throughout of the UN's potential role. One of the reasons he wished to eschew the robust military measures advocated by his colleagues was his desire not to be placed in "an unfavourable position in the UNO." Of course, in response to the Indian military buildup against Junagadh, it was conceivable that Pakistan might appeal to the UN and that the latter might issue some directions. "If so," Nehru observed, "we shall naturally abide by these directions."[29] Clearly, he was keen to ensure the steps taken by India were in conformity with the UN's stance on the matter. Following Junagadh's decision to rescind its accession to Pakistan, the Indian cabinet was prepared to hold a plebiscite under UN supervision.[30]

The problem in Kashmir was the obverse of Junagadh.[31] Here, the Hindu maharaja of Kashmir, whose population was largely Muslim and whose state was of importance to both Pakistan and India, dithered in the matter of accession. Forced by a Pakistan-abetted tribal invasion of his state, in October 1947 the Maharaja joined India, thus locking Pakistan and India in a bitter and violent dispute. On Kashmir, too, Nehru offered to undertake a UN-supervised plebiscite. But he was clear from the outset that this could happen after the Pakistani raiders had withdrawn and status quo ante restored in Kashmir. Although Pakistan rejected this offer, Nehru decided to refer the matter to the UN Security Council. As seen earlier, Nehru was no great admirer of the Security Council, but he believed that the alternative to UN reference was an all-out war with Pakistan, which he wished to avoid.

The Kashmir dispute was referred under Article 35 of the UN charter. India claimed that Pakistani nationals and tribesmen had attacked its state of Jammu and Kashmir. It requested the Council to take steps to prevent Pakistan from continuing its actions. Pakistan denied complicity and in turn alleged that India had pocketed the accession of Kashmir by fraud and violence.

The Security Council's attitude toward Kashmir was largely shaped by the British delegation led by the commonwealth secretary, Philip Noel-Baker. Like his counterpart in the foreign office, Noel-Baker believed that

Britain's position in the Middle East was doddering: in scurrying from Palestine, the British had already alienated the Arabs. The latter might be further inflamed if Britain wobbled on Kashmir. "It was important to avoid the danger of antagonising the whole of Islam by appearing to side with India against Pakistan." Besides, Noel-Baker believed that with a majority of Muslims, Kashmir quite properly belonged to Pakistan. Consequently the British delegation brushed aside India's complaint and asserted that fighting could stop only if arrangements for a fair plebiscite were reached. This would entail the induction of Pakistani troops into Kashmir and the establishment of a "neutral" administration. These ideas, of course, were antithetical to New Delhi's stance.

These developments led Nehru to conclude that Britain and the US had "played a dirty role" and set in motion his steady disenchantment with the UN's role on Kashmir. The subsequent induction of the Pakistan army into the fighting in Kashmir convinced him that his original idea of a plebiscite was impractical, for Pakistan would not withdraw its forces prior to the plebiscite. By the summer of 1948, Nehru veered to the idea of partitioning Kashmir as the best alternative. Interestingly, following its visit to the subcontinent during this period, the UN Commission on India and Pakistan unanimously concluded partition was "the only eventual solution." Because Pakistan was resolutely opposed to it and because it was beyond their remit, the commission decided not to recommend it, but they would allude to it in their report.[32]

Thus India's attitude toward the UN on Kashmir did not, as Mazower suggests, stem from a reflexive desire of an independent state to uphold the status quo. After all, it was India that took the lead in referring the dispute to the UN. The British, and to a lesser extent American, stance appeared to Nehru as overtly biased against India. This, coupled with the lack of realism in the numerous proposals for a plebiscite advanced by UN mediators, led Nehru to begin stonewalling the UN's efforts. In any event, the Kashmir imbroglio did not spell an end to Nehru's attempts to use the UN both to shape the agenda of world politics and to advance India's interests. During the 1950s and early 1960s India continued to play an important role on such issues as race relations, decolonization, mediation, and UN efforts in Korea and Vietnam and, above all, in Congo. That these efforts were not an airy idealism divorced from India's own interests was most forcefully demonstrated when the UN General Assembly approved India's military action against Portuguese Goa—an action that was almost unanimously condemned by the NATO states.

Nearly five decades after Nehru's death, India today boasts of a much larger pool of military and economic resources. It is not surprising that as India's military and economic might has increased, Indians have come to set much store by "hard" power. As one influential account of recent Indian foreign policy puts it, India now relies on the argument of power rather than the power of argument.[33] This is perhaps inevitable. But a rising India can ill afford to overlook the role of norms, legitimacy, and institutions in the pursuit of its interests. As New Delhi charts its way through a turbulent international order, reflecting on its early engagement with the UN might provide intellectual and practical tools for the challenges that lie ahead.

Notes

1. Mark Mazower, *No Enchanted Palace: The End of Empire and the Ideological Origins of the United Nations* (Princeton University Press, 2009), 25–27, 149–89.

2. Manu Bhagavan, "A New Hope: India, the United Nations and the Making of the Universal Declaration of Human Rights," *Modern Asian Studies* (2008): 3, n4. Also see, idem, *The Peacemakers: India and the Quest for One World* (New Delhi: HarperCollins, 2012).

3. Two recent works have highlighted this aspect of Nehru's foreign policy. Srinath Raghavan, *War and Peace in Modern India: A Strategic History of the Nehru Years* (Palgrave Macmillan, 2010); Andrew Kennedy, *The International Ambitions of Mao and Nehru: National Efficacy Beliefs and the Making of Foreign Policy* (Cambridge: Cambridge University Press, 2011).

4. Marika Sherwood, "India at the Founding of the United Nations," *International Studies* 33:4 (1996): 408.

5. Interview with Evelyn Wrench, December 1941, *The Collected Works of Mahatma Gandhi* (New Delhi: Publications Division Government of India, 1999), 98 vols. (electronic book) (hereafter *CWMG*), vol. 81, p. 348. Available at http://www.gandhiserve.org/e/cwmg/cwmg.htm.

6. Statement to the Press, April 17, 1945, *CWMG*, vol. 86, pp. 188–90.

7. Sherwood, "India at the Founding of the United Nations," 408–12.

8. For an overview of these issues, see John Darwin, *Britain and Decolonisation: The Retreat from Empire in the Post-War World* (Palgrave Macmillan, 1988), 67–166.

9. Darwin, *Britain and Decolonisation*, 89–90; Anita Inder Singh, *The Limits of British Influence: South Asia and the Anglo-American Relationship, 1947–56* (New York: St. Martin's Press, 1993), 16–21; R. J. Moore, *Escape from Empire: The Attlee Government and the Indian Problem* (Oxford: Clarendon Press, 1983), 61–65.

10. "Situation in India and Its Possible Effect upon Foreign Relations," memorandum by Secretary of State for Foreign Affairs, June 14, 1946; annexure to the memorandum titled "Situation in India and the United Nations Organisation," in Nicholas Mansergh, E. W. R. Lumby, and Penderel Moon, eds., *Constitutional Relations between Britain and India: The Transfer of Power, 1942–47*, vol. 7, pp. 930–37.

11. For a brilliant account of the imperial system, see John Darwin, *The Empire Project: Rise and Fall of the British World-System* (Cambridge: Cambridge University Press, 2009).

12. Chris Bayly and Tim Harper, *Forgotten Wars: The End of Britain's Asian Empire* (London: Allen Lane, 2007).

13. Note, September 7, 1946, *Selected Works of Jawaharlal Nehru* (hereafter *SWJN*), 2nd series, vol. 1, pp. 441–44.

14. Note, September 5, 1946, ibid., 438–40.

15. Note, September 16, 1946, ibid., 451.

16. On these ideological cross-currents see, Mazower, *No Enchanted Palace*, 28–65.

17. Jawaharlal Nehru, *Discovery of India* (n.p., 1946), 41.

18. Note, September 15, 1946, *SWJN*, vol. 1, pp. 445–47.

19. Mazower, *No Enchanted Palace*, 171–85.

20. Note, November 15, 1946, ibid., 446.

21. Message to Vijayalakshmi Pandit, December 9, 1946, ibid., 468.

22. Telegram to Hansa Mehta, February 1, 1947, *SWJN*, vol. 2, p. 485.

23. Note, September 5, 1946, *SWJN*, vol. 1, p. 438. Also see Note, September 15, 1946, ibid., 447–49.

24. M. Crowder, "Tsekhedi Khama, Smuts and South-West Africa," *Journal of Modern African Studies* 25:1 (1987): 25–42.

25. Bhagavan, "New Hope," 1–37.

26. Bhagavan misreads this as suggesting that Nehru wanted the same rights for nationals and non-nationals. This is erroneous: Nehru only sought equal treatment for all non-nationals.

27. Note, January 14, 1947, *SWJN*, vol. 1, pp. 470–71.

28. Telegram to Hansa Mehta, February 1, 1947, *SWJN*, vol. 2, p. 485.

29. Note on Junagadh by Nehru, September 29, 1947, F200/246, Mountbatten Papers, British Library.

30. Extracts from Minutes of an Emergency Meeting of the Cabinet held on November 10, 1947, F200/90D, Mountbatten Papers, British Library.

31. This account of Kashmir draws on Raghavan, *War and Peace in Modern India*, 101–46.

32. Record of talk with Josef Korbel on September 27, 1948, DO 134/5, The National Archives, Kew, London.

33. C. Raja Mohan, *Crossing the Rubicon: The Shaping of India's New Foreign Policy* (Palgrave Macmillan, 2004).

Chapter 6

Palestine and Israel at the United Nations: Partition, Recognition, and Membership

Debra Shushan

Here are the sole remaining representatives of the Semitic race. They are in the land in which that race was cradled. . . . With good will and a spirit of cooperation, may arise a rebirth, in historical surroundings, of the genius of each people.

—Report to the General Assembly, UN Special Committee on Palestine

The UN's actual role in critical situations was, to a considerable extent, pioneered in Palestine.

—Sir Brian Urquhart, UN Undersecretary-General for Special Political Affairs, 1974–86

The histories and legacies of Israel, Palestine, and the United Nations are deeply enmeshed. The UN played a crucial role in the attempted partition of Palestine and the recognition of Israeli independence. This early test of its authority and efficacy helped shape the nascent international organization. Throughout the duration of the Arab-Israeli conflict, the UN's role in determining the disposition of this disputed land has been underappreciated.[1] In this essay I begin with a look at the origins of the Arab-Jewish struggle in Palestine, and then demonstrate the impact the UN had by tracing its effect on Palestine's fortunes from the end of the British mandate through the partition resolution and subsequent acceptance of Israel's bid for UN membership. I then examine the legacy and lessons of UN involvement through this period, closing with a consideration of the recent Palestinian bid for UN membership through the lens of 1947.

THE STRUGGLE FOR PALESTINE: ENTER THE UN

The United Nations took over the question of Palestine in 1947 as the problem solver of last resort. At the time, Arabs and Jews were struggling over the territory, the war-weary British faced imperial overstretch and desired to wash their hands of the troublesome mandate for Palestine they had assumed under the League of Nations, and none of the other ostensible great powers wished to assume responsibility for crafting a solution.[2] Having declared that "His Majesty's Government are not prepared to continue indefinitely to govern Palestine themselves merely because Arabs and Jews cannot agree upon the means of sharing its government between them,"[3] the United Kingdom requested on April 3, 1947, that the UN General Assembly make recommendations concerning the future government of Palestine with a view to bringing about an "early settlement."[4] The letter from the UK delegation referenced Article 10 of the UN Charter,[5] according to which the General Assembly may discuss and make recommendations concerning any matter within the purview of the UN, provided that the Security Council is not already considering the matter.

Prior to its consideration by the General Assembly, the struggle between the Arab and Jewish communities in Palestine had amassed a substantial history. The modern political Zionist movement began in Europe in the late nineteenth century.[6] The resurgence in anti-Jewish violence in Russia in the 1880s, along with the experience of unvarnished anti-Semitism in France during the Dreyfus Affair in the subsequent decade, convinced some that Jews would never find safety and equality in Europe. Against a backdrop of European nationalist movements, influential opinion makers including Leo Pinsker and Theodor Herzl found their answer in nationalism. Pinsker argued for the "regeneration" of the Jewish nation, arguing that emancipation from being "everywhere aliens" in the Diaspora required that Jews acquire "a home of their own."[7] Herzl called for establishment of Jewish sovereignty over "a portion of the globe large enough to satisfy the reasonable requirements of a nation"[8] and was agnostic regarding the location.[9] For the majority within the small Zionist movement, however, only the ancestral homeland of the Jewish people, Eretz Yisrael (the Land of Israel), would do. The first Zionist Congress meeting at Basel, Switzerland, in 1897 announced: "Zionism aims at establishing for the Jewish people a publicly and legally assured home in Palestine."

As Jewish immigration began, the stage was set for confrontation between the Zionists and the native Arab population of Palestine. Incorporated into the Ottoman Empire in 1516 along with the rest of Greater Syria, Palestine's fate was in question given Ottoman decline and European powers' designs on the region. When Istanbul allied with Germany in World War I, Britain promised Sharif Hussein of Mecca an independent Arab state if Hussein would lead an Arab revolt against Turkish rule. Dispute would later en-sue over whether the Hussein-McMahon correspondence of 1916 had stipulated that Palestine would be included in that Arab state.[10] Meanwhile, Britain conspired with France to divide control over Ottoman territories after the war. The resulting Sykes-Picot Agreement stipulated that much of Palestine[11] would become part of an "independent" Arab state under British protection. Palestine became the "thrice-promised land" when the British government issued the Balfour Declaration, calling for the "establishment in Palestine of a national home for the Jewish people" provided that "nothing shall be done which may prejudice the civil and religious rights of existing non-Jewish communities in Palestine."[12]

The League of Nations, established after World War I to prevent future wars, devised the mandate system to address the issue of "territories and colonies which as a consequence of the late war have ceased to be under the sovereignty of the states which formerly governed them," including areas that had been part of the Ottoman Empire. Article 22 of the League's Covenant provided for entrusting the peoples of these territories who are "not able to stand by themselves under the strenuous conditions of the modern world" to the "tutelage . . . of advanced nations," which would act on behalf of the League of Nations and report to it annually. Britain and France became mandatory powers for the former Ottoman territories, with Britain taking the mandate for Palestine. Under the British mandate, the Jewish population of Palestine grew from 83,790 (less than 8 percent) in 1922 to 608,225 (roughly one-third) in 1946. Jewish immigration constituted the greatest factor in this increase, with an estimated 376,000 Jewish immigrants entering Palestine between 1920 and 1946.[13] Immigration was particularly heavy during the 1930s due to Nazi persecution; between 1931 and 1936, Jews grew from 18 to nearly 30 percent of the total population of Palestine.[14] As Jewish immigration grew, strife between the Arab and Jewish communities also increased, with outbreaks of violence in 1920, 1921, 1929, 1933, and a protracted Arab uprising from 1936 to 1939 that targeted both Jews and the British administration.[15] When Britain curbed Jewish immigration to assuage Arab concerns, Jewish resistance to British rule mounted, with many Jews enraged that their brethren attempting to escape the Holocaust and its aftermath were turned away from Palestine.[16]

Britain, as the mandatory power, found itself in a quagmire of its own making. In 1937, a report by the Royal Commission on Palestine (also known as the Peel Commission) found:

An irrepressible conflict has arisen between two national communities within the narrow bounds of one small country. There is no common ground between them. Their national aspirations are incompatible. . . . The conflict has grown steadily more bitter since 1920 and the process will continue. . . . The continuance of the present system means the gradual alienation of two peoples who are traditionally the friends of Britain.[17]

Ten years later and battle weary from World War II, Britain decided to quit. On February 18, 1947, Foreign Secretary Ernest Bevin announced in the House of Commons that the government had "reached the conclusion that the only course now open to us is to submit the problem to the judgment of the United Nations."[18]

UNSCOP RECOMMENDS PARTITION

The UN proceeded with its charge by forming a preparatory committee to study the Palestine situation and make recommendations to the General Assembly. Trygve Lie, the Norwegian who served as the UN's first Secretary-General, thought it best that the preparatory committee consist of eight members, including the five permanent members (P5) of the Security Council. He found, however, that "the Big Five were not enthusiastic."[19] Instead and following "some sparring,"[20] the General Assembly on April 28, 1947, adopted an Australian resolution which provided that the United Nations Special Committee on Palestine (UNSCOP) would consist of eleven members outside the P5. Australia, Canada, Czechoslovakia, Guatemala, India, Iran, the Netherlands, Peru, Sweden, Uruguay, and Yugoslavia were appointed to UNSCOP.[21]

UNSCOP proceeded with its investigation, which included visits to Jerusalem, Beirut, Amman, and displaced persons camps for Jewish refugees in Germany and Austria. It culled testimony from the Jewish Agency for Palestine, the governments of seven Arab states, and the British government, among others. The Arab Higher Committee—which had been formed at the initiative of the Grand Mufti of Jerusalem in 1936 and included prominent members of the Arab clans in Palestine—refused UNSCOP's invitations to cooperate.[22] In November 1947, UNSCOP presented its recommendations to the General Assembly. Its report included a majority plan recommending partition and a minority plan which called for a single federal state.[23]

The majority report contained three main provisions. First, it called for the partition of Palestine into two political entities: an Arab state and a Jewish state. Given the boundaries proposed in the plan,[24] each state would have three territorial sections, which would be linked together at two points of connection. The Arab state—consisting of the Western Galilee, the hill country of Samaria and Judea on the West Bank of the Jordan River, and the Mediterranean coastal plain in the South extending along the Egyptian border—would be almost entirely Arab with only a small Jewish minority. The Jewish state—made up of the Eastern Galilee, the Mediterranean coastal plain from Haifa to Jaffa, and a large swath of territory in the South including the Negev Desert—would contain a substantial Arab minority. Recognizing this demographic reality, the plan required protection of minority rights, including free exercise of religion, respect for family law and personal status of minorities, the right of each community to administer its own schools in its own language, and restrictions on expropriating property owned by minorities.[25] Second, the majority plan provided for an international trusteeship for Jerusalem and the surrounding areas, including Bethlehem. In accordance with Article 81 of the UN Charter, the UN would serve as the administering authority for this region holy to three faiths "for the reason that the Trusteeship Council, as a principal organ of the United Nations, affords a convenient and effective means of ensuring both the desired international supervision and the political, economic, and social well-being of the population of Jerusalem."[26] Third, the Arab and Jewish states and the international trusteeship for Jerusalem would be joined in an economic union to ensure the economic viability of partitioned Palestine. The economic union would include a common currency; customs union; cooperative oversight of public infrastructure, including railways and ports; and joint economic development.[27] The dissenters to the majority plan declared that it was "impracticable, unworkable, and could not possibly provide for two reasonably viable States."[28]

Instead, the minority provided a plan under which Palestine would become a single federal state composed of Arab and Jewish states with an overarching federal government. Crucially, while the plan would allow Jewish immigration into the Jewish state during a three-year transitional period, it would limit the influx to the "absorptive capacity" of the Jewish state, to be determined by an international commission. The minority report makes clear that "the homeless persons of Europe" are an "international responsibility" and that "no claim to a right of unlimited immigration of Jews into Palestine, irrespective of time, can be entertained"; in particular, Jews would not be allowed to immigrate in such numbers that would make them the majority population of Palestine. Calling partition an "anti-Arab solution," the minority report claimed that its own proposed solution "would be the most in harmony with the basic principles of the Charter of the United Nations," especially pertinent in this case in which the "moral and political prestige of the United Nations is deeply involved."[29]

The UN General Assembly approved the majority plan for partition of Palestine on November 29, 1947. The roll call vote indicated thirty-three in favor, thirteen opposed, and ten abstentions.[30] While resolution 181 was not entirely pleasing to the Zionist movement, particularly because it called for drastic restrictions on Jewish immigration, the Jewish Agency under the stewardship of David Ben-Gurion accepted it and the Jewish community in Palestine celebrated the vote.[31] For the Arab Higher Committee and members of the Arab League, who had rejected partition outright, the General Assembly vote came as a blow. Speaking immediately after the vote, Prince Faisal Al-Saud, the future king of Saudi Arabia, declared that his country had no intention of abiding by the UN decision:

> The Government of Saudi Arabia registers, on this historic occasion, the fact that it does not consider itself bound by the resolution adopted today by the General Assembly. Furthermore, it reserves to itself the full right to act freely in whatever way it deems fit, in accordance with the principles of right and justice.[32]

Saudi Arabia was not alone; representatives of Iraq, Syria, and Yemen made similar statements.[33] After the passage of the partition resolution, leaders of the Arab states laid the groundwork for the establishment of the Arab Liberation Army (ALA). In a letter to the UN Secretary-General, a representative of the Arab Higher Committee made clear, "The Arabs of Palestine . . . will never submit or yield to any Power going to Palestine to enforce partition. The only way to establish partition is first to wipe them out—man, woman, and child."[34] Meanwhile, the Arab Higher Committee and the Jewish Agency made their own military preparations as intercommunal violence between Arabs and Jews erupted in Palestine.[35] The British indicated they would not enforce the partition resolution and prepared to pull their forces out of Palestine by May 15, 1948.[36]

FAILURE OF PARTITION AND UN RECOGNITION OF ISRAEL

To facilitate the transfer of authority from the British mandatory administration to the new Arab and Jewish states, the UN formed a new Palestine

Commission of "five lonely pilgrims," with representatives from Bolivia, Czechoslovakia, Denmark, Panama, and the Philippines. In its first report to the Security Council, the Palestine Commission warned of the infiltration into Palestine of outside Arab troops, including members of the ALA. Given the prospect that "the period immediately following the termination of the Mandate will be a period of uncontrolled, widespread strife and bloodshed in Palestine," the Palestine Commission requested that the Security Council provide the "armed assistance which alone would enable the Commission to discharge its responsibilities."[37] Secretary-General Trygve Lie enthusiastically worked to establish a United Nations land force, which he proposed to form from "minimum units" contributed by members of the P5. Although Lie did not believe that the UN, as a general proposition, should be able to enforce political settlements, he argued that Palestine was a special case because the mandatory power in charge had turned over the territory to the UN to decide its future. In the event, the United States and United Kingdom declined to provide troops; Lie concluded that only the Soviet Union seemed committed to implementing partition.[38]

Without an international force to impose partition upon the withdrawal of British forces, events in Palestine took a different course. The Jewish leadership in Palestine, with future prime minister David Ben-Gurion at the helm, declared Israel's independence on the afternoon of May 14, effective at midnight with the termination of the British mandate. Within days, the armies of several surrounding Arab states invaded Palestine. The resulting war expanded the territory of Israel beyond what had been allotted to the Jewish state under resolution 181 and displaced 726,000 Palestinian Arab refugees.[39] Jordan seized most of the remaining territory that the UN had reserved for an Arab state, annexing the West Bank and East Jerusalem in 1950; Egypt took control of the Gaza Strip. The result, in the words of John Strawson, "was to be a partition of Palestine without Palestine itself."[40]

As for Israel, the new state received de facto recognition from the United States and de jure recognition from the Soviet Union within a week of proclaiming independence. In November 1948, Israel presented its application for UN membership in accordance with Article 4 of the UN Charter, which invites all "peace-loving states" that accept the obligations contained in the Charter to become members. The letter submitted by Israeli Foreign Minister Moshe Shertok[41] included a declaration that "the State of Israel hereby unreservedly accepts the obligations of the United Nations Charter and undertakes to honour them from the day when it becomes a Member of the

United Nations."[42] The General Assembly voted to admit Israel to membership in the UN on May 11, 1949, while alluding to Israel's responsibilities under resolutions 181 and 194, the latter of which called for UN control of Jerusalem and return of refugees.[43]

The UN played an important role in mediating between Israel and the Arab states during the 1948 war, facilitating the armistice agreements that brought armed hostilities to a close. On May 20, 1948, the Security Council appointed Count Folke Bernadotte of Sweden as UN mediator to Palestine. Bernadotte helped secure two short-term cease-fires and had just prepared recommendations for a lasting settlement when he was assassinated in Jerusalem by the Jewish militant group Lehi (also known as the Stern Gang) on September 17, 1948.[44] After helping to secure the 1949 armistice agreements between Israel and Egypt, Jordan, Lebanon, and Syria, Bernadotte's successor, Dr. Ralph Bunche of the United States, received the Nobel Peace Prize in 1950.[45]

UN INVOLVEMENT IN PALESTINE/ISRAEL: LEGACY AND LESSONS

Founded with the goal of keeping the postwar peace, the UN took on the unenviable task of determining the future governance of Palestine when the British mandatory power had exhausted its resources and patience. In the process, the organization experienced many "firsts":

> At various points since its founding, Israel has been separated from each of its neighbors by a UN peacekeeping operation; three of these operations remain in place.[46] The Arab-Israeli theater was the site of the first UN mediator,[47] the first UN observer mission,[48] the first UN peacekeeping mission,[49] and the first UN specialized agency,[50] still its largest. Even the white and black markings that adorn UN vehicles the world over have their origins in the Middle East, where UN blue and white was avoided so as not to give rise to an appearance of bias by replicating the colors of the Israeli flag.[51]

What can we learn from the successes and failures of the UN in its attempts to promulgate a solution to the struggle between Arabs and Jews over Palestine/Israel? I suggest three lessons.

1. *UN success requires cooperation of and coordination with great powers.* In the case of the UN's attempt to impose partition in Palestine, this was not forthcoming. The lack of interest among the P5 in serving as members of the UN Special Committee on Palestine was an early indication of insufficient great power commitment. Instead, eleven small and middle-sized states were appointed

to UNSCOP. In Brian Urquhart's assessment, "It is astonishing that such a mediocre body should have been entrusted with a problem of such importance."[52] Meanwhile, key great power stakeholders were intransigent or equivocating. The cooperation of the United Kingdom, as the mandatory power in Palestine, was essential but elusive. In his memoir, Secretary-General Lie frequently expresses frustration with the lack of British cooperation with UN efforts, as well as with American flip-flopping (due to apparent divisions among US policy makers regarding the Palestine issue). Lie rebukes the Security Council's lack of action in response to the Arab invasion of Israel after the latter's independence declaration: "The United States did not say a word; and in the Council as a whole (with the exception of the Soviet Member)[53] there seemed to be a conspiracy of silence reminiscent of the most disheartening head-in-the-sand moments of the Chamberlain appeasement era."[54] Great powers must cooperate with the UN if its efforts are to be successful. Likewise, in its role as an agent, the UN must be attentive to the powerful states that constitute its principal, the international community of states.[55]

2. *UN success requires buy-in from local stakeholders.* Opposition to partition by Arab states and especially by Palestinian Arabs was a formidable obstacle to the efforts of UNSCOP, just as Jewish opposition to UNSCOP's minority plan would likely have scuttled any attempt to implement it. Both the majority and minority portions of the report submitted by UNSCOP contained optimistic forecasts for how local interests would change over time once a new reality had been imposed from outside. The minority plan offers this wishful note, "It is entirely possible that if a federal solution were firmly and definitively imposed, the two groups, in their own self-interest, would gradually develop a spirit of co-operation in their common State."[56] For better or worse, no solution is likely to be *imposed* on the parties concerned "definitively" enough. Their cooperation in reaching and implementing an agreement that meets the minimum requirements of each side is essential in achieving a solution to this long-running conflict.

3. *UN success requires organizational capacity.* States delegate authority to international organizations (IOs) because these organizations help states achieve aims—like preserving peace and security—better and more efficiently than states can on their own. Centralization and independence are two characteristics that make IOs effective.[57] With a skilled and centralized administrative apparatus, IOs can develop substantive expertise in areas such as peacekeeping, while independence confers "the authority to act with a

degree of autonomy, and often with neutrality, in defined spheres."[58] The attempted partition of Palestine brought to light a key deficiency in the UN's organizational capacity, namely the lack of an independent international policing force. Elsewhere in this volume, Michael Doyle notes that the original vision for the UN Charter included provisions for a standing force to be under a joint command appointed by the Security Council and that the failure to constitute such a force reflected a victory of discretionary state sovereignty over supranationalism. Secretary-General Lie advanced the view that the Security Council possessed the authority to raise a police force since Article 24 of the UN Charter had charged the Council with "primary responsibility for the maintenance of international peace and security." Lie was particularly keen to leverage the Palestine case to push such an interpretation of the Charter and constitute a UN land force to be deployed for peacekeeping in Palestine.[59]

Much to Secretary-General Lie's consternation, the failure to persuade the P5 to contribute armed personnel for the establishment of a UN land force both hampered the efforts of the UN in Palestine and limited the UN's effectiveness more broadly.[60] In lieu of armed peacekeepers, the Security Council approved the dispatch of unarmed observers to Palestine (the United Nations Truce Supervision Organization, or UNTSO) to facilitate a cease-fire between the belligerents in late May 1948. Lie's successor, Dag Hammarskjöld, furthered these efforts at UN capacity-building. In 1956, while Hammarskjöld was Secretary-General, the UN deployed its first armed peacekeepers (the UN Emergency Force, or UNEF) to defuse the Suez Crisis.[61] The UN still lacks its own military force, but its Department of Peacekeeping Operations relies on contributions of manpower from member states and currently maintains almost 100,000 troops, military observers, and police personnel serving around the world.[62]

THE UN AND PALESTINIAN STATEHOOD GOING FORWARD

On September 23, 2011, Palestinian Authority President Mahmoud Abbas presented to Secretary-General Ban Ki-moon an application for membership in the United Nations on behalf of the State of Palestine. Just as Moshe Shertok's application on behalf of Israel had done in 1948,[63] the letter from Abbas referenced the instructions in the General Assembly's partition resolution (181) urging "sympathetic consideration" regarding UN membership for the Arab and Jewish states carved out of the former Palestine mandate.[64] Israeli Prime Minister Binyamin Netanyahu, speaking before the General Assembly, responded, "The Palestinians should first make peace with Israel and then get their state. . . . After such a peace agreement is signed, Israel will not be the last country to welcome a Palestinian state as a new member of the United Nations. We will be the first."[65] Palestinians blame Israel for the failure of peace talks to date and have declined to continue negotiations while Israel builds settlements in the occupied territories. As of mid-2013, the UN Security Council, which chooses whether or not to recommend admission by the General Assembly, has not taken action on the Palestinian bid; the Council has stated that it is "unable to make a unanimous recommendation."[66] The Obama administration has indicated willingness to veto Palestinian UN membership if the question comes to a vote before the Security Council.[67]

With its membership bid stalled in the Security Council, the Palestinian Authority turned to the General Assembly, requesting an upgrade in its status to "non-member observer State." Casting ballots on November 29, 2012, the sixty-fifth anniversary of its vote to partition Palestine, the General Assembly voted to approve the Palestinian request with a resounding tally of 138 members in favor, 9 against, and 41 abstentions.[68] In remarks to the Assembly prior to the vote, President Abbas stated, "We did not come here seeking to delegitimize a State established years ago, and that is Israel; rather we came to affirm the legitimacy of the State that must now achieve its independence, and that is Palestine."[69]

With the events of 1947–48 in the background, the return of the Palestinian issue to the United Nations prompts the following observations. First, the Palestinian bid for UN membership indicates respect for international law and the will of the community of states. From its establishment, the Zionist movement made its goal securing a home for the Jewish people in Palestine that would be recognized by "public law."[70] The passage of resolution 181, the establishment of Israeli diplomatic relations with other states, and Israel's admission to the UN fulfilled that goal. In 1948, Arab states defied the UN and took up arms rather than allow Palestine's partition. Today, however, the Palestinian Authority is seeking recognition through international legal channels and appealing for the belated partition of mandatory Palestine into two states. That is a positive development and one which the international community would do well to encourage; this is particularly important given the continued refusal of Hamas, the Islamist ruling party in Gaza, to recognize Israeli statehood.

Second, the Palestinian bid has important symbolic repercussions, and some practical ones as well. Following the November 2012 vote by the

General Assembly, Palestine became one of two non-member states that maintain permanent observer missions to the UN (the other is the Holy See). Especially significant, the UN now officially recognizes the Palestinian mission as representing the "State of Palestine." For President Mahmoud Abbas, the General Assembly vote brought a short-term boost in popularity at a time when attention had shifted to Gaza, which withstood eight days of Israeli military strikes following an increase in Hamas rocket launches into Israel. While changing the practical reality of Palestinian statelessness will still require an agreement between Israelis and Palestinians, the upgrade of Palestine's status by the General Assembly generates some tangible consequences for both the Palestinian Authority and the UN itself. The Palestinian Authority may pursue membership in specialized UN bodies; it has already received full membership in the UN Educational, Scientific, and Cultural Organization (UNESCO).[71] Of particular importance, the Palestinian Authority may attempt to join the International Criminal Court and push for condemnation of Israeli practices in the West Bank and Gaza. In the words of chief Palestinian negotiator Saeb Erakat, following the General Assembly's vote "Palestine will become a country under occupation."[72] Consequences for UN bodies that extend membership to Palestine may include funding cuts by the United States. Following UNESCO's decision to make Palestine a full member, the US followed through on a threat to freeze its financial contributions to the organization. The loss of 22 percent of its budget, according to UNESCO's director-general, has led to the organization's "worst ever financial situation" and is "crippling our capacity to deliver."[73]

Third, Palestine's recent bid for UN membership confirms the Security Council's image as a conservative body bent on preserving the status quo, whereas the General Assembly appears more progressive and open to a multiplicity of voices. In this volume, Edward Luck notes this dichotomy, with the Council behaving more as a "League of the Satisfied" and the Assembly focusing on universality of membership. The General Assembly's recognition of Palestinian statehood and upgrading of Palestine's status is starkly contrasted against the stalling of the Palestinian membership request by the Security Council, stymied by the threat of a US veto.

Fourth, the international standing of the United States has been sullied in this diplomatic battle over Palestinian membership in the UN, particularly in the Middle East, where Arab attitudes toward the US were already negative.[74] With its threatened veto of Palestinian UN membership, slashing of UNESCO funding, and threat to cut off American foreign aid to the Palestinian Authority, Washington is further alienating itself from a more democratic Arab world, in which Arab publics are likely to have a greater say in formulating the foreign policies of their respective states. Meanwhile, in renewed efforts by Secretary of State John Kerry to rejuvenate the Arab-Israeli peace process, the US claim to be an honest broker will further strain credulity and tarnish American efforts at mediation.

Finally, absent an agreement on a two-state solution to the Israeli-Palestinian conflict, time is working in favor of rendering partition obsolete. Since its victory in the 1967 war, Israel has held de facto control over the former Palestine mandate, from the Jordan River to the Mediterranean Sea. While a majority of Israelis and Palestinians favor division into two states for two peoples,[75] endorsing partition as the best available solution to their impasse, Israeli settlement construction and encroachment into predominantly Arab territory will continue to increase the difficulty of separation.[76] Given the current course, pressure for a binational state is likely to grow, especially among Palestinians who had previously invested hope in the Palestinian-Israeli peace process but find themselves "living a one-state reality."[77]

The United Nations was central to the attempt to partition Palestine into Arab and Jewish states over sixty-five years ago, and the Arab-Israeli conflict has helped shape the UN in turn. For better or worse and whether the former territory of mandatory Palestine is destined to become two states or one, the United Nations will remain deeply embroiled in the Israel/Palestine saga. Secretary-General Ban Ki-moon recently pledged: "I will continue to do my utmost to achieve a negotiated two-State solution. . . . We cannot afford another year without courageous action." [78]

Notes

Epigraph: Brian Urquhart, "The United Nations in the Middle East: A Fifty-Year Retrospective," *Middle East Journal* 49, no. 4 (1995): 573.

1. Bruce D. Jones, "The Middle East Peace Process," in *The UN Security Council: From the Cold War to the Twenty-First Century,* ed. David M. Malone (Boulder, CO: Lynne Rienner Publishers, 2004).

2. The United States was divided internally on Palestine, and particularly so regarding the question of Jewish statehood. The Soviet Union, at the time, strongly supported an end to the British mandate and the formation of a Jewish state, consonant with its opposition to European colonialism. France was embroiled in its own interests in the region (particularly in North Africa) and chose to avoid active involvement. Urquhart, "United Nations in the Middle East," 574.

3. Quoted in United Nations Special Committee on Palestine, "Report to the General Assembly," A/364, September 3, 1947. United Nations Information System on the Question of Palestine (UNISPAL) Documents Collection. Located at unispal.un.org.

4. United Kingdom Delegation to United Nations, UK letter to Acting Secretary-General, April 3, 1947, A/286, UNISPAL Documents Collection.

5. Ibid.

6. Howard M. Sachar, *A History of Israel: From the Rise of Zionism to Our Time*, 2nd ed. (New York: Alfred A. Knopf, 1996).

7. Leo Pinsker, *Auto-Emancipation: An Appeal to His People by a Russian Jew* (1882). Excerpted in Arthur Hertzberg, ed., *The Zionist Idea: A Historical Analysis and Reader* (Philadelphia: Jewish Publication Society, 1997).

8. Theodor Herzl, *A Jewish State: An Attempt at a Modern Solution of the Jewish Question*, trans. J. de Haas (New York: Maccabean, 1904). 26.

9. In Herzl's view, Argentina and Palestine might be equally suitable. Joseph Chamberlain, Britain's colonial secretary, suggested to Herzl in 1902 that he consider modern-day Kenya (then referred to as Uganda). According to John Strawson, Herzl's enthusiasm regarding the proposal, which was rejected by the Zionist Congress, had more to do with Herzl's satisfaction over the implicit recognition of the Zionist movement by the UK than with the substance of the East Africa proposal. See John Strawson, *Partitioning Palestine: Legal Fundamentalism in the Palestinian-Israeli Conflict* (London: Pluto Press, 2010), 22–23.

10. The British side of the dispute is recorded in Winston Churchill, "The Churchill White Paper," June 3, 1922, UNISPAL Documents Collection.

11. Exceptions included much of northern Palestine, including Jerusalem, which would be under "international administration," and the ports of Haifa and Acre, which would be subject to British control. A map dividing the Ottoman Empire's Middle East territories into an independent Arab state (or states) under British and French protection, European-occupied areas (with swaths under control by the British, French, and Russians), and an international zone is included in "Sykes-Picot Agreement," May 16, 1916, UNISPAL Documents Collection.

12. United Kingdom Foreign Office, "Balfour Declaration," November 2, 1917, UNISPAL Documents Collection.

13. Population statistics were reported by the British mandatory administration and appear in United Nations Special Committee on Palestine, "Report to the General Assembly," chapter 2, paragraphs 13–16, UNISPAL Documents Collection. In absolute numbers, the Arab population of Palestine also grew considerably during the British mandate. According to the UNSCOP report, the increase in the Arab population was due almost entirely to high fertility rates coupled with a substantial decline in death rates due to improvements in public health and living conditions.

14. Ibid.

15. Palestine Royal Commission, "Summary of the Report of the Palestine Royal Commission," C.495.M.336.1937.VI., November 30, 1937, UNISPAL Documents Collection; Gudrun Kramer, *A History of Palestine: From the Ottoman Conquest to the Founding of the State of Israel*, trans. Graham Harman and Gudrun Kramer (Princeton: Princeton University Press, 2008), 264–95.

16. United Nations Special Committee on Palestine, "Report to the General Assembly," chapter 2, paragraphs 91–92.

17. Palestine Royal Commission, "Summary of the Report of the Palestine Royal Commission."

18. Government of the United Kingdom, "The Political History of Palestine under British Administration," A/AC.14/8, October 2, 1947, UNISPAL Documents Collection.

19. Trygve Lie, *In the Cause of Peace: Seven Years with the United Nations* (New York: Macmillan, 1954), 160.

20. Ibid., 161.

21. United Nations Special Committee on Palestine, "Report of the First Committee," A/307, May 13, 1947, UNISPAL Documents Collection.

22. United Nations Special Committee on Palestine, "Report to the General Assembly," chapter 1.

23. Eight members of UNSCOP (Australia, Canada, Czechoslovakia, Guatemala, the Netherlands, Peru, Sweden, and Uruguay) endorsed the majority report. The three members that endorsed the minority report (India, Iran, and Yugoslavia), Trygve Lie noted in his memoir, all had "influential Moslem populations." Lie, *In the Cause of Peace*, 162.

24. United Nations Special Committee on Palestine, "Report to the General Assembly," chapter 6, part 2. A map of the proposed boundaries is located in Annex A to the report and is available at domino.un.org/maps/m0103_1b.gif.

25. Ibid., chapter 6, part 1.

26. Ibid., chapter 6, part 3.

27. Ibid., chapter 6, part 1.

28. Ibid., chapter 7, paragraph 4.

29. Ibid., chapter 7.

30. States voting in favor included: Australia, Belgium, Bolivia, Brazil, Byelorussian Soviet Socialist Republic, Canada, Costa Rica, Czechoslovakia, Denmark, Dominican Republic, Ecuador, France, Guatemala, Haiti, Iceland, Liberia, Luxembourg, Netherlands, New Zealand, Nicaragua, Norway, Panama, Paraguay, Peru, Philippines, Poland, Sweden, Ukrainian Soviet Socialist Republic, Union of South Africa, Union of Soviet Socialist Republics, United States of America, Uruguay, and Venezuela. The following opposed the resolution: Afghanistan, Cuba, Egypt, Greece, India, Iran, Iraq, Lebanon, Pakistan, Saudi Arabia, Syria, Turkey, and Yemen. These states abstained: Argentina, Chile, China, Colombia, El Salvador, Ethiopia, Honduras, Mexico, United Kingdom, and Yugoslavia. See United Nations General Assembly, "Future Government of Palestine—GA Debate, Vote on Resolution 181—Verbatim Record," A/PV.128, November 29, 1947, UNISPAL Documents Collection.

31. Strawson, *Partitioning Palestine*, 123.

32. United Nations General Assembly, "Future Government of Palestine—GA Debate, Vote on Resolution 181—Verbatim Record."

33. Ibid.

34. Quoted in Lie, *In the Cause of Peace*, 165.

35. Strawson, *Partitioning Palestine*, 122–25.

36. United Nations Palestine Commission, "Communication Received by Mr. Federspiel from the United Kingdom Delegation Concerning Termination of the Mandate, Contracts of Employment and Compensation Terms," A/AC.21/UK/42, February 25, 1948, UNISPAL Documents Collection.

37. United Nations Palestine Commission, "First Special Report to the Security Council: The Problem of Security in Palestine," A/AC.21/9, February 16, 1948, UNISPAL Documents Collection.

38. Lie, *In the Cause of Peace*, 166–69.

39. This figure is a UN estimate. The official Israeli estimate is that 530,000 Palestinians fled; some Palestinian estimates have claimed that as many as 1 million Palestinians were expelled during the war. Strawson, *Partitioning Palestine*, 137. The classic account which draws on declassified Israeli, British, and American papers to debunk myths on both sides is Benny Morris, *The Birth of the Palestinian Refugee Problem, 1947–1949* (Cambridge: Cambridge University Press, 1987).

40. Strawson, *Partitioning Palestine*, 150.

41. After independence, Shertok Hebraized his name, changing it to Sharett. However, he signed this letter with his original last name, Shertok.

42. Provisional Government of Israel, letter dated November 29, 1948, from Israel's Foreign Minister to the Secretary-General, S/1093, UNISPAL Documents Collection.

43. United Nations General Assembly, "194 (III). Palestine—Progress Report of the United Nations Mediator," A/RES/194 (III), December 11, 1948; United Nations General Assembly, "Admission of Israel to the United Nations—GA Debate—Verbatim Record," A/PV.207, May 11, 1949; United Nations General Assembly, "Israel Membership in the UN—GA Resolution," A/RES/273 (III), May 11, 1949, UNISPAL Documents Collection.

44. Lie, *In the Cause of Peace*, 185–90; Cary David Stanger, "A Haunting Legacy: The Assassination of Count Bernadotte," *Middle East Journal* 42, no. 2 (1988).

45. Benjamin Rivlin, "Ralph Johnson Bunche: Brief Life of a Champion of Human Dignity, 1903–1971," *Harvard Magazine*, November/December 2003.

46. The three remaining operations are: the UN Truce Supervision Organization (UNTSO), established in 1948; the UN Disengagement Observer Force (UNDOF), which has supervised the implementation of the Israeli-Syrian disengagement agreement in the Golan Heights since 1974; and the UN Interim Force in Lebanon (UNIFIL), which was created in 1978 to supervise Israeli withdrawal from Lebanese territory.

47. Count Folke Bernadotte.

48. The Palestine Liberation Organization (PLO) has maintained an observer mission at the UN since 1974. See United Nations, *The Question of Palestine and the United Nations* (New York: United Nations Department of Public Information, 2008), 26.

49. UNTSO.

50. The United Nations Relief and Works Agency for Palestine Refugees in the Near East (UNRWA) began its operations in May 1950 and continues to provide services to eligible individuals among the 5 million registered Palestinian refugees.

51. Jones, "Middle East Peace Process," 391.

52. Urquhart, "United Nations in the Middle East."

53. For an analysis of the reasons behind the Soviet Union's strong support for partition and expeditious recognition of Israeli statehood, see Arnold Krammer, "Soviet Motives in the Partition of Palestine, 1947–48," *Journal of Palestine Studies* 2, no. 2 (1973).

54. Lie, *In the Cause of Peace*, 175.

55. On the concept and functioning of principal-agent relationships between states and international organizations, see Darren G. Hawkins et al., eds., *Delegation and Agency in International Organizations* (New York: Cambridge University Press, 2006).

56. United Nations Special Committee on Palestine, "Report to the General Assembly," chapter 7.

57. Kenneth W. Abbott and Duncan Snidal, "Why States Act through Formal International Organizations," *Journal of Conflict Resolution* 42, no. 1 (1998).

58. Ibid., 9. On IO independence, see also Yoram Z. Haftel and Alexander Thompson, "The Independence of International Organizations: Concept and Applications," *Journal of Conflict Resolution* 50, no. 2 (2006).

59. Lie, *In the Cause of Peace*, 166–69.

60. For a discussion of Lie's efforts in this regard, see the editors' introduction to Andrew W. Cordier and Wilder Foote, eds., *Public Papers of the Secretaries-General of the United Nations*, vol. 1: Trygve Lie, 1946–1953 (New York: Columbia University Press, 1969).

61. Carl Bildt, "Dag Hammarskjöld and United Nations Peacekeeping," *UN Chronicle* no. 2 (2011). Available at http://www.un.org/en/peacekeeping/documents/un_chronicle_carl_bildt_article.pdf.

62. United Nations Department of Peacekeeping Operations, UNDPKO website, www.un.org/en/peacekeeping/about/.

63. Provisional Government of Israel, letter dated November 29, 1948, from Israel's Foreign Minister to the Secretary-General.

64. State of Palestine, "Application of Palestine for Admission to Membership in the United Nations," S/2011/592, September 23, 2011, UNISPAL Documents Collection.

65. Quoted in Peter Goodspeed, "Netanyahu Chides UN, Seeks Renewed Talks with Abbas," *National Post*, September 23, 2011.

66. UN News Service, "General Assembly Grants Palestine Non-member Observer State Status at UN," *UN News Centre*, November 29, 2012.

67. Reuters, "Abbas Presses Palestinian UN Bid, Despite Warnings," msnbc.com, September 20, 2011.

68. Ethan Bronner and Christine Hauser, "U.N. Assembly, in Blow to U.S., Elevates Status of Palestine," *New York Times*, November 29, 2012.

69. Quoted in UN News Service, "General Assembly Grants Palestine Non-member Observer State Status at UN."

70. Strawson, *Partitioning Palestine*, 1.

71. Harriet Sherwood, "US Pulls UNESCO Funding after Palestine Is Granted Full Membership," *Guardian*, October 31, 2011.

72. Quoted in Bronner and Hauser, "U.N. Assembly."

73. UNESCO Director-General Irina Bukova, quoted in Reuters, "UNESCO Chief Says U.S. Funding Cuts 'Crippling' Organization," October 11, 2012, www.reuters.com.

74. For recent poll results, see Zogby International, *Arab Attitudes, 2011* (Arab American Institute Foundation, 2011).

75. According to Palestinian political scientist and pollster Khalil Shikaki, at least 70 percent of Palestinians and Israelis support a two-state solution. Khalil Shikaki, "The Future of Israel-Palestine: A One-State Reality in the Making," *NOREF Paper*, Norwegian Peacebuilding Resource Centre (May 2012), 3. pcpsr.org/strategic/occasionalpapers/futureofisraelpalestine.pdf.

76. Michael A. Cohen, "Think Again: The Two-State Solution," foreignpolicy.com (September 14, 2011).

77. Shikaki, "Future of Israel-Palestine," 3.

78. United Nations General Assembly, "Status of Palestine in the United Nations: Report of the Secretary General," A/67/738, March 8, 2013, UNISPAL Documents Collection.

Chapter 7

Namibian Independence:
A UN Success Story

Jean Krasno

The independence of Namibia from South Africa in 1989–90 is often cited as a United Nations success, and it indeed set a precedent for later peace operations. Many aspects of the Namibia case were repeated in later UN efforts to assist countries transitioning to democracy, activities not possible during the Cold War. Although there were many useful lessons learned from the UN Namibia operation, several features of the Namibia-UN experience make it unique and difficult to replicate. The UN began the frustrating process of seeking, and then demanding, independence for Namibia as far back as 1949. Four decades later, in 1989, the UN Transition Assistance Group for Namibia (UNTAG) was implemented, and the UN oversaw the territory's final transition into statehood.

The UNTAG operation, begun a year before the fall of the Berlin Wall, was clearly a side effect of the thaw between East and West. One might say that Namibia found itself at a pivotal cusp between the struggles of the past and the advent of UN peacebuilding operations in countries undergoing a transition from oppressive governments to the birth of representative democracies and the rule of law. UNTAG, first conceived in the 1978 Security Council resolution 435, was given the responsibility to oversee free and fair elections and to create an environment that would allow a multiparty system to operate openly and safely. Yet, Namibia, earlier known as South

West Africa, had a long history of brutal repression first under German occupation and later under South Africa and its Apartheid system. Understanding that history and the early role of the UN is an important part of this story.

EARLY HISTORY

The first peoples to inhabit the region that is now Namibia were the Bushman and Nama, with the Herero and Ovambo arriving later in the sixteenth and eighteenth centuries.[1] The Germans arrived in what was then called South West Africa during the late nineteenth century and declared the territory a German colony in 1884. The German period of colonial control was known for its brutality. As a result, the Herero and Nama, who occupied the most productive land in north-central Namibia, staged a number of uprisings, particularly during 1903–6, in response to German settlers taking over their communal lands. The Herero uprising of 1904 resulted in the genocide of the Herero people; about 65,000, or three-quarters of the group, were exterminated.

By 1915, during World War I, the British, through South Africa, defeated the Germans in South West Africa and took over the colony. At the end of the war, South West Africa was given as a mandate to South Africa to prepare the territory for independence. Instead, South Africa was determined to incorporate the territory within its own borders. The legacy of German occupation and the Herero genocide campaign carried over into the continued resistance of the indigenous people against their new South African occupiers. Herero chief Hosea Kutako was an early leader in the resistance against South African rule and led an effort to petition the United Nations on behalf of Namibian independence. Mosé Tjitendero, the first speaker of the National Assembly after independence, also Herero, explains, "Our history was intricately tied to the United Nations, and there was a firm belief that the United Nations will definitely free us."[2]

Beginning in the 1950s, the South African administration moved the indigenous peoples from their homes into townships, as they had done in South Africa. By 1968, with many of their homes bulldozed they were forced to move into a township just outside Windhoek, called Katutura, which in the Herero language means "we have no permanent abode."[3] The coloureds (people from India or other mixed backgrounds) were moved to a separate area between Katutura and Windhoek. The two townships were separated by a wide expanse of highways so that it would be easy to patrol any movement from one area to another. In Katutura, the tribal groups were separated, and the addresses on the small, box-like houses were marked by a number that was preceded by a letter standing for the first letter of the ethnic group, for example, H for Herero, O for Ovambo, D for Damara, and so forth. Separate councils were established for each group, as well as separate schools. This divide-and-conquer strategy, common in colonial Africa, was reinforced by an allocation system whereby councils, representing different tribal groups, had to compete for funds.

There was only one high school for the Namibian people. The school, called Agustinium, was located in Okahanja about seventy-five kilometers north of Windhoek. This school turned out to be the educational foundation and, one could say, the breeding ground for the resistance movement. Theo-Ben Gurirab, later Namibia's foreign minister, who attended Agustinium explains:

> The people who were associated with setting up that educational and training facility in Namibia were Lutherans to begin with and some money had been made available to those missionaries to set up the school. Its importance for me, more than the connection with the church, is that it was at that time the point of convergence of all the African students, those who were eligible or who had an opportunity one way or another to attend schooling and to have come together. . . . What initially we did not realize ourselves was that by this arrangement, it was possible to bring together at one place the future leaders of Namibia from all parts of the country.[4]

Theo-Ben Gurirab, Mosé Tjitendero, Peter Katjavivi (later ambassador to the EU), Hage Geingob (who became prime minister), among others, attended the school. Blacks were not allowed to study science or math and certainly not politics. But black teachers and political activists secretly came to the school at night from Windhoek to teach the students about political issues and educate them in forming an independence movement. In the 1960s, many African colonies, Ghana and Congo, for example, were gaining their independence. However, as the students began to face harassment from the South African administration and were prohibited from attending college in South West Africa, many decided to leave and study abroad with the intention of returning to run the country. Eventually, this group of young resistance leaders formed the movement called the South West Africa People's Organization, or SWAPO.

At the time, the UN and various US-based foundations were offering scholarships for Africans to study in the United States, and Hage Geingob

was given a scholarship to Temple High School in Philadelphia; later he be-
gan his college studies at Fordham University in New York City. He chose
New York because in 1964 he was appointed by the leader of SWAPO, Sam
Nujoma, to represent the independence movement at the United Nations.[5]
Many other young resistance leaders won similar UN scholarships to study
in the US or in other countries.

THE ORGANIZATION OF AFRICAN UNITY

The Organization of African Unity (OAU) was founded on May 25, 1963.
Within about a year of its founding, the OAU established the Coordinating
Committee for the Liberation of Africa, known as the Liberation Committee,
headquartered in Dar es Salaam. The committee called together leaders of
the national liberation movements from African countries that were not yet
independent. The committee asked the movement leaders to draw up plans
for how they proposed to achieve freedom and independence for their nations and peoples. The leaders were then asked to prepare programs of action, setting out their objectives and goals.[6] From South West Africa, there
were two movements represented: SWAPO and SWANU (South West Africa
National Union). Moses Katjiuongua was one of the prominent leaders of
SWANU. Both movements presented their programs of action. A key SWAPO
leader, Theo-Ben Gurirab explains:

> In our case, SWAPO, we said in addition to the United Nations mobilizing the
> international community for supportive assistance, we would also organize a
> military resistance body. We specifically asked the Liberation Committee and
> the OAU member states to assist us to train our combatants to launch the
> armed struggle. SWANU felt that the objective conditions in Namibia and the
> practicalities of how to get from whatever to Namibia was such that they did
> not think the time was right for launching an armed struggle.[7]

Initially both movements received support from the OAU, but the OAU ultimately decided that SWAPO was carrying out most of the campaigning and
had gained recognition and support beyond the OAU membership. Thus in
1972, at the summit held in Rabat, Morocco, the OAU decided to concen-
trate its resources in SWAPO, and that year it recognized the organization as
the sole and authentic representative of the Namibian people. SWANU was
not derecognized per se, but SWAPO became the focal point of support.

At the United Nations, the OAU had observer status, but more important,
its members were voting participants in the UN General Assembly (GA).

These independent African countries formed the Africa Group at the UN, which had enough members to have influence in GA voting. This enabled the African countries to introduce resolutions in the GA and to lobby to get them passed. The OAU introduced the concept of recognizing SWAPO as the sole and authentic representative of the Namibian people to the GA, and SWAPO was given observer status at the UN in 1972. Having observer status at the UN meant that SWAPO representatives could be at the UN every day, following and shaping decisions on the status of Namibia and also keeping its independence on the agenda of the international community. The OAU's use of GA voting as established by the Charter—one country, one vote with no veto—demonstrated that the UN offered a proactive avenue that otherwise would not have existed.

Before observer status was granted, Hage Geingob, who had been representing SWAPO in New York, had often been unable to enter the UN building as he had no official security pass. He would have to get friends from other African countries to say he was coming to see them, just to be able to enter and talk to people about Namibian issues. After SWAPO was given observer status and he was issued an official pass, Geingob says, "I nearly cried when I saw the SWAPO seat there, on the floor."[8] Hage Geingob was the first to be allowed to take the seat, and he says he was very proud, especially after having been locked out.[9] That same year, Geingob was assigned to the UN Secretariat as associate officer in the Department of Political Affairs under the Office of the Commissioner for Namibia. At that point, Theo-Ben Gurirab became the official observer for SWAPO in the General Assembly. By 1978, SWAPO was given permanent observer status, equal to that of the OAU, the OAS, and the Holy See, and was the only people's organization other than the Palestine Liberation Organization (PLO) to have this status.

THE UNITED NATIONS INTERNATIONAL COURT OF JUSTICE

The General Assembly took a very proactive role in asserting Namibia's right to independence, but another main body of the UN, the International Court of Justice (ICJ), obstructed the process. The GA, in an attempt to further legitimize the Namibian campaign, sought legal support from the ICJ. In 1949, the General Assembly passed resolution 338 seeking an advisory opinion from the ICJ in The Hague on the Namibian issue. The League of Nations had granted South Africa mandatory powers to administer South West Africa in order to prepare the territory for independence. When the UN was created, the mandated territories were to be put under the tutelage of the

Trusteeship Council and prepared for independence. South Africa refused to do this and, contrary to its responsibility under the mandate, had incorporated South West Africa into South Africa, giving the South West African white farmers representative status in the South African parliament. The General Assembly was seeking an opinion from the court that South Africa's actions were illegal. But a year later, the ICJ, skirting the issue, declared that because the territory was given as a mandate by the League of Nations, not the UN, the United Nations did not have authority in this instance. The court reaffirmed that South West Africa was a territory under international mandate by the Union of South Africa.

Since it had not achieved the desired outcome from its request for an advisory opinion in 1949, in 1960 the GA tried again. This time, along with the OAU, it persuaded Ethiopia and Liberia, as former members of the League of Nations, to bring the Namibia case before the ICJ as a lawsuit against South Africa. The case took several years, and the decision was not handed down until 1966. Roelof (Pik) Botha, who later became South Africa's foreign minister, was on South Africa's legal team, which claimed that there was no discrimination against the Namibian people, that separate facilities for them did not violate their needs. The court sided with South Africa, as Pik Botha describes:

> I remained a member of the legal team until the judgment on 18 July '66. We won the case in the sense that the court "rejected" the claims of Ethiopia and Liberia, saying that they did not have sufficient legal interest in the charges they made, or in the claims.[10]

The ICJ again failed to give the General Assembly what it wanted, saying that Ethiopia and Liberia did not have sufficient legal interest because they did not border Namibia and hence were not directly affected by the situation there. The court also added that the right to sue was exclusive to the League itself, not its members. Of course, the League no longer existed. At the creation of the United Nations, all former mandates of the League of Nations had been formally handed over to the UN, which was given responsibility for their eventual independence. This put the court in direct contradiction to the trust given to the UN to oversee the independence of Namibia as a former mandate of the League. Rosalyn Higgins, later a member of the ICJ and a legal scholar, states that this was a very difficult period for the court because of the legacy of the South West African cases due to the fact that the "law and politics are here so closely interwoven."[11]

Following this convoluted response by the ICJ, in 1966 the GA passed resolution 2145. The resolution terminated South Africa's mandate and placed South West Africa under the direct responsibility of the United Nations. The GA "declared that South Africa had failed to fulfill its obligations under the Mandate to ensure the moral and material well-being of the people of the Territory."[12] It was not until 1971, in an advisory opinion, this time requested by the UN Security Council, that the ICJ, reflecting political changes in the international arena, finally stated that the continued occupation by South Africa in Namibia was illegal.

THE COUNCIL FOR NAMIBIA

In May 1967, the GA established the Council for South West Africa to administer the territory and to include as much as possible the people of the territory in the decision-making process. The administrative functions would be carried out by a commissioner who would be appointed by the GA upon the recommendation of the UN Secretary-General. The following year the General Assembly decided that, according to the wishes of the people, South West Africa would be called Namibia and the council would be called the Council for Namibia. The council, originally composed of eleven member states, was expanded several times and by 1978 had thirty-one members.[13] The presidency of the council rotated from time to time, under somewhat changing terms. The Council for Namibia established a commissioner to carry out its work, and the Office of the Commissioner was placed in the Department of Political Affairs. Over the years there were six commissioners; Martti Ahtisaari, who later became the Special Representative of the Secretary-General for UNTAG, served as commissioner from 1977 to 1981. The last commissioner was Bernt Carlsson who served from 1987 until independence.[14]

The Council for Namibia was unique. No other country or territory has had such a council to represent its needs and grievances in this manner, performing many of the functions of a state. The goal was to contact the South African authorities and lay down procedures for the orderly transition to independence. Of course, South Africa refused to recognize the Council for Namibia, and the council was not allowed to set up its work inside the territory. Nevertheless, it moved forward with its program to support the struggle of the Namibian people, encouraging states to comply with UN resolutions (particularly sanctions against South Africa), establishing training and educational programs for Namibians, and representing Namibian interests in international organizations and conferences. The council, for example, signed on behalf of the Namibian people the Convention on the Law of the Sea, for the purpose of protecting the fishing and resources of Namibia's coast. The council also was the legal representative of Namibia at the UN Conference on Succession of States in Respect of Treaties, held in Vienna in 1977. In addition to organizing its own seminars and conferences, the Council for Namibia also attended meetings of the OAU and the Non-Aligned Movement (NAM) countries.[15] The council also provided Namibians with travel and identity documents that were recognized by member states. This was essential because South Africa had refused to give indigenous Namibians such documents.

The Council for Namibia acted as the trustee for the United Nations Fund for Namibia, established in 1972. The fund depended primarily on voluntary contributions but also received each year an allocation from the regular budget of the UN, ranging from $50,000 in 1971 to $1.5 million in 1986. In 1986, the fund had some $9 million. The fund also supported the Institute for Namibia, another unique creation of the Council for Namibia.

The UN Institute for Namibia was established in 1976 in Lusaka, Zambia, to enable Namibians to develop the skills that would be required once the people took over the administration of the country. This was clearly in reaction to troubles encountered in previous transitions to independence in Africa, particularly in Congo, where only seventeen Congolese had ever attended college by the time of independence in 1960 and the Congolese minister of health was selected for the position because he was the only indigenous person to have been inside a hospital. The Namibia program included education, research, sharing of information, and the formulation of policies and plans for establishing new governmental structures and laws once independence was achieved. Hage Geingob became the director of the institute and moved from New York to Lusaka to take over his duties. Mosé Tjitendero became the assistant director, charged with training teachers and magistrates. It was anticipated that when South Africa left Namibia, the South Africans who had been administering the country would leave and the public service would collapse. The purpose of the institute was to ensure that Namibians would be able to take over running the country.[16]

The challenge faced by all the actors in the drive for Namibian independence—including SWAPO, the council, and the institute—was the task of building a nation, as Mosé Tjitendero explains, "out of political, ethnic, linguistic, and cultural diversity."[17] SWAPO leaders had been negotiating and writing the constitution for over a decade prior to independence and the election of the Constitutional Assembly in 1989, which had been mandated to write the Namibian constitution. Once the elected Constitutional Assembly completed its task in the spring 1990, this body became the National Assembly. Tjitendero had been a secretary of the SWAPO Constitutional Committee. In exile, the members of the committee had a number of meetings, inviting experts from different countries to review drafts of the constitution and give advice. By the time of elections in Namibia in 1989, they had revised the constitution three times.

In the interest of pluralism, they based the constitution on proportional representation so that even the smallest parties could be represented. The constitution also included language about preserving private property to quell any fears of a Communist-style nationalization of farms or industries. SWAPO wanted a presidency with executive powers elected for a fixed term and a unicameral assembly. Once the Constituent Assembly was elected in 1989, SWAPO did not have the two-thirds majority needed to pass provisions on its own. Therefore, it had to negotiate with opposition parties. The trade-off for being allowed to keep the executive presidency was giving in on the creation of a bicameral legislature. That was the only major change made in the draft constitution that had been negotiated over the years in exile.[18] The final constitution called for a president to be elected for a five-year term, a prime minister, and a two-bodied legislature—with a National Council of twenty-six seats, two from each of the thirteen regions, and a National Assembly with seventy-two popularly elected seats, through a process of party proportionality.

UN RESOLUTIONS

Beginning in 1949, General Assembly resolutions led the way in calling for Namibian independence and for free and fair elections based on multiparty participation. Its role in condemning South Africa, revoking its mandate for South West Africa in 1966 and then establishing the Council for Namibia, is evidence of its constant efforts to resolve the issue. The Security Council, however, entered the picture much later and was slow to take a strong stand. The first important Security Council resolution did not come until 1976, resolution 385. Adopted on January 30, 1976, by unanimous agreement, resolution 385 demanded that South Africa accept provisions for the United Nations to begin the establishment of the necessary machinery within Namibia to conduct free and fair elections under UN supervision.

The next year a decisive break came with the election of Jimmy Carter as president of the United States and as a consequence the positioning of Andrew Young, and later Donald McHenry, leaders of the black movement in the United States, as ambassadors to the UN. Along with Cyrus Vance as secretary of state, these men had a different approach to African issues from their predecessors. The Carter administration's influence on UN issues, in this case Namibia, demonstrates the effect domestic politics can have on decisions taken inside and outside the UN on issues before the Organization. The Carter people initiated the Western Five Contact Group on Namibia, consisting of the three Western permanent members of the Security Council—the US, UK, and France—along with West Germany and Canada, the two non-permanent members at the time (1977–78). The Western Five Contact Group conducted numerous negotiations, visiting South Africa for meetings, culminating in the 1978 adoption of Security Council resolution 435, which established the United Nations Transition Assistance Group for Namibia (UNTAG).

While the West in general abhorred Apartheid and South Africa's illegal actions in Namibia, many also feared SWAPO's leanings toward the Communist world, where it had received much of its support. But South Africa's intransigence and flagrant violations of human rights had become an embarrassment, and world opinion was pressing for action. Nevertheless, the United States wanted to be sure that any decision by the Security Council would be a product of the West that avoided input by the Soviet Union and China, now represented by the People's Republic of China. More important, South Africa had refused to negotiate with the UN Security Council. Therefore, the Western Five Contact Group operated outside the Security Council. In a visit to South Africa, the contact group managed to convince South Africa that the pressure to impose economic sanctions was growing.[19] In addition, Martti Ahtisaari, then commissioner for Namibia acting for the Council for Namibia, along with several advisers, made a trip to Namibia in August 1978 to investigate what role the UN would play in an eventual mission to oversee independence. As a result of the reports by the contact group and the Ahtisaari delegation, on September 29, 1978, the Security Council passed resolution 435, establishing UNTAG.

The initial optimism that blossomed with the passage of 435 soon wilted as a number of factors continued to thwart Namibia's independence. Primarily, South Africa still believed it had other options: (1) that it could defeat SWAPO militarily and (2) that it could foster a white-dominated government structure in Namibia that would be accepted by the international community. South Africa believed, and had convinced others to also believe, that if these things were not accomplished and elections held immediately, SWAPO would clearly win any elections and would impose socialist policies that might include the nationalization of white-owned industries (such as the diamond mines) and farms. South Africa needed time to build alternative political parties within Namibia to oppose SWAPO. Importantly, South Africa also believed that the UN had been supporting SWAPO for years and was therefore not impartial. The personality of South African president P. W. Botha, who also oversaw the Apartheid system at home, was also a factor.

A 1979 statement to the UN Security Council by the Council for Namibia transmitted by the president of the Council for Namibia, Paul Lusaka, described the situation:

> In contravention of United Nations resolutions and the will of the international community, South Africa is clearly bent upon imposing a puppet regime on Namibia through which it intends to perpetuate its colonial exploitation of the people and resources of Namibia and, to this end, South Africa has, furthermore, continued to arrest and detain Namibian patriots who are part of the leadership of the South West Africa People's Organization (SWAPO) within the Territory.[20]

SWAPO, the UN General Assembly, the OAU, and human rights advocates continued their frustration with South Africa.

FROM CARTER TO REAGAN

Unfortunately President Carter did not see resolution 435 implemented during his presidency. The election of conservative Ronald Reagan, whose anti-Soviet policies were to dominate US foreign policy for the next eight years, brought an end to hopes for Namibia, at least for the time being. Again, UN members saw US domestic politics intervene in issues of concern to the General Assembly. When Carter lost the election in 1980, his administration attempted a last-ditch effort and called a meeting in Geneva in January 1981 to negotiate a draft plan for a Namibian constitution. This included a "bill of rights" and other mechanisms for protecting private property that were later included in the final constitution adopted after independence.

The Reagan and Botha administrations found common ground in delaying Namibia's independence, and the Reagan administration encouraged a position of "linkage" that tied the withdrawal of Cuban forces from Angola with Namibian independence. There were some 50,000 Cuban troops in Angola, there to protect the socialist Angolan government from attacks by rebel UNITA forces led by Jonas Sivimbi and backed by South Africa. "The U.S. policy was used by the South Africans as a very important delaying tactic, enabling them to argue that they were actively engaged in negotiations with the United States, while in fact they were attempting to draw out negotiations and pursue an internal settlement."[21]

Security Council resolution 566 of 1985, in paragraph 7, continues to express the council's mood of frustration. The Security Council:

> 7. *Rejects once again* South Africa's insistence on linking the independence of Namibia to irrelevant and extraneous issues as incompatible with resolution 435 (1978), other decisions of the Security Council and the resolutions of the General Assembly on Namibia, including General Assembly resolution 1514 (XV) of 14 December 1969.[22]

A CONFLUENCE OF FACTORS BRINGS ABOUT A BREAKTHROUGH

With Cuban troops still fighting in Angola, linkage continued to ensure the status quo in Namibia through 1988; however, a confluence of factors merged at that time, forcing the issue to a head. In 1988, at the battle at Cuito Cuanavale in Angola, the South African Defense Forces suffered heavy casualties at the hands of the Angolan government and Cuban forces, and a number of white South African soldiers were killed. When news of these casualties reached the South African public, people began to question the cost of the war in Angola, both in lives and money spent. The National Party, as the ruling party, came under heavy criticism and feared losing its domestic support. South African leaders were feeling pressure to pull out of Angola. At the same time, a number of spontaneous uprisings were taking place inside Namibia as people became increasingly frustrated by South African discrimination and brutality. From the South African perspective, it was becoming increasingly more difficult to maintain control on both fronts.

In addition, changes were taking place politically on a global level. Under Mikhail Gorbachev, the Soviet Union was seeking ways to improve its relationship to the West. The atmosphere in the UN Security Council reflected the global mood. The Soviets and Americans had cooperated in bringing about the end to the Iran-Iraq war by 1988, and hope was mounting that the deadlock in the Security Council was coming to an end. Economic conditions in the Soviet Union were such that it could no longer afford to pay for Cuban troops in Angola, and Reagan was beginning to find a partner in Gorbachev rather than an enemy. By July 1988 negotiations on removing Cuban troops from Angola were making headway, and in December the agreement was finalized. Having accepted the linkage policy, South Africa was now left with the other half of the deal: Namibian independence.

Other US domestic factors were also coming into alignment. The 1988 election brought George Herbert Walker Bush into the presidency, replacing Reagan. Soon after the election in November, even before taking office, Bush put his foreign policy team in place and instructed them to seek out peaceful solutions to conflicts in both Africa and Central America, namely El Salvador. In South Africa, hard-liner P. W. Botha was replaced as president by F. W. de Klerk who, a year later, released Nelson Mandela from prison, where he had spent some twenty-seven years. With this convergence of events, the atmosphere was ripe for Namibia finally to gain its independence.

THE ESTABLISHMENT OF UNTAG AND A TROUBLED START

The Tripartite Accord signed in New York on December 22, 1988, established a settlement plan, cease-fire, and withdrawal of Cuban troops, which the UN was asked to oversee. To monitor implementation, the agreement also created a joint commission, consisting of Angola, Cuba, and South Africa with the US and the Soviet Union as observers. On January 16, 1989, the UN Security Council passed resolutions 628 and 629 that set April 1 as the start date for UNTAG.

Unfortunately, in the following weeks an argument broke out over the budget for the mission. The Africa Group backed by the Non-Aligned Movement wanted to maintain the original budget contained in resolution 435 of 1978, with troop levels set at 7,500. Western countries led by the US wanted to reduce the budget and troop levels by about one-third. The Western countries believed that South Africa was ready to cooperate and the higher budget was not needed. But the African countries still did not trust South Africa and felt that the violence on the ground would call for a greater show of force. A compromise was finally brokered by Secretary-General Javier Pérez de Cuéllar by which the implementation of 435 would begin at the lower level of 4,650 troops at a budget of $416 million but with an increase in police monitors from 350 to 500, with the caveat that increases could be made if necessary.

The budget was not approved until March 1, 1989, only one month from the start date. It was important not to move the date, set at April 1, because seven months were needed to prepare for elections, which had to take place before the rainy season began at the end of November, when most of the roads in Namibia would become impassable. By April 1, there were only a handful of UN troops in place, and none in the north of Namibia.

On April 1, as Special Representative Martti Ahtisaari, the head of the mission, arrived in Namibia, a crisis erupted that could have ended the operation. Whether it was a misunderstanding or a miscalculation, SWAPO leader Sam Nujoma sent some of his soldiers across the border from Angola into Namibia, ostensibly to turn in their weapons and demobilize to UN bases they thought had been established in northern Namibia. South Africa reported this to Martti Ahtisaari quite differently, calling it a SWAPO incursion, and demanded that the South African Police and the Defense Force be released from base to "put down the incursion." With no UN troops or observers in the north, Ahtisaari was caught with no independent information, and after consulting with Pérez de Cuéllar, gave his permission to the South African demands. SWAPO fighters, unable to find the UN bases, suddenly found themselves under attack. What South Africa had sent, already stationed in the north, were the paramilitary special forces known as the "Koevoet" (in Afrikaans meaning "crowbar"), who had historically been given the role of torturing and killing SWAPO fighters. Their policy had been "take no prisoners."[23] With the Koevoet joined by the South African Defense Force, about 314 SWAPO were killed and about 38 captured. Some 30 South Africans were killed.

With no independent information of its own on the situation in the north, the UN took several days to assess the crisis and the disinformation coming from Pretoria. The crisis had to be resolved and the mission put back on track before the outbreak of violence scuttled the operation. It was in the interest of both the United States and the Soviet Union to get the issue off the international agenda. The Soviets no longer were able to pay for troops in Angola, and the US was under pressure on human rights grounds to end South African repression and Apartheid in Namibia. The five members of the Joint Commission met on April 8–9 at a resort called Mount Etjo in Namibia and reached a cease-fire agreement. The Cubans convinced Sam

Nujoma to recall his troops to Angola and the South Africans agreed to return their forces to base.[24]

AN ATMOSPHERE OF INTIMIDATION

What continued to be misunderstood outside Namibia was the fact that although the South African government had agreed to independence, there were many South Africans and whites in Namibia who did not go along with the decision and tried to either sabotage the process in general or manipulate it through intimidation in an attempt to maintain white control. They continued to use the Koevoet and other methods to cause violence, disinformation, and intimidation. Also, it must be remembered that the UN did not administer the election process. That power was given to the South African administrator general in Namibia, Louis Pienaar, who had the power to set the rules for the registration of voters and all the voting procedures. UNTAG had the ultimate authority to declare the elections "free and fair," but this was an agonizing process of constant negotiation with Pienaar. Every policy, whether on rules for the electoral registration or on voting would emanate from the Office of the Administrator General. Of course, most of the laws on the books discriminated against the Namibian people, and there was a constant struggle to get them changed in time for the elections. All this had to be approved by UNTAG, the various Namibian political parties, and ultimately the UN Security Council. Then the administrator general would often not approve the changes made by UNTAG and the other groups. When there was a roadblock, Ahtisaari and/or his deputy, Joseph Legwaila (UN ambassador from Botswana), would go to Pretoria with Pienaar, sometimes on his airplane. Ambassador Legwaila has described their conversations with the South Africans, particularly with Pik Botha, the foreign minister:

> "There is a danger that the process will be scuttled if you insist on the following things in this proclamation and there is a danger that you might be faced with a meeting of the Security Council to debate your stalling tactics," and so on. "Is that what you want?" We always got a positive response from the government of South Africa if we went to Pretoria. We never went to Pretoria and came back empty-handed. When we went to Pretoria, we always made sure that we dramatized the situation. That is, "You will be faced with a situation where we fail. And if we fail, what happens?" And I remember, Pik Botha would always shout, "No, no, no, we must not allow this process to fail. What will happen to South Africa if it fails?" I used to say, "Thank God."[25]

Of course, UNTAG would not go to Pretoria unprepared. Pérez de Cuéllar would call ahead and prepare the South African government, de Klerk and Pik Botha, for the arrival and make clear what pressures would be brought to bear on South Africa, namely, further sanctions, if the Namibia process failed. They always took Pienaar with them so he could not later deny the decisions that were made.

THE PIVOTAL ROLE OF UN INDIVIDUALS

In Namibia, as well as in other peacekeeping operations, there are many examples of the personal courage of UN individuals. Fred Eckhard, who later became Kofi Annan's spokesman, explains that he went to the north of Namibia shortly after the April crisis had erupted. The UN had agreed to escort SWAPO soldiers back across the Angola border and had set up small tents at various places along the border. Where Fred was stationed, there was no flagpole, so they just hung the UN flag from a tree. The South Africans then set up a modern military encampment with armored vehicles, trucks, and the like right next door. Fred describes a wounded SWAPO member coming to the UN tent and asking for protection. The South Africans de-manded that the UN hand him over for interrogation. The British major in charge of the UN site refused. The South Africans pointed their automatic weapons at the UN officer, and he still said, "Over my dead body." The South Africans said they would be back in one hour to collect the "prisoner." Fred explains that the UN major tried to contact the UN commander in Windhoek, hundreds of miles away, but could not reach him by phone. When the South Africans returned, he pretended that he had reached head-quarters. He drew a line in the sand, and said to them, "You cross that line and we'll shoot." To everyone's relief, the South Africans left.[26]

Binta Dieye, a UN staff member from Senegal, volunteered to go to Na-mibia, as an African, enthusiastic about Namibia finally gaining its independence. When she arrived she convinced Ahtisaari to allow her to set up the UN office in the black township of Katutura. After the April 1 crisis, many Namibians did not trust the UN, and Dieye worked hard to gain their confi-dence. The South West African Police, SWAPOL, were still brutally intimi-dating black Namibians. Namibian refugees were beginning to return to register to vote, and SWAPOL had been using high-pressure hoses and other force tactics to keep people from coming to the airport to welcome people home. Hundreds of people from Katutura were planning to go to the airport to welcome the returnees, and this was a test for Dieye.

I went to the airport, and SWAPOL was there armed to the teeth, and there were hundreds of people from Katutura who had gone to the airport, hundreds of black people, and it was essential for me: I had to show that they could be protected. . . . I kept walking between the crowd and the police, the SWAPOL, back and forth, back and forth, to make myself very visible. . . . But just the fact that I was not afraid and I was there—it was pure luck that the SWAPOL police did not turn them back—the crowd waited patiently when the returnees came, the first plane came and they started dancing and chanting. That was really for me the first turning point. From then on, they would come to the district, the center, to report any time there was a problem. Up to that time, they did not trust me that much.[27]

CONCLUDING THOUGHTS

On November 14, 1989, the vote count was completed, and SWAPO had won a little over 57 percent of the total that entitled them to forty-one seats in the seventy-two-member Constitutional Assembly; DTA (Democratic Turnhalle Alliance), the white-led and South African–supported party, was next with twenty-one seats, with five other parties winning the remaining seats. SWAPO did not have the two-third majority needed to ratify the constitution on its own and had to make some compromises, as Mosé Tjitendero described above. The new constitution was completed in early 1990, and Namibia celebrated its independence on March 21, 1990.

The deputy special representative for UNTAG, Joseph Legwaila, stated, "To tell you the truth, I think UNTAG was a trailblazer for United Nations peacekeeping and peacemaking."[28] The deployment of UN troops from countries all over the world, along with UN police (done only once before in Cyprus), UN administrative staff, and election monitors were unique but would be a formula used over and over again. The country was divided into ten regions with forty-two district UN offices[29] to observe the registration of voters, monitor the South African police, educate everyone across the country—on the farms and in the cities—about the upcoming important election, monitor the elections at 358 polling stations, count the votes, and always watch to be sure the process was free and fair. A code of conduct was created by the UN that all the parties helped develop and agreed upon. After Namibia, a code of conduct was always part of any complex UN operation, along with establishing regional and district offices. Ultimately, some 4,500 UN troops from 50 countries were deployed, 1,500 civilian police, and some 2,000 international and local staff. The total number of UN police was increased from the original 360 due to the ongoing intimidation carried out by the South West African police (SWAPOL) and the Koevoet, who continued to disobey the mandate. Despite these increases and all the dispute over the budget that delayed the deployment of UN troops, the entire operation came in under budget at $368.6 million.[30]

What is unique about Namibia is the ten-year wait that delayed the implementation of resolution 435. Even before 435, the Council for Namibia, the UN Institute for Namibia, and the Fund for Namibia were created and successfully implemented, along with considerable thought on several drafts of the future constitution. What today we would call "peacebuilding" happened before the actual UN operation in the country. The UN peace operations in Namibia established the in-country process of electoral assistance and troop deployment first, followed by peacebuilding. Part of the reason for the success of UNTAG was the effort that went into preparing the Namibians to govern. In addition, the UNTAG leadership—Ahtisaari, Legwaila, and others—orchestrated a system that brought about success, even in the face of obstruction and intimidation by those who did not want UNTAG to succeed nor a SWAPO-run Namibia. Problems were reported up and down the chain of command and generally settled in favor of the process. The courage and dedication of individuals also played an important role. Most Namibians are still poor and the country suffers from the debilitating effects of HIV/AIDS as do its neighbors in South Africa and Botswana. Nevertheless, due to the long-term dedication of the United Nations, Namibia is independent, democratic, and continues to be peaceful and politically stable.

Notes

1. Roger Hearn, *UN Peacekeeping in Action: The Namibian Experience* (Commack, NY: Nova Science Publishers, 1999), 35–39.

2. Interview with Mosé Tjitendero by Jean Krasno in Windhoek, Namibia, March 10, 1999, available in the Yale Archives and Manuscripts Library within Sterling Memorial Library at Yale under the Yale-UN Oral History, 3.

3. Interview with Moses Katjiuongua by Jean Krasno in Windhoek, Namibia, available in the Yale Archives and Manuscripts Library within Sterling Memorial Library at Yale under the Yale-UN Oral History, 1.

4. Interview with Theo-Ben Gurirab by Jean Krasno at the United Nations in New York, November 3, 1999, available in the Yale Archives and Manuscripts Library under the Yale-UN Oral History, 1. Gurirab was, at the same time, Namibian foreign minister and president of the UN General Assembly.

5. Ibid., 8.

6. Ibid.

7. Ibid., 7–8.

8. Interview with Geingob, 11–12.

9. Ibid.

10. Interview with Roelof (Pik) Botha by Jean Krasno in Johannesburg, South Africa, March 5, 2001, available in the Yale Archives and Manuscripts Library within Sterling Memorial Library at Yale under the Yale-UN Oral History, 4.

11. Rosalyn Higgins, "The International Court and South West Africa: The Implications of the Judgment," *International Affairs* 42, no. 4 (1966): 573.

12. Report on the United Nations Council for Namibia, *The United Nations Council for Namibia: A Summary of Twenty Years of Effort by the Council for Namibia on Behalf of Namibian Independence* (New York: UN Publication, 1987), 1.

13. Ibid. In 1987, two years before Namibia's independence and when the council finished its work, the members were: Algeria, Angola, Australia, Bangladesh, Belgium, Botswana, Bulgaria, Burundi, Cameroon, Chile, China, Colombia, Cyprus, Egypt, Finland, Guyana, Haiti, India, Indonesia, Liberia, Mexico, Nigeria, Pakistan, Poland, Romania, Senegal, Turkey, the Soviet Union, Venezuela, Yugoslavia, and Zambia.

14. A list of the UN commissioners for Namibia includes: 1967–69, Constantine Stavropoulos (acting commissioner); 1970–71, Agha Abdul Hamid (acting commissioner); 1972–73, Agha Abdul Hamid; 1974–76, Sean MacBride; 1977–81, Martti Ahtisaari; 1982–87, Brajesh C. Mishra; 1987–89, Bernt Carlsson.

15. Ibid., 9.

16. Interview with Tjitendero, 8–12.

17. Ibid., 7–8.

18. Ibid., 8.

19. R. Jaster, "The 1988 Peace Accords and the Future of South-western Africa,"Adelphi Papers 253 (London: International Institute for Strategic Studies, autumn 1990), 11.

20. Letter dated May 11, 1979, and attached Annex, UN document A/33/564, and S/13325, May 15, 1979, paragraph 2 of the Annex found on the UN's website www.un.org.

21. Hearn, *UN Peacekeeping in Action*, 44.

22. UN Security Council resolution 566 of June 19, 1985, UN document S/17442, September 6, 1985.

23. Brian Harlech-Jones, *A New Thing? The Namibian Independence Process, 1989–1990* (Windhoek, Namibia: EIN Publications, 1997), 40.

24. Unpublished letter of December 14, 1999, by Cedric Thornberry, UNTAG staff member present at Mount Etjo on April 9, 1989.

25. Yale-UN Oral History Interview with Legwaila Joseph Legwaila, ambassador to the UN from Botswana, by Jean Krasno in New York, May 11, 1999, available at the Yale Archives and Manuscripts Library within Sterling Memorial Library at Yale under the Yale-UN Oral History, 33–34.

26. Yale-UN Oral History Interview with Fred Eckhard by Jim Sutterlin in New York, February 16, 1999, available at the Yale Archives and Manuscripts Library within Sterling Memorial Library at Yale, 10–12.

27. Yale-UN Oral History Interview with Hawa Binta Dieye by Jim Sutterlin in New York. June 23, 1998, available at the Yale Archives and Manuscripts Library within Sterling Memorial Library, 5–6.

28. Interview with Legwaila, 17.

29. *The Blue Helmets: A Review of United Nations Peace-Keeping*, 3rd ed. (New York: United Nations Publications, 1996), 210.

30. Ibid., 228.

Part III

THE UNITED NATIONS IN THE
CONTEMPORARY WORLD

Chapter 8

A History of UN Peacekeeping

James Dobbins

Peacekeeping has become the United Nations' lead product, making the largest claim on the organization's budget, employing the largest number of its personnel, and occasioning the most public attention, debates in the General Assembly and Security Council aside. This emphasis on keeping the peace is consistent with the founders' hopes for this organization, but the manner in which these activities have evolved has diverged considerably from that original vision.

The United Nations Charter provides for a Military Committee made up of senior officers from the five permanent members of the Security Council. The expectation in 1945 was that these powers would collaborate to keep, and if necessary to enforce, international peace, acting through this committee to oversee such military operations as might be authorized by the Security Council. This intention was never fulfilled. For the first forty-four years of the organization's existence, the major powers proved unable to so collaborate. Indeed competition among the permanent members of the Security Council was itself, throughout much of this period, the leading threat to international peace and security. The UN served, nevertheless, as an occasional venue for defusing confrontations between East and West and was used periodically to put the lid on localized conflicts that threatened to escalate to superpower confrontation.

COLD WAR PEACEKEEPING

These limited East-West accommodations never, with one exception, advanced to the point where the major powers could agree to conduct joint military operations to enforce or keep the peace. The exception was the Security Council decision in 1950 to dispatch troops under American command to defend South Korea from attack by the North. This initiative was approved during an ill-conceived and never repeated Soviet boycott of that body. China was at that point represented in the Council by the government in Taipei, not Beijing. This was in fact the reason the Soviets were boycotting Council meetings. In the absence of the two Communist major powers, the Western-dominated Council was able to agree that American and allied troops should fight in Korea under a United Nations flag. In modern parlance, the Korean intervention was a UN-mandated American-led coalition of the willing, much like Desert Storm in 1991 and Operation Enduring Freedom in 2001.

The Korea anomaly aside, neither the United States nor the Soviet Union participated significantly in UN-authorized military operations during the Cold War. Instead, UN peacekeeping relied primarily on troops from smaller or at least less powerful countries. These troops operate under the day-to-day control not of the great powers sitting on the Military Committee, or even of the larger Security Council, but rather of the Secretary-General and his professional, mostly civilian staff. While the Security Council agreed to authorize all such missions, and the General Assembly to finance them, neither body provided operational oversight. A division of labor thus emerged in which the great powers decided, the lesser powers manned, and the richer states paid for these operations.

Over its first forty-four years the UN launched fifteen peacekeeping missions, two in the 1940s (both of which are still in existence), two in the 1950s, six in the 1960s, three in the 1970s, and two more in the last decade of the Cold War, prior to 1989. Most of these missions were small and limited in scope, usually confined to observing cease-fires and helping to separate adversarial forces. Conflicts during this era tended to be not so much settled as suspended. Both Washington and Moscow viewed regional disputes through the prism of their global competition. Neither would support any resolution that might be thought to advantage the other. Yet at the same time both superpowers were occasionally prepared to collaborate to the extent of containing conflicts that might escalate into a dangerous confrontation.

Thus Cold War disputes were more often frozen than settled. Berlin, Germany, Europe, Cyprus, Palestine, Korea, Vietnam, and China were all divided, and either superpower or United Nations troops were used to maintain all these divisions (unsuccessfully in the case of Vietnam).

During these years several UN military observer missions were dispatched to the Middle East, and two were deployed between India and Pakistan. The largest interpositional mission was deployed to separate Cypriot and Turkish forces in Cyprus in 1964. That mission continues today, as do several other Cold War–era missions in the Middle East and South Asia. Of these, only the Cyprus mission can be said to have had an enduring success, but even that dispute remains merely in suspension.

Only one Cold War mission prefigured the larger and more ambitious nation-building operations that became the norm after 1989: the United Nations operation in the Congo. That state failed almost from the moment of its birth. Within days of its independence the army mutinied, the remaining white administrators fled, the government and the economy collapsed, Belgian paratroops invaded, and the mineral-rich province of Katanga seceded. These developments cast a serious shadow over prospects for the successful and peaceful completion of Africa's decolonization, which at that point was just gathering momentum. On July 14, 1960, acting with unusual speed on the basis of an almost unprecedented US-Soviet consensus, the Security Council passed the first of a series of resolutions authorizing the deployment of UN-led military forces to assist the Republic of the Congo in restoring order and, eventually, in suppressing the Katangese rebellion.

Given the unprecedented nature of its mission and the consequent lack of prior experience, existing doctrine, designated staff, or administrative structure to underpin the operation, the United Nations performed remarkably well. Significant forces began to arrive within days of the Security Council's authorization, performance matched in few subsequent UN peacekeeping missions. The United Nations was quickly able to secure the removal of Belgian forces. Over the next three years, UN troops forced the removal of foreign mercenaries and suppressed the Katangan rebellion, and civil elements of the mission provided a wide range of humanitarian, economic, and civil assistance to the new Congolese regime. Measured against the bottom-line requirements of the international community—that decolonization proceed, colonial and mercenary troops depart, and the Congo remain intact—the United Nations was largely successful.

Democracy did not feature heavily in the various Congo resolutions passed by the UN Security Council; there was, in any case, no agreement during the Cold War on the definition of that term. The Congo never became a functioning democracy, but large-scale civil conflict was averted for more than a decade following the United Nations' departure, and the country more or less held together for another three decades, albeit under a corrupt and incompetent dictatorship.

UN achievements in the Congo came at considerable cost in men lost, money spent, and controversy raised. The United Nations' apparent complicity in the apprehension and later execution of Prime Minister Patrice Lumumba overshadowed for many its considerable accomplishments. As a result of these costs and controversies, neither the United Nations' Secretariat nor its member nations were eager to repeat the experience. For the next twenty-five years the United Nations restricted its military interventions to interpositional peacekeeping, policing cease-fires, and patrolling disengagement zones in circumstances where all parties invited its presence and armed force was to be used by UN troops only in self-defense.

HEALING COLD WAR WOUNDS

Today most Americans and Europeans tend to recall the Cold War as a tense and occasionally scary era, but one that was also generally peaceful. This was not the experience of the rest of the world. The number of armed conflicts around the world increased steadily throughout these four and a half decades, peaking at over fifty wars, mostly civil, under way at the beginning of the 1990s. In Africa, Asia, and Latin America East-West tensions fed the flames of local wars that smoldered on for years in places like Cambodia, Angola, Mozambique, El Salvador, and Nicaragua. Tens of millions were killed.

The end of the Cold War presented the United Nations with new opportunities and new challenges as the United States and the Soviet Union began to disengage from proxy wars in Latin America, Africa, and Asia and were finally prepared to work together in pressing former clients to resolve outstanding differences.

The early post–Cold War UN-led operations in Namibia, Cambodia, El Salvador, and Mozambique followed similar patterns. The international community, with US and Soviet backing, first brokered a peace accord. The Security Council then dispatched a UN peacekeeping force to oversee its implementation. In each case the responsibilities of the UN mission included initiating an expeditious process of disarmament, demobilization, and reintegration; encouraging political reconciliation; holding democratic elections; and overseeing the inauguration of a new national government. Operations in each of these countries were greatly facilitated by war-weary populations, great power support, and neighboring country cooperation. The United Nations became adept at overseeing the disarmament and de-mobilization of willing parties. The reintegration of former combatants was everywhere more problematic, for nowhere did the international commu-nity provide the necessary resources. Economic growth accelerated in most cases, largely as a result of the cessation of fighting. Peace, growth, and de-mocracy were often accompanied by an increase in common crime, as old repressive security services were dismantled and demobilized former com-batants were left without a livelihood.

All four of these operations culminated in reasonably free and fair elec-tions. All four resulted in sustained periods of civil peace, which endured after the United Nations withdrawal. Cambodia enjoyed the least successful democratic transformation and experienced the greatest renewal of civil strife, although at nothing like the levels that preceded the UN intervention. Cam-bodia was also the first instance in which the United Nations became respon-sible for actually governing a state in transition from conflict to peace. The United Nations was ill prepared to assume such a role. For its part, the govern-ment of Cambodia, although it had agreed to UN administrative oversight as part of the peace accord, was unwilling to cede effective authority. As a result, the United Nations' control over Cambodia's civil administration was largely nominal.

The end of the Cold War did not lead to an activation of the long mori-bund Military Committee or to a major-power domination of UN peace-keeping. Since the UN's birth in 1945, more than one hundred new states had been created. These newer members had no desire to be policed by the great powers, nor were the permanent members of the Security Council eager to embrace such a role. As a result, the lesser powers continued to man most peacekeeping missions and the professional Secretariat to run them. But a less divided Security Council did begin to authorize larger and more frequent missions with more far-reaching objectives. From, on average, once every four years during the Cold War, the frequency picked up after 1989 to one new mission, on average, every six months, a pace the organi-zation has maintained ever since.

The scope of such missions also expanded. No longer was the UN's role confined to separating combatants. Most of these new missions were intended to overcome divisions, not just suspend hostilities. Adversarial forces were not just separated, but disarmed, demobilized and reintegrated in society. Elections were to be held, new governments formed, societies healed, and economies rebuilt. And the United Nations was expected to oversee or perform all these functions.

Despite the substantial successes of its early post–Cold War operations in Namibia, Mozambique, Cambodia, and El Salvador, a number of weaknesses in the United Nations' performance emerged in the early 1990s that would hobble later missions launched in more difficult circumstances. Deficiencies included the slow arrival of military units, the even slower deployment of police and civil administrators, the uneven quality of military components, the even greater unevenness of police and civil administrators, the United Nations' dependence on voluntary funding to pay for mission-essential but nonmilitary functions, such as the reintegration of combatants and capacity-building in local administrations, the frequent mismatches between ambitious mandates and modest means, and the premature withdrawal of missions, often following immediately upon the successful conclusion of a first democratic election.

REBUILDING FAILED STATES

The UN's initial post–Cold War winning came to an abrupt end in Somalia and the former Yugoslavia. In both those instances UN-led peacekeeping forces were inserted into societies where there was no peace to keep. In both cases UN forces eventually had to be replaced by larger, more robust American-led peace enforcement missions.

While the Cold War had divided some societies, it provided the glue that held others together. Even as former East-West battlegrounds like Namibia, Cambodia, El Salvador, and Mozambique were able, with UN assistance, to emerge as viable nation states, other divided societies, such as Somalia, Yugoslavia, and Afghanistan, which had been held together by one superpower or the other, and sometimes by both, began to disintegrate as these external supports were removed. Not surprising, the United Nations had a harder time holding together collapsing states than brokering reconciliation in coalescing ones.

The original UN mission in Somalia was undermanned and overmatched by warring Somali clan militias. The US-led multinational force that replaced it was built on a core of 20,000 American soldiers and marines. This force was quickly able to overawe local resistance and secure the delivery of famine relief supplies, its principal mission. Washington then chose to withdraw all but 2,000 of its troops. The United States passed overall responsibility back to the United Nations while also supporting a radical expansion of that organization's mandate. The previous UN and US forces had confined their mission to securing humanitarian relief activities. Even as the United States withdrew 90 percent of its combat forces and saw them replaced by a smaller number of less well-equipped UN troops, it joined in extending the mission of those remaining forces to the introduction of grass-roots democracy, a process that put the United Nations at cross-purposes with every warlord in the country. The result was a resurgence of violence to levels that residual US and UN troops proved unable to handle.

Insuperable difficulties also arose in the former Yugoslavia, where UN peacekeepers were again deployed into an ongoing civil war without the mandate, the influence, or the firepower needed to end the fighting. UN deficiencies contributed to the failure of its efforts in Bosnia, as they had in Somalia, but again at least equal responsibility lies with its principal member governments: with Russia, for its stubborn partisanship on behalf of Serbia; with the United States, for its refusal to commit American forces or to support the peacemaking initiatives of those governments that had; and with Britain and France, the principal troop contributors, for failing to enforce the mandate they had accepted to protect the innocent civilians entrusted to their care.

The inadequacies of UN missions in both Somalia and Bosnia, when contrasted with the more robust American-led multinational efforts that succeeded them, led to a general conclusion that while the United Nations might be up to peacekeeping, peace enforcement was beyond the organization's capacity. This conclusion, not uncongenial to the United Nations' leadership, had been belied by that organization's performance thirty years earlier in the former Belgian Congo where the UN had conducted several military offensives and suppressed one coup d'état and two separatist insurgencies. Its later conduct of small but successful peace enforcement missions in Eastern Slavonia from 1996 to 1998 and in East Timor, beginning in 1999, demonstrates that the United Nations was perfectly capable of executing a robust peace enforcement mandate in circumstances where the scale is modest, the force included a core of capable First World troops, and the venture has strong international backing.

Eastern Slavonia was the last Serb-held area of Croatia at the end of the conflict between these two former Yugoslav republics. Here the United Nations once again became responsible for governing a territory in transition, in this case from Serb to Croat control. This particular operation was generously manned, well led, abundantly resourced, and strongly supported by the major powers, whose influence in turn assured the cooperation of neighboring states. Not surprisingly, given these advantages, the UN peace enforcement mission in Eastern Slavonia was highly successful.

NATION BUILDING IN THE NEW MILLENNIUM

In the closing months of 1999, the United Nations found itself charged with governing both Kosovo and East Timor. The latter operation proved an ideal test case for UN capabilities. Like Eastern Slavonia, East Timor was small in both territory and population, but international resources, in terms of military manpower and economic assistance were unusually abundant. Major power influence secured neighboring states' cooperation. A UN-authorized coalition of the willing, led by Australia, secured initial control of the territory and then quickly turned the operation over to UN management. Remaining combatants were disarmed, new security forces established, a local administration recreated, elections held, and a democratically elected government inaugurated within the first two years.

Even in this showcase operation, certain chronic UN deficiencies were exhibited. International police and civil administrators were slow to arrive and of variable quality. Once ensconced, UN administrators were a trifle slow to turn power back to local authorities. In 2005, under financially motivated pressure from Security Council members, including notably the United States, the UN withdrew its remaining forces, only to have to reinsert them in 2006 after large-scale rioting broke out.

In less benign circumstances, the UN's characteristic limitations became apparent. In Sierra Leone inadequate UN forces were inserted under unduly optimistic assumptions, encountered early reverses, and eventually suffered the ultimate humiliation of being captured and held hostage in large numbers. Poised on the verge of collapse, the Sierra Leone operation was rescued by the United Kingdom and then turned around thanks in large measure to extraordinary personal efforts by UN Secretary-General Kofi Annan. British forces arrived, extricated UN hostages, intimidated insurgent forces, and began to train a more competent local military. The United States threw its logistic and diplomatic weight behind the operation. The regime in neighboring Liberia, highly complicit in Sierra Leone's civil war, was displaced. Additional manpower and economic resources were secured. So bolstered, the United Nations was able to oversee a process of disarmament and demobilization and hold reasonably free elections.

Subsequently the United Nations has also overseen successful transitions to democracy in neighboring Liberia. It has helped broker and sustain a still very tenuous peace between northern and southern Sudan. In conjunction with the African Union, UN peacekeepers have greatly improved security in the Darfur region of that same country. The UN force in the Congo, currently some 20,000 strong, is the largest of that organization's current peacekeeping operations. Although security in that country has improved, the UN force there continues to face daunting challenges in an impoverished country of 68 million inhabitants (making it considerably more populated than Iraq and Afghanistan combined) beset by the variety of internal conflicts and surrounded by interfering neighbors.

HAS NATION BUILDING PROVED COST-EFFECTIVE?

In addition to the horrendous human costs, war inflicts extraordinary economic costs on societies. On average, a study by Paul Collier and Anke Hoeffler indicates, civil wars reduce prospective economic output by 2.2 percent per year for the duration of the conflict. However, once peace is restored, economic activity resumes and in a number of cases, the economies grow. Collier and Hoeffler look at the cost and effectiveness of various policy options to reduce the incidence and duration of civil wars and find post-conflict military intervention to be highly cost-effective, in fact, the most cost-effective policy examined.[1]

The sharp overall decline in deaths from armed conflict around the world over the past decade also points to the efficacy of nation building. During the early 1990s deaths from armed conflict were averaging over 200,000 per year. By 2003 this number had come down to 27,000, a fivefold decrease. This positive trend has been sustained since, although the decline has been less rapid. Interestingly, the part of the world that has seen the most dramatic drop in overall violence has been Africa, where the United Nations is the dominant provider of international security forces.[2]

Thus the world has not become a more violent or disorderly place since the end of the Cold War, or even since 9/11, rather the reverse. More conflicts are being ended each year than are starting, and those ended are restarting less frequently. In this, international activism and United Nations peacekeeping have made significant contributions. These positive trends may not be apparent to most Americans since US armed forces are heavily involved in two ongoing conflicts.

The cost of UN nation building tends to look quite modest, particularly when compared to the cost of these larger and more demanding US-led operations. For several years the United States spent some $4 billion per month to support its military operations in Iraq. This is roughly what the United Nations was spending to run all nineteen of its then-current peacekeeping missions for a year; further, the United States funds only a quarter of that total. Thus the totality of its annual share of UN peacekeeping costs the United States roughly the same as it was paying for one week of operations in Iraq.

EVALUATING OTHER PEACEKEEPING PROVIDERS

The United Nations no longer has a monopoly on international peacekeeping. NATO mounted its first such mission in 1995 in Bosnia. The European Union sent its first military force abroad to Macedonia in 2003 and has since conducted larger peacekeeping operations in the Democratic Republic of the Congo and Chad. The EU has also, in 2005, replaced the NATO peacekeeping force in Bosnia with one of its own. The African Union has become the peacekeeper of last resort for that continent, assuming responsibilities for operations that are too risky for anyone else to touch.

Each of these institutions has its own strengths and weaknesses. The UN has the widest experience; NATO has the most powerful forces; the EU has the most developed array of civil competencies; and the African Union is the least risk averse.

The United Nations has the most widely accepted legitimacy and the greatest formal authority. Its actions, by definition, enjoy international sanction. Alone among international organizations, it can require financial contributions even from those opposed to the intervention in question. The United Nations has the most straightforward decision-making apparatus and the most unified command-and-control arrangements. The UN Security Council is smaller than its NATO, EU, or AU equivalents and is the only one that makes all its decisions by qualified majority; only five of its members have the capacity to block decisions unilaterally. Once the Security Council determines the purpose of a mission and decides to launch it, further operational decisions are left largely to the Secretary-General and his professional staff, at least until the next Security Council review, generally six months hence. In UN operations, the civilian and military chains of command are unified and integrated, with unequivocal civilian primacy and a clear line of authority from the Secretary-General through the local civilian representative to the local force commander.

The UN is also a comparatively efficient force provider. The United Nations currently deploys almost 100,000 soldiers and police officers in nineteen separate missions. In its specialized agencies, it possesses a broad panoply of civil as well as military capabilities needed for nation building.

All UN-led operations are planned and directed by a few hundred military and civilian staffers at UN headquarters in New York. Most UN troops come from developing countries, whose costs per deployed soldier are a small fraction of those of any Western army. NATO, by contrast, is capable of deploying powerful, heavily equipped, highly mobile forces and of using them to force entry where necessary. But NATO has no capacity to implement civilian activities; it depends on the United Nations, the European Union, and other institutions and nations to perform all the nonmilitary functions essential to the success of any nation-building operation.

NATO decisions are by consensus; consequently, all members have a veto. Whereas the UN Security Council normally makes one decision with respect to any particular operation every six months and leaves the Secretary-General relatively unconstrained to carry out that mandate during the intervals, the NATO council's oversight is more continuous, its decision making more incremental. Member governments consequently have a greater voice in operational matters, and the NATO civilian and military staffs and local commanders have correspondingly less.

Like NATO, and unlike the UN, EU decision making in the security and defense sector is by consensus. The European Union has a much leaner military and political staff than NATO, in part because it can call on NATO, if it chooses, for planning and other staff functions. The EU, like the UN but unlike NATO, can draw upon a wide array of civilian assets essential to any nation-building operation. Like NATO soldiers, EU soldiers are much more expensive than their UN counterparts. EU decision-making mechanisms, like those of NATO, offer troop-contributing governments more scope for micromanaging military operations on a day-to-day basis than do the UN's.

The African Union disposes the least capable military forces and the least developed capacity for their command, control, and sustainment. The organization is completely reliant on non-African donors to finance its peacekeeping activities. In practice this means that while the United States and Europe between them foot about half the bill for UN peacekeeping, they pay nearly 100 percent of the AU's peacekeeping costs.

The AU does possess one advantage. Its members are those most affected by the conflicts in what is the world's most conflict prone region. Proximity means that these states get the bulk of the refugees, criminality, terrorism, disease, and commercial disruption that comes from having a failed state on their doorstep. As a result of this vulnerability, AU member governments are often ready to move faster and under more discouraging conditions than are those who dominate the capable but more distant organizations like the EU, NATO, or the UN. This willingness to go where others fear to tread has led to a rather perverse division of labor in which the most powerful peace-keeping provider (NATO) was, until its intervention in Libya, completely unengaged in Africa; the second most powerful (the EU) does only the easi-est of missions, most recently in Chad; the UN does most of the rest, leaving the least capable organization to deal with the most hopeless situations, to wit Somalia and, until recently, Darfur.

THE US AND UN WAYS OF NATION BUILDING

The United States is also a provider of nation-building-type missions, having led coalitions of the willing into Somalia, Haiti, Afghanistan, and Iraq. The American approach to these missions differs considerably from that of the United Nations, reflecting its different character and capabilities. The United Nations is an international organization entirely dependent on its members for the wherewithal to conduct nation building. The United States is the world's only superpower, commanding abundant resources of its own and access to those of many other nations and institutions.

When compared to American-organized efforts, UN operations have al-most always been undermanned and under resourced. This is not because UN managers believe smaller is better, although some do, but because mem-ber states are rarely willing to commit the manpower or the money any prudent military commander would desire. As a result, small, weak UN forces are routinely deployed into what they hope, on the basis of best-case assumptions, will prove to be post-conflict situations. Where such assump-tions prove ill founded, UN forces have had to be reinforced, withdrawn, or, in extreme cases, rescued.

Throughout the 1990s the United States adopted the opposite approach to sizing its nation-building deployments, basing its plans on worst-case as-sumptions and relying on an overwhelming force to quickly establish a stable environment and deter resistance from forming. In Somalia, Haiti, Bosnia, and Kosovo, US-led coalitions originally intervened in numbers and with capabilities that discouraged even the thought of resistance. In Somalia, this American force was quickly drawn down. The resultant casualties reinforced the Clinton administration's determination to establish and retain a substantial overmatch in its future nation-building operations.

Unfortunately, the administration of George W. Bush did not initially follow this precedent. In the aftermath of the September 2001 terrorist attacks, American tolerance of military casualties significantly increased. In sizing its stabilization operations in Afghanistan and Iraq, the new American leadership abandoned the strategy of overwhelming preponderance (sometimes labeled the Powell Doctrine after former chairman of the Joint Chiefs of Staff General Colin Powell) in favor of the "small footprint" or "low profile" force posture that had previously characterized UN operations.

Throughout the 1990s the United States slowly got better at nation building. The Haitian operation was better managed than Somalia, Bosnia better than Haiti, and Kosovo better than Bosnia. This learning curve was not sustained into the current decade. The Bush administration was initially disdainful of nation building, viewing it as an unsuitable activity for US forces. When compelled to engage in such missions, first in Afghanistan and then Iraq, the administration sought to break with the strategies and institutional responses that had been honed throughout the 1990s to deal with these challenges. The result, in both cases, was a failure to translate rapid and overwhelming conventional military victories into enduring peace. In both cases the initially small American-led force proved unable to establish a secure environment. Spoiler elements were not deterred, instead they were given time and space to organize violent resistance movements. In both cases the original US force levels had to be significantly increased, but not before what might have been conducted as robust peace-enforcement missions evolved into full-scale counterinsurgency operations.

The United Nations has largely avoided the institutional discontinuities that have marred US performance. UN nation-building missions have been run over the past twenty years by an increasingly experienced cadre of international civil servants. Similarly in the field, many peacekeeping operations are headed and staffed by veterans of earlier operations. Only in the last couple of years has the US government begun to establish its own doctrine for the conduct of its nation-building endeavors (labeled "stabilization" and "reconstruction missions" in official USG jargon), and to build a cadre of professionals prepared to serve in one such endeavor after another.

It would appear that the low-profile, small-footprint approach to nation building is much better suited to UN-style peacekeeping, where there is a preexisting peace settlement and an invitation by the parties for third-party intervention, than to the more demanding US-style peace enforcement. The United Nations has an ability to compensate, to some degree at least, for its "hard" power deficit with "soft" power attributes of international legitimacy and local impartiality. The United States does not have such advantages in situations where America itself is a party to the conflict being terminated, or where the United States has acted without an international mandate. Military reversals may also have greater consequences for the United States than for the United Nations. To the extent that the United Nations' influence depends more on the moral than the physical, more on its legitimacy than its combat prowess, military rebuffs do not fatally undermine that central attribute. To the extent that America leans more on "hard" rather than "soft" power to achieve its objectives, military reverses strike at the very heart of its deterrent credibility and thus potential influence.

The United Nations and the United States also tend to enunciate their nation-building objectives very differently. UN mandates are highly negotiated, densely bureaucratic documents. UN spokespersons tend toward understatement in expressing their goals. Restraint of this sort is more difficult for American officials, who must build congressional and public support for costly and sometimes dangerous missions in distant and unfamiliar places. As a result, American nation-building rhetoric tends toward the grandiloquent. The United States often becomes the victim of its own rhetoric when its higher standards are not met.

Thus UN-led nation-building missions tend to be smaller than American, to take place in less demanding circumstances, to be more frequent and therefore more numerous, and to define their objectives more circumspectly. By contrast, American-led nation building has taken place in more demanding circumstances, has required larger forces and more robust mandates, has received more economic support, has espoused more ambitious objectives, and sometimes encountered greater resistance.

CONCLUSION

The UN's founders envisaged its military operations as being led and largely conducted by its most powerful members. The Security Council has on rare occasions mandated just such peace enforcement missions, most recently in Libya. Peacekeeping, on the other hand, has evolved rather differently, being authorized by the major powers but funded by the membership as a whole, directed by the UN Secretary-General and his professional staff, and drawing for its manpower largely on smaller, or at least less powerful, and, in recent decades, largely non-Western states.

Among the several international organizations active in the field of peacekeeping, the United Nations now provides the most suitable institutional framework for peacekeeping and nation-building-type missions in circumstances in which a permissive entry is possible and no more than 20,000 troops are required. The UN has the widest experience in the field, a comparatively low cost structure, a comparatively high success rate, and the greatest degree of international legitimacy. Other possible options are likely to be either much more expensive, e.g., US-, EU-, or NATO-led coalitions, or less capable, e.g., the African Union. NATO-, EU-, or American-led forces should be looked to only where a forced entry is a necessary prerequisite (the UN doesn't do invasions), or a much larger initial force is needed to establish order, or the UN Security Council cannot agree.

UN peacekeeping operations would be more capable still if American and European militaries participated, as they did substantially in the early 1990s. Among the permanent members of the Security Council, China is now the largest troop contributor. Once the American and European military commitment in Afghanistan is scaled back, it should be hoped that these nations will return to UN peacekeeping.

Notes

1. Paul Collier and Anke Hoeffler, "The Challenges of Reducing the Global Incidence of Civil War," Centre for the Study of African Economies, Department of Economics, Oxford University, Copenhagen Challenge Paper, April 23, 2004.

2. For discussion of levels of armed conflict and resultant casualties over the past fifty years, see "Human Security Report, 2005" and "Human Security Briefs" of 2006 and 2007, produced by the Human Security Centre at the University of British Columbia under the direction of Andrew Mack.

Chapter 9

Fighting the Last War:
The United Nations Charter in the Age
of the War on Terror

Oona A. Hathaway

W e the Peoples of the United Nations Determined to save succeeding generations from the scourge of war, which twice in our lifetime has brought untold sorrow to mankind . . . do hereby establish an international organization to be known as the United Nations."[1] These are the words with which the United Nations Charter begins. When they were penned in the spring of 1945, the world was struggling to emerge from the second devastating global conflagration in several decades. Over 50 million people were dead, and countless cities lay in ruins.

The delegates who gathered in San Francisco to finalize the Charter dreamed of putting an end to such wars. The words they chose make clear that the recent wars were very much on their minds. The Charter declared, "All Members shall refrain in their international relations from the threat or use of force against the territorial integrity or political independence of any state, or in any other manner inconsistent with the Purposes of the United Nations."[2] The power to address any threats to international peace and security would be vested in a new Security Council, led by representatives of the five leading Allied powers.

Crafted as it was to prevent another world war, the Charter was well suited to respond to threats to sovereign states by other sovereign states—at least as long as none of the privileged five permanent Security Council members opposed action. But the system the Charter created to respond to such threats was extremely rigid. The permanent seats on the Security Council were exactly that—permanent. That left the organization less able to respond to the changing political and economic realities of the postwar era. Moreover, the United Nations Charter focused on preventing one particular kind of threat to global peace and security—belligerent sovereign states. This singular aim meant that the organization created and governed by the Charter was not well prepared for the global security landscape of the twenty-first century, in which non-state actors pose unprecedented threats.

The spread of devastatingly destructive weapons technology and the rise of non-state actors capable of inflicting large-scale damage across national boundaries have placed the United Nations under new pressures. At the same time, the human rights revolution that emerged on the heels of the Charter has posed challenges to the Charter's limits on states' use of force. The framework created by the Charter has thus far proven slow to adapt to these challenges. Whether or not the system put in place by the Charter is able to "save succeeding generations from the scourge of war," as its authors hoped, will depend on its capacity to effectively respond to these changes.

In this essay I examine three key challenges that have emerged at the dawn of the twenty-first century as a result of the changing security, political, and legal environment. First, the rise of the doctrine of preemptive self-defense threatens to turn the right to defend into a right to attack. Since the attacks on the United States on 9/11, many have argued that states' inherent right to self-defense—preserved in Article 51 of the United Nations Charter—permits states to use force to preempt the extreme threats posed by such weapons. Taken to an extreme, the doctrine of preemptive self-defense thus threatens to unravel the Charter's prohibition on the use of force. Second, armed conflicts today often occur between states and transnational non-state actors. Can the United Nations remain relevant in an age of non-state warfare? Finally, the international human rights revolution has tested the limits on the use of military force to address human rights abuses and humanitarian disasters. Is it possible for the United Nations to prevent war *and* protect human rights? The United Nations Charter, forged by the anvil of World War II, must prove itself able to meet these modern challenges if it is to successfully govern the use of military force as the twenty-first century unfolds.

CHALLENGE 1: CAN THE UNITED NATIONS PREVENT THE RIGHT TO DEFEND FROM BECOMING A RIGHT TO ATTACK?

The September 11, 2001, terrorist attacks on the World Trade Center changed how ordinary Americans viewed global threats. In the now-familiar events of the day, nineteen members of al Qaeda hijacked four commercial passenger jets. Two flew into the twin towers of the World Trade Center in New York City, killing nearly three thousand people. A third crashed into the Pentagon, and a fourth, with passengers wrestling to retake control, crashed into a field in rural Pennsylvania.

The United States quickly responded by launching the "war on terror" and, with it, the invasion of Afghanistan, which had harbored al Qaeda for years. Dubbed "Operation Enduring Freedom," the military operation's immediate aim—one quickly accomplished—was to depose the Taliban-led Afghan government that had allowed al Qaeda leader and 9/11 mastermind Osama bin Laden to operate freely in the country.[3] The United States vigorously defended the legality of its actions. John Negroponte, then permanent representative of the US to the UN, explained, "In response to these attacks, and in accordance with the inherent right of individual and collective self-defense, United States armed forces have initiated actions designed to prevent and deter further attacks on the United States."[4]

The United States found strong legal support for this position in the United Nations Charter, which expressly preserves states' right to self-defense. Article 51 of the Charter provides, in part: "Nothing in the present Charter shall impair the inherent right of individual or collective self-defence if an armed attack occurs against a Member of the United Nations, until the Security Council has taken measures necessary to maintain international peace and security."[5] The express preservation of the right to self-defense in Article 51 acknowledges the reality that the Security Council might not react immediately to attacks on member states. States are thus permitted to respond provisionally—"until the Security Council has taken measures" to address the threat.[6]

As conceived by the authors of the UN Charter, however, the right of self-defense was not unlimited. In addition to requiring that the state act only "until" the Security Council has taken measures, the Charter expressly provides that any act of self-defense shall be immediately reported to the Security Council.[7] There is a substantive limitation as well: a member has a right to self-defense "if an armed attack occurs."

The "war on terror"—which opened with an attack on "nations, organizations, or persons" responsible for the September 11 attacks and those who harbored them—clearly began as an act of self-defense consistent with the UN Charter. But as the war progressed, the self-defense justification offered by the Bush administration began to take on a life of its own. That new self-defense justification was no longer tethered to any particular armed attack. According to administration lawyers, an act of self-defense need no longer be simply reactive—responding to a prior attack—as the UN Charter clearly contemplated. It might be proactive as well.

The 2002 US National Security Strategy memo described this new stance, which has since come to be called the Bush Doctrine: "While the United States will constantly strive to enlist the support of the international community, we will not hesitate to act alone, if necessary, to exercise our right of self-defense by acting pre-emptively against such terrorists, to prevent them from doing harm against our people and our country."[8] Making the case for the need for preemptive strikes, the memo continued,

> Given the goals of rogue states and terrorists, the United States can no longer solely rely on a reactive posture as we have in the past. The inability to deter a potential attacker, the immediacy of today's threats, and the magnitude of potential harm that could be caused by our adversaries' choice of weapons, do not permit that option. We cannot let our enemies strike first.[9]

Four years later, this message was reaffirmed in the 2006 National Security Strategy memo, which added, "If necessary . . . under long-standing principles of self-defense, we do not rule out the use of force before attacks occur, even if uncertainty remains as to the time and place of the enemy's attack. When the consequences of an attack with WMD are potentially so devastating, we cannot afford to stand idly by as grave dangers materialize. This is the principle and logic of preemption."[10]

The United States relied on this principle of preemptive self-defense in the war against Iraq that began in 2003.[11] Iraq had not actually attacked the United States, but that did not prevent the Bush administration from arguing that action was justified by self-defense: "Iraq's demonstrated capability and willingness to use weapons of mass destruction, the risk that the current Iraqi regime will either employ those weapons to launch a surprise attack against the United States or its Armed forces or provide them to international terrorists who would do so, and the extreme magnitude of harm that would result to the United States and its citizens from such an attack, combine to justify action by the United States to defend itself."[12]

By April 9, 2003, Saddam Hussein's regime had fallen. Coalition forces began the search for the weapons of mass destruction that had provided the rationale for the preemptive war. They found nothing. All evidence indicated that Hussein had abandoned his weapons development program after the 1991 Gulf War.[13] High-ranking officials began to invoke humanitarian and regional security justifications for the invasion. Some argued that the mere possibility that Saddam Hussein might acquire weapons of mass destruction in the future was sufficient rationale for the United States to attack—stretching the preemptive self-defense argument to even greater lengths.[14]

This expansion of preemptive self-defense is at least in part an inevitable response to new threats borne of new destructive technologies. The spread of weapons of mass destruction means that states cannot always wait to respond to attacks before acting but sometimes must attempt to preempt them—with force, if necessary. Yet little systematic attention has been given to when and how such threats in fact justify preemptive force—and what to do when the suspected threat turns out to be nonexistent.

This problem has become all the more challenging and pressing in light of new technological developments that allow state and non-state actors to pose new threats. Cyberattacks, for example, have become more common and more threatening—and many arguably constitute an illegal "use of force" under Article 2.4 of the Charter. But they are rarely so severe that they constitute an "armed attack," giving the victim state the right to respond with force under Article 51.[15] This has raised questions of what, if anything, states can do in response to attacks that fall in the space between Article 2.4 and Article 51—how, if at all, can they respond to attacks that constitute an illegal use of force but do not amount to an "armed attack"? In response to the problem, the Obama administration has indicated support for the aggressive legal position that "the inherent right of self-defense potentially applies against any illegal use of force" and that "there is no threshold for a use of deadly force to qualify as an 'armed attack' that may warrant a forcible response."[16]

This much is clear: the once very limited self-defense exception now threatens to swallow the Charter's rule prohibiting the "threat or use of force" by states. The Charter thus finds itself perched on a precipice. The self-defense justification for the use of force holds the potential to undo the central aim of the Charter—to bring an end to the "scourge of war." For if an armed attack is no longer necessary to justify a use of force in self-defense, then self-defense is unmoored from its most salient substantive limit. To prevent the exception from swallowing the rule, much closer attention will need to be paid to the proper scope of the self-defense justification in this new security environment. Reformers will need to confront whether it is possible to permit states to respond to threats from weapons of mass destruction and new technologies without unleashing the "scourge of war" that the Charter sought to control.

CHALLENGE 2: CAN THE UNITED NATIONS REMAIN RELEVANT IN AN AGE OF TRANSFORMED WARFARE?

Threats to peace today are different not only in kind from those of sixty-five years ago but also in their source. Many of the greatest threats come not from states but from non-state actors with international reach. There have always been threats to states from non-state actors, of course. But what makes today's threat from non-state actors new—and of greater concern to states than ever before—is the new weapons and communications technology that makes it possible for non-state actors to do unprecedented harm: a handful of individuals can wreak immense destruction on even the most powerful states.

Technological change does not simply affect the weapons used in military conflict. It changes the way entities organize, communicate, and fight. Developments in communications technology, particularly the Internet, have facilitated a shift from traditional warfare between territorially defined states to war—in both real space and cyberspace—between states and more loosely organized communities.[17] As Jarrett Brachman, an expert on al Qaeda and online jihaddism observes, "Al-Qaeda's transformed from a terrorist organization that uses the media into a media organization that uses terrorism. Al-Qaeda realized it was constrained operationally but that it could get other people to do its job for it, if it could just rally them up enough."[18] Non-state actors facing an opponent that possesses both technological dominance and overwhelming conventional weapons capability will fight asymmetrically. These actors will not organize themselves into traditional military units, nor distinguish themselves from civilians because to do so invites rapid identification and hence defeat. The weak frequently refuse to play by the rules or organizational logic of the strong (that is, the traditional laws of war) because to do so would ensure failure.

States have reacted by pursuing non-state actors that they believe pose a threat, regardless of whether they are located within or outside their own territory. The result has been a growing number of transnational conflicts between states and non-state actors. This increasingly prominent form of armed conflict is very different from the state-to-state conflict the authors of the Charter had in mind at the time of its drafting.

The US conflict with al Qaeda is the most prominent such conflict in recent years. There has arguably been "protracted armed violence"[19] between the United States and al Qaeda since the 1998 bombings by al Qaeda of the US embassies in Nairobi and Dar es Salaam. This violence has also included the retaliatory US missile strikes against al Qaeda facilities in Afghanistan and suspected al Qaeda–linked facilities in Sudan in 1998; the 2000 bombing of the USS *Cole*; the attacks of September 11, 2001; and the subsequent assault by the United States upon al Qaeda in Afghanistan and Pakistan, including in particular the Battle of Tora Bora and the ongoing targeted killings in Pakistan's federally administered tribal areas. This conflict meets all the traditional standards of armed conflict but one—the United States' enemy is not itself a state entity but is instead a non-state actor with transnational reach.[20]

The United Nations has responded to the current armed conflict between the United States and al Qaeda by recognizing that the dispute represents a threat to international peace. The day after the September 11, 2001, attacks, the Security Council passed resolution 1368, which repeatedly invoked the threat to international peace posed by the September 11 attacks. The resolution expressly recognizes the "inherent right of individual or collective self-defense in accordance with the Charter" and "unequivocally condemns in the strongest terms the horrifying terrorist attacks which took place on 11 September 2001 in New York, Washington, D.C. and Pennsylvania and *regards* such acts, like any act of international terrorism, as a threat to international peace and security."[21] In a later resolution, the Security Council reiterated its determination that the September 11 attacks, "like any act of international terrorism, constitute a threat to international peace and security."[22] Together, these resolutions demonstrated a clear willingness by the United Nations to regard a threat by a non-state actor as a threat to the peace justifying UN action.

Despite its condemnation of the September 11 attacks and its recognition of the threat to international peace and security posed by international terrorism the United Nations has taken only limited steps to respond to those threats. The second Security Council resolution passed in the weeks after

September 11 called for states to freeze the assets of suspected terrorists and to put in place more effective border controls. It also set up a counterterrorism committee to oversee state compliance with the resolution.[23] The resolution has, in fact, been criticized for its sweeping character. Described as "more legislative in character than anything that the Security Council had previously attempted,"[24] the resolution called on states to change their domestic laws to allow for a more coordinated response to terrorism.

Yet the resolution and the work of the committee it created did not directly address a key problem: many terrorist threats are orchestrated and financed by non-state actors operating outside the state they intend to attack. And it did little to help states understand the legal limits of their possible courses of action. States have three legally available options for responding to terrorist threats posed by transnational non-state actors. First, they can encourage the home state to act against the suspected terrorists, thus cutting off their ability to launch an attack. Second, they can seek the consent of the home state to the use of armed force against the non-state actors operating within the home state's territory. Third, they can use armed force against the non-state actors within the home state's territory without seeking consent, but only so long as that attack can be justified as a legal act of self-defense under Article 51. What rules govern the choice between these options and what legal rules would apply once the actions are commenced—including whether and how the laws of armed conflict apply to what some have taken to calling "transnational non-international armed conflicts"—remain uncertain. The United Nations has done little to address these questions and the Charter is silent on them, thus leaving it to states and international organizations to tussle over the issues on their own.

CHALLENGE 3: IS IT POSSIBLE FOR THE UNITED NATIONS TO PREVENT WAR *AND* PROTECT HUMAN RIGHTS?

The authors of the Charter were concerned first and foremost with preventing war between states. The document they designed thus prohibited states from using force unilaterally, except in cases of self-defense. And it gave the power to respond to threats to peace and security to a Security Council, where the five permanent members each possessed a veto. At the time of the Charter's founding, it was already clear that those five members were unlikely to agree on much, meaning the Security Council would likely authorize the use of force very infrequently—and that was just fine by most of those at the San Francisco Conference, who had seen enough war for a lifetime.

But the UN Charter did not emerge alone into the postwar era. It was accompanied by a new and growing human rights movement, championed by none other than former first lady Eleanor Roosevelt. Advocates of human rights—including several representatives of small nations and the more than forty nongovernmental organizations attending the conference as consultants and observers—failed to gain the attention at the San Francisco Conference that they had hoped.[25] But they did succeed in writing their aims into the Charter's Preamble. The Preamble declared that the member states pledged "to reaffirm faith in fundamental human rights, in the dignity and worth of the human person, in the equal rights of men and women and of nations large and small," to "establish conditions under which justice and respect for the obligations arising from treaties and other sources of international law can be maintained," and to "promote social progress and better standards of life in larger freedom."[26] Yet the text of the Charter did not make clear how these lofty goals would be achieved or how they would be reconciled with the promise that "nothing contained in the present Charter shall authorize the United Nations to intervene in matters which are essentially within the domestic jurisdiction of any State."[27]

The first step forward was the adoption of the ambitious and far-reaching Universal Declaration of Human Rights of 1948. A sort of international bill of rights covering everything from slavery to torture to freedom of assembly, the declaration came to serve as a rallying point and agenda of the fledgling human rights movement. Where there were once only a handful of international agreements dealing with states' treatment of their own citizens within their own territory, now there are hundreds. As Eleanor Roosevelt—who became the central force behind the Universal Declaration of Human Rights—later recounted, "Many of us thought that lack of standards for human rights the world over was one of the greatest causes of friction among the nations, and that recognition of human rights might become one of the cornerstones on which peace could eventually be based."[28]

The Universal Declaration helped spark a revolution. The number of human rights treaties has grown steadily each year since its creation. The declaration was followed in quick succession by the Convention against Genocide; the Geneva Conventions governing the use of armed force; the International Covenant on Civil and Political Rights; the Covenant on Economic, Social, and Cultural Rights; the Convention against Torture, among many other universal and regional agreements. Now international law covers an astonishing array of topics, from civil and political rights, to the right to be free from racial and gender discrimination, to the rights of children, to the protection of economic, social, and cultural well-being. In addition to the over one hundred universal human rights instruments—universal because any recognized state may join them—there are hundreds of regional agreements. It is not without reason, then, that former UN Secretary-General Kofi Annan dubbed this "the Age of Human Rights."[29]

Yet this revolution was on a collision course with the UN Charter. The Charter prohibited states from using force, placing authority to respond to threats to the peace in the hands of a Security Council, whose structure almost guaranteed inaction in all but the most extraordinary circumstances. And the Charter protected states from interfering in "matters which are essentially within the domestic jurisdiction of any State." The human rights revolution, on the other hand, questioned absolute state sovereignty—and recognized that states did not always live up to fundamental obligations to protect their citizens' most basic rights. Moreover, it challenged states to recognize their responsibility to those outside their borders as well. This was embodied most clearly in the declaration in the Convention against Genocide that state parties "confirm that genocide, whether committed in time of peace or in time of war, is a crime under international law which they undertake to prevent and to punish."[30]

The unspeakable horrors of the 1994 Rwanda genocide laid bare the problem. In April of that year, President Habyarimana of Rwanda and several top government officials died when their plane was hit by a surface-to-air missile during its approach to Kigali airport. A conflagration unfolded over the next 100 days, resulting in the deaths of an estimated 800,000 people. Ten Belgian UN troops were killed in the opening days of the conflict, and the United Nations responded by withdrawing the 2,500 UN peacekeepers in the country, leaving the genocide to unfold unimpeded. No country intervened on its own. The international community simply stood by and watched in horror as events unfolded.[31]

At the same time Rwanda was imploding, a genocide was beginning to unfold in the heart of Europe. The disintegration of Yugoslavia in 1991 brought with it years of war between the former Yugoslav republics. As in Rwanda, the United Nations had peacekeeping troops on the ground. The United Nations also went one step further and authorized a no-fly zone to prevent military attacks on civilians.[32] But, again, as in Rwanda, the small UN force was incapable of preventing any significant outbreak of violence.

On July 11, 1995, just a year after the Rwandan genocide, Bosnian Serb forces overran the small, lightly armed UN peacekeeping force protecting the safe area of Srebrenica. Ratko Mladić, commander of the Bosnian Serb army, declared, "Finally after the rebellion of the Dhaijas, the time has come to take revenge on the [Muslims] in this region."[33] It was a promise he kept to horrifying effect: his forces separated Muslim men and boys and led them to slaughter. All together, they killed roughly 7,000 Muslims—the largest mass murder in Europe since World War II. The UN peacekeeping forces—understaffed, underfunded, poorly armed, and unprepared for any serious fighting—were powerless to stop the massacre. This time, however, the United States and its NATO allies decided they could no longer sit on their hands. In August 1995, NATO planes flew 3,400 sorties in what was called "Operation Deliberate Force," which was authorized by a series of Security Council resolutions and undertaken in consultation with the UN Secretary-General.[34] Three months later, the war came to an end with the Dayton Peace Agreement.

But that was not the end of the violence. Mass violence again broke out in 1998. The massacre of forty-five unarmed civilian Albanians—including three women, a twelve-year-old boy, and several elderly men—at Račak by Serb paramilitary forces at the start of 1999 brought renewed international attention to the conflict. Serbian forces stepped up a campaign of ethnic cleansing against Kosovo Albanians in which thousands were killed and hundreds of thousands forced to flee to Albania, Macedonia, and Montenegro.

In response, NATO began a bombing campaign against Serbia to halt what it called a "campaign of terror" against ethnic Albanians in Kosovo by Yugoslav military forces and Serb paramilitary groups. This time, however, the action did not have United Nations approval. Well aware that Russia, a member of the Security Council's permanent five members, would veto any UN-approved operations, the NATO allies decided not to seek Security Council approval for the action.

This signaled the inevitable clash between two of the most significant postwar agendas of the international community: the prohibition on unilateral, unauthorized war-making by states and the human rights revolution. The action was clearly inconsistent with the UN Charter.[35] After all, the Charter prohibits use of force under Article 2.4. The only permitted exceptions are if the target state consents, a state is acting in self-defense, or if the action is approved by the Security Council under Chapter VII—none of which was true in this case. Yet that prohibition was in direct conflict with newly binding human rights obligations on states, particularly the Convention against Genocide's affirmative obligation on state parties to "undertake to prevent and to punish" genocide.[36] That affirmative obligation was later given strong voice by Secretary-General Kofi Annan, who had been the head of UN peacekeeping operations during the 1994 Rwandan genocide. He endorsed the concept of a "responsibility to protect," noting that, "What is clear is that when the sovereignty of States and the sovereignty of individuals come into conflict, we as an international community need to think hard about how far we will go to defend the former over the latter. Human rights and the evolving nature of humanitarian law will mean little if a principle guarded by States is always allowed to trump the protection of citizens within them."[37]

The conflict that Kofi Annan identified almost a decade ago remains today. And the solution to the conflict remains just as unclear. That is nowhere more clear at the time of this writing than in Syria, where the United Nations has proven unable to respond to the massacre of tens of thousands of people by their own government—because the United Nations Security Council has been incapacitated by veto threats from China and Russia. This has exposed once again a central fault line between the prohibition on war, on the one hand, and the promises of the human rights revolution, on the other. A central challenge facing the Charter in the coming years will be to address that conflict in a way that preserves both closely held values.[38]

———————————

> More than an end to war, we want an end to the beginning of all wars—yes, an end to this brutal, inhuman and thoroughly impractical method of settling the differences between governments.[39]

Franklin Delano Roosevelt penned these words the night of April 11 for an address he was scheduled to deliver three days hence. Although he never gave the address—he died of a cerebral hemorrhage the next day—his words captured the hopes of a generation.

Today, more than sixty-five years later, the Charter has done its part to prevent a third world war—and in this respect has fulfilled the greatest dreams of the generation that created it. Yet the world faces security challenges never imagined by the Charter's authors. A dirty bomb in the hands of a terrorist could destroy a city in a moment. Loosely organized groups that exist independent of any state government have declared their intent to destroy states, effectively declaring war against them—and those states have responded in kind.[40] And states sometimes engage in horrific abuse of their own citizens—abuse can no longer be hidden behind the thin veneer of state sovereignty thanks to the human rights revolution.

Each of these challenges has the potential to strengthen or undermine the regime built in 1945. To remain strong and relevant, the United Nations must reach beyond what those who created it envisioned. It cannot ignore these challenges but must lead the effort to engage them head-on. Only then will it stop fighting the last war and begin fighting the next.

Notes

1. United Nations Charter, Preamble.

2. United Nations Charter, Article 2.4.

3. Congress authorized the president to pursue "nations, organizations, or persons" responsible for the September 11 attacks and those who "harbored such organizations or persons." Authorization for Use of Military Force, Pub. L. 107–40, S.J. Res. 23 (Sept. 18, 2001).

4. Letter dated October 7, 2001, from the Permanent Representative of the United States of America to the United Nations addressed to the President of the Security Council, UN Doc. S/2001/946. The UK Permanent Representative sent a similar letter stating, "These forces have now been employed in exercise of the inherent right of individual and collective self-defense, recognized in Article 51, following the terrorist outrage of 11 September, to avert the continuing threat of attacks from the same source." Letter dated October 7, 2001, from the Chargé d'Affaires a.i. of the Permanent Mission of the United Kingdom of Great Britain and Northern Ireland to the United Nations addressed to the President of the Security Council, UN Doc. S/2001/947. All UN documents cited can be found via the UN's Official Document System available at http://www.un.org/en/documents.

5. United Nations Charter, Article 51.

6. This provision also allows collective defense arrangements to continue to lawfully operate alongside the UN Charter—a key concern of Latin American states at the time the Charter was concluded. See Tom Ruys, *"Armed Attack" and Article 51 of the U.N. Charter: Evolutions in Customary Law and Practice* (Cambridge University Press, 2010), 62; Inter-American Reciprocal Assistance and Solidarity (Act of Chapultepec), Mexico, March 6, 1945, 60 Stat. 1831.

7. "Measures taken by Members in the exercise of this right of self-defence shall be immediately reported to the Security Council and shall not in any way affect the authority and responsibility of the Security Council under the present Charter to take at any time such action as it deems necessary in order to maintain or restore international peace and security." United Nations Charter, Article 51.

8. George W. Bush, "The National Security Strategy of the United States of America" (2002), 6. Available at http://www.state.gov/documents/organization/63562.pdf.

9. Ibid., 15.

10. Ibid., 12.

11. For more on the Iraq war, see Bruce Ackerman and Oona A. Hathaway, "Limited War and the Constitution: Iraq and the Crisis of Presidential Legality," *Michigan Law Review* 109 (2011): 447–517.

12. Authorization for Use of Military Force against Iraq, Resolution of 2002, H.J. Res. 114, 107th Cong., Preamble (2002). There remains some legal debate over whether the United Nations authorized the war in Iraq. The Security Council unanimously passed resolution 1441, calling for new inspections in Iraq. Most nations understood that this resolution alone would not support military action. But the Bush administration claimed a right to act under the resolution. See, e.g., John C. Yoo, "International Law and the War in Iraq," *American Journal of International Law* 97 (2003): 563 (arguing that the action

was authorized by the Security Council but that the use of force could also be justified as an exercise of self-defense).

13. Charles Duelfer, who was then an advisor to the director of Central Intelligence for Iraqi Weapons, authored a more than 1,000-page report in 2004 in which he concluded that Iraq's WMD program had been destroyed in 1991 and was not active at the time of the 2002 invasion by the United States. Iraq Survey Group, Central Intelligence Agency, Iraq Survey Group Final Report (2004), http://www .globalsecurity.org/wmd/library/report/2004/isg-final-report/. Duelfer testified to the same effect at a Senate hearing before the Armed Services Committee on October 6, 2004. The Report of the Special Advisor to the Director of Central Intelligence for Strategy Regarding Iraqi Weapons of Mass Destruction Programs: Hearing Before the S. Comm. on Armed Servs., 108th Cong. (2004), 46, 58, http://homepage .ntlworld.com/jksonc/docs/duelfer-sasc-20041006.html (statement of Charles A. Duelfer, Special Advisor to the Director of Central Intelligence for Iraqi Weapons of Mass Destruction).

14. The administration thus expanded its use of what it called "preemptive self-defense"—generally understood to apply where there is an imminent threat of armed attack—to include what might be more properly called "preventive self-defense"—actions taken to prevent an imminent threat from developing. For more on the shifting justifications offered for the Iraq war, see Marc Sandalow, "Record Shows Bush Shifting on Iraq War: President's Rationale for the Invasion Continues to Evolve," *San Francisco Chronicle*, Sept. 29, 2004, A1. See also Ackerman and Hathaway, "Limited War and the Constitution," 447.

15. Oona A. Hathaway et al., "The Law of Cyber-Attack," *California Law Review* (2012).

16. Harold Hongju Koh, "International Law in Cyberspace" (Sept. 18, 2012; available at http://www .state.gov/s/l/releases/remarks/197924.htm). It's far from clear whether this statement, which was made, after all, in a speech, endorses a low threshold for Article 51 self-defense, envisions active countermeasures outside the Article 51 framework, or instead endorses the view that any "deadly use of force" is, by definition, an "armed attack" under Article 51.

17. John Arquilla and David Ronfeldt, *The Advent of Netwar* (Rand, 1996).

18. On the Media, "The Worst Job in Al Qaeda," June 4, 2010, http://www.onthemedia.org/transcripts /2010/06/04/02.

19. Prosecutor v. Tadić, Case No. IT-94–1, Decision on the Defense Motion for Interlocutory Appeal on Jurisdiction, ¶ 70, Oct. 2, 1995, International Criminal Tribunal for the former Yugoslavia.

20. See Harold Hongju Koh, "The Obama Administration and International Law," March 25, 2010; available at http://www.state.gov/s/l/releases/remarks/197924.htm. ("We live in a time, when, as you know, the United States finds itself engaged in several armed conflicts. . . . In the conflict occurring in Afghanistan and elsewhere, we continue to fight the perpetrators of 9/11: a non-state actor, al-Qaeda [as well as the Taliban forces that harbored al-Qaeda].")

21. SC Res. 1368, UN Doc. S/RES/1368 (Sept. 12, 2001).

22. SC Res. 1373, UN Doc. S/RES/1373 (Sept. 28, 2001).

23. Ibid.

24. Kim Scheppele, *The International State of Emergency* (Harvard University Press, forthcoming 2013), 16.

25. See, e.g., Mary Ann Glendon, *A World Made New* (Random House, 2001), 10–16.

26. UN Charter, Preamble.

27. UN Charter, Article 2.7.

28. Eleanor Roosevelt, "The Promise of Human Rights," *Foreign Affairs* 26 (April 1948), 470, 473.

29. Kofi A. Annan, "The Age of Human Rights," Project Syndicate, http://www.project-syndicate .org/commentary/ann1.

30. Convention on the Prevention and Punishment of the Crime of Genocide (entered into force 1951), art. 1. Available at http://treaties.un.org/doc/Publication/UNTS/Volume%2078/volume-78-I-1021 -English.pdf.

31. Report of the Secretary-General on the Situation in Rwanda (S/1994/640, May 31, 1994), UN and Rwanda 1993–1996, p. 291.

32. Security Council resolutions 781 and 786 (October 9 and November 10, 1992) established a ban on unauthorized military flights over Bosnia. Security Council resolution 816 (March 31, 1993) authorized member states and regional organizations to take "all necessary measures" to ensure compliance with the no-fly zone.

33. Samantha Power, *A Problem from Hell* (Harper Perennial, 2003), 191 (quoting Ratko Mladić).

34. Walter Dellinger, Proposed Deployment of United States Armed Forces into Bosnia, memorandum opinion for the counsel to the president, Nov. 30, 1995, http://www.justice.gov/olc/bosnia2.htm #N_1_.

35. Daniel H. Joyner, "The Kosovo Intervention: Legal Analysis and a More Persuasive Paradigm," *European Journal of International Law* 13, no. 3 (2002): 597–619 Indeed, the General Assembly actually condemned NATO's intervention, "reaffirming . . . that no State may use or encourage the use of economic, political or any other type of measures to coerce another State in order to obtain from it the subordination of the exercise of its sovereign rights." GA Res. 54/172, UNGAOR, 54th Sess., UN Doc. A/RES/54/172 (1999).

36. Convention on the Prevention and Punishment of the Crime of Genocide (entered into force 1951), art. 1.

37. Kofi Annan, "Secretary-General Addresses International Peace Academy Seminar on 'The Responsibility to Protect'" (2002), http://www.un.org/News/Press/docs/2002/sgsm8125.doc.htm.

38. For an attempt at resolving this conflict, see Oona A. Hathaway et al., A Consent-Based Approach to Humanitarian Intervention (2013).

39. Franklin Delano Roosevelt, undelivered Jefferson Day address, April 11, 1945 (scheduled for delivery April 14, 1945). Available at http://www.presidency.ucsb.edu/ws/?pid=16602.

40. Osama bin Laden declared in 1998: "By God's grace . . . we have formed with many other Islamic groups and organizations in the Islamic world a front called the International Islamic Front to do jihad against the crusaders and Jews. . . . And by God's grace . . . the men . . . are going to have a successful result in killing Americans and getting rid of them." Nic Robertson, "Previously Unseen Tape Shows bin Laden's Declaration of War," Aug. 19, 2002, http://articles.cnn.com/2002–08–19/us/terror .tape.main_1_bin-international-islamic-front-osama?_s=PM:US. The United States responded by effectively declaring war against al Qaeda in the 2001 Authorization for the Use of Military Force.

Chapter 10

Science and Politics on a Warming Planet: The IPCC and the Representation of Future Generations

Joseph Lampert

The first line of the UN Charter frames the project as the international community—"We the Peoples of the United Nations"—committing to the well-being of "succeeding generations." While that line focuses on avoiding "the scourge of war," the Charter did not simply establish a peacekeeping organization. Indeed, a significant legacy of the Charter is the creation of a world body that provides an institutional framework within which member states and nongovernmental organizations can respond to concerns not contemplated by its founders and engage in the kinds of activities that might make good on the idea of promoting "social progress and better standards of life in larger freedom," along with other aspirational aims enshrined in the Preamble. An instance of this was initiated in December 1988, when the General Assembly adopted a resolution calling on the World Meteorological Organization (WMO) and the United Nations Environment Programme (UNEP) to establish the Intergovernmental Panel on Climate Change (IPCC). This proved to be a significant step in both the scientific and political processes of understanding and addressing the problem of climate change, though the subsequent efforts of the panel have faced some difficult challenges.

This essay briefly recounts the creation and history of the IPCC and argues that the IPCC's current role—with its focus on knowledge assessment and grounded in a stance of policy-neutral science—is not sufficient for addressing a central legitimacy challenge of climate change politics. The General Assembly resolution calling for the establishment of the IPCC frames the normative implications of climate change in these terms: "Climate change affects humanity as a whole and should be confronted within a global framework so as to take into account the vital interests of all mankind."[1] This reflects the democratic principle that all interests affected by a policy or decision should be included in the decision-making process. Yet the institutional framework put into place via the United Nations Framework Convention on Climate Change (UNFCCC) has no mechanism for representing the interests of future generations—that portion of humanity whose vital interests are most significantly affected by a warming planet. I suggest that scientific expertise can help to fill this gap and propose that recasting the IPCC as a reviewing agency, charged with trusteeship over the interests of future generations affected by a warming planet, will bring climate change politics into better accord with democratic principles of legitimacy and will contribute to saving "succeeding generations" from more than the scourge of war.

FROM SCIENTIFIC INQUIRY TO INSTITUTIONAL DEVELOPMENT

The establishment of the IPCC in 1988 can be understood as an effort by the global community to formulate an institutional and policy response to a problem that is difficult to understand and global in its implications. The panel was created against the backdrop of a long process of scientific inquiry. While there was once significant uncertainty about anthropogenic climate change, there is now virtually no credible scientific dissent on the matter.[2] The evidence has gradually accumulated over the last hundred years or so.[3] The Swedish chemist Svante Arrhenius first hypothesized the warming potential of industrial gases in 1896, but for the first half of the twentieth century scientists believed that the oceans absorbed the increase in carbon dioxide (CO_2) emissions. Confirmation that CO_2 was in fact building up in the atmosphere did not come until Charles Keeling began measuring atmospheric concentrations of the gas at the Mauna Loa Observatory in Hawaii in 1958. The resulting "Keeling curve" vividly demonstrates the fact that CO_2 is, in fact, accumulating in the atmosphere.[4] This is significant because the more CO_2 there is in the atmosphere, the more it will trap the incoming energy from the sun, leading to a warmer planet.[5] Indeed, over the past 100 years (1906–2006) the average global temperature has increased .74 degrees Celsius, and eleven of the twelve years from 1995 to 2006 are among the twelve warmest years on record. Other indicators of climate change, such as rising sea levels and decreasing snow and ice coverage confirm that the Earth is getting warmer, which risks an increase in the frequency of extreme weather events, such as heat waves, heavy precipitation, and tropical storms. The science shows that the warming of the planet will bring about a set of complex changes in the global climate with profound implications for human well-being.[6]

The first steps from scientific inquiry into climate change toward an institutional response started to take shape in the late 1970s and 1980s as various scientific conferences and research networks increasingly focused on the impacts of climate change and raised the issue of policy responses. Significant among these was a series of conferences held in Villach, Austria, under the auspices of the WMO, the UNEP, and the International Council of Scientific Unions (ICSU). The report from the Villach 1985 conference stated that "scientists and policymakers should begin active collaboration to explore the effectiveness of alternative policies and adjustments."[7]

It was not until the late 1980s that the science of climate change began to have a significant public impact. An initial move was the establishment of the Advisory Group on Greenhouse Gases (AGGG), made up of members nominated from the WMO, the UNEP, and the ICSU and charged by those organizations with knowledge assessment on the issue of climate change. At the same time, the director of the UNEP wrote to the United States secretary of state to bring the US into the process. As a producer of much of the expertise on climate change, and as one of the largest emitters (second only to China, which has a far larger population) of greenhouse gases (GHG), the United States has played—and continues to play—a significant role in the politics of climate change. Fueled by (domestic) interagency disagreement, the concerns of influential industrial interests, and the implications a climate accord could have for the economy, the US was skeptical of an expert-driven panel unconstrained by government oversight. Accordingly, an intergovernmental panel emerged as the preferred solution, rather than a purely expert-driven body such as the AGGG.[8] In December 1988 the General Assembly adopted the resolution charging the WMO and the UNEP to establish the IPCC, citing, among other issues, the concern "that certain human activities could change global climate patterns, threatening present and future generations with potentially severe economic and social consequences."[9]

The primary work of the IPCC is the production of assessment reports, which synthesize and summarize the state of scientific knowledge of climate change, its impacts on society and possibilities for adaptation, and potential mitigation strategies. Each of these areas corresponds to one of three working groups, which consist of experts nominated by governments and NGOs, and each of which produces a section of the report. These reports have been issued roughly every five to six years (1990, 1995, 2001, 2007, 2013, 2014), and they undergo an extensive peer review process—by the team of authors assigned to each chapter, the lead authors of the working groups, outside experts, and by government representatives to the IPCC. The 2007 report, for example, was produced by over 500 authors and reviewed by over 2,000 other experts. Those involved in producing the reports reflect a wide array of scientific perspectives on the issue of climate change.[10] Each report also includes a "Summary for Policymakers," which is subject to line-by-line approval by government representatives. As one observer characterized the process of producing the Second Assessment Report of 1995, "This was peer review at 10 times the normal level of scrutiny."[11] In short, by all accounts the process followed by the IPCC conforms to the standards of scientific practice.

The First Assessment Report (1990) warned that global warming should be taken seriously but emphasized the uncertainties in the science. With each subsequent report the certainty of the science has become clearer, to the point that in the most recent (2013) report the IPCC writes that "warming of the climate system is unequivocal" and "it is *extremely likely* that human influence has been the dominant cause of the observed warming since the mid-20th century."[12] That *"extremely likely"* is a significant phrase, representing an assessed probability of greater than 95 percent. It also signals that scientific certainty has advanced since the 2007 report's conclusion that the rise in temperatures is only "very likely" (90 percent probability) due to human activity. The IPCC is not alone in this conclusion; every major scientific organization in the US has produced similar statements.[13] In short, although the evidence for anthropogenic climate change has been slow to accumulate and has been the subject of scientific controversy in the past, there is now virtually no legitimate scientific disagreement on the matter.

BRIDGING SCIENCE AND POLITICS

Currently, the IPCC is primarily an expert advisory body, producing the regular assessment reports as well as occasional special reports, which policy makers rely on when formulating domestic policy and in the effort to negotiate global climate policy. The body maintains an explicit stance of policy-neutrality, and it does not make policy proposals. Proponents of this approach argue that it is the most productive way for science to inform the policy-making process in a legitimate manner—that weighing in on policy matters would undermine the credibility of the science. Indeed, many scholarly commentators on the practice of science observe that scientists and scientific organizations attempt to do "boundary work" to separate scientific questions from questions of value or policy, in order to maintain the credibility of science and the legitimate role it plays in politics.[14] The boundary between science and politics may be constructed—and that construction is influenced by prevailing norms and attitudes about science and its place in the political process—but being conscientious about it, the argument goes, preserves the distinctive contribution that science makes to politics, in much the same way that the Supreme Court strengthens its role in the American political system by separating "political" questions from the legal ones over which it has authority. However, policy-neutrality is not the only form this boundary could take for the IPCC, and reconfiguring the manner in which the institution bridges science and policy will be explored below.

In fact, when the panel was established it was originally charged with a much broader role in global climate policy formulation. The General Assembly resolution that called upon the WMO and the UNEP to establish the IPCC outlined its mandate as providing

a comprehensive review and recommendations with respect to:
a. The state of knowledge of the science of climate and climatic change;
b. Programmes and studies on the social and economic impact of climate change, including global warming;
c. Possible response strategies to delay, limit or mitigate the impact of adverse climate change;
d. The identification and possible strengthening of relevant existing international legal instruments having a bearing on climate;
e. Elements for inclusion in a possible future international convention on climate.[15]

Items D and E get beyond the assessment responsibilities outlined in A, B, and C, sketching a considerable role for the IPCC in formulating policy. And in the first couple of years of its existence steps were taken to do just this, as the WMO and the UNEP formed the WMO/UNEP Task Force on a Convention on Climate Change, the purpose of which was to begin to formulate the provisions that would go into a global climate convention. The creation of this task force reflected an effort by officials at the UNEP to replicate the success of the Montreal Protocol, the treaty that bans chemicals that deplete the ozone layer, in which scientific experts had direct input into the negotiations on the treaty, along with government delegations. This approach also echoed the AGGG, which had experts going beyond providing assessments of climate change science to make value judgments about tolerable levels of GHG emissions and rises in global temperatures.[16]

However, as the IPCC process got under way in the late 1980s, and it became clear that a climate change convention would likely be in the offing, developing countries began to express reservations about the IPCC. Concerned that a science-driven response to climate change would not recognize the developmental dimensions of the issue (e.g., the implications of GHG regulations for developing economies and raising standards of living), they objected to the IPCC also serving as the negotiating body for a climate treaty. The US also did not want experts to drive the policy-making process on an issue with much higher political stakes than ozone depletion. These countries prevailed upon the General Assembly, which, in 1990, created the Intergovernmental Negotiating Committee (INC) to house the policy process away from the science.[17] In short, the mission of the IPCC in its early years morphed from a body with some policy-making aspirations as a contributor to the treaty-making process to an advisory panel charged primarily with issuing assessment reports.

This is not to say that the IPCC has not had an influence on climate change politics and policy. Most observers agree that the IPCC has been quite influential, if not at shaping policy then at shaping the knowledge base and providing the underlying motivation for action on climate change. As Clark Miller has argued, one of its great successes is in facilitating and sustaining a view of the environmental challenges posed by climate change in global terms, rather than in local or regional terms, and in fostering a global epistemic community that produces knowledge that policy makers, governments, and NGOs rely upon.[18] The global stature of the panel and the central role it has played in increasing our understanding of the climate was recognized when it was awarded, with Al Gore, the 2007 Nobel Peace Prize. In short, the IPCC has become an important knowledge broker on climate science and is widely viewed as the authoritative voice on the matter.

This situation has led one observer to conclude that the influence of the IPCC on policy has been "largely symbolic in terms of triggering and sustaining policy concern and considerably less in shaping subsequent action."[19]

The First Assessment Report, issued in 1990, helped to spur the negotiations on the UNFCCC, agreed to in 1992. The UNFCCC established a body composed of all parties to the convention, known as the Conference of the Parties (COP), which meets once a year, with the purpose of negotiating the details of climate regulation and to ensure compliance. A report issued by COP 2 pointed to the Second Assessment Report (1995) in urging the UN-FCCC parties to negotiate legally binding commitments on GHG emission reductions, which were eventually agreed to in the form of the Kyoto Protocol at COP 3 in 1997. Again, the IPCC did not directly participate in or influence the negotiations, but policy makers and activists drew on the authoritative assessment reports to motivate the process.[20]

CONTEMPORARY CHALLENGES

The IPCC, then, has certainly been successful in producing credible, authoritative reports that synthesize the state of climate science and, in doing so, sustaining climate change as a salient issue. Nevertheless, the panel and the broader global effort to confront climate change face significant challenges that demand a new institutional framework for addressing the problem, particularly in light of the questionable success of the Kyoto measures and the lack of progress in negotiating a successor regime. The first set of challenges has to do with communication and management and can be addressed within the current global climate change regime. A second, deeper challenge has to do with a legitimacy gap in the current approach to climate change itself, which does not include an adequate institutional mechanism to represent future generations. I briefly address the first issue in this section and take up the second in the following section.

The first challenge is shaped in part by public misunderstanding of climate science and of the practice of science itself.[21] Climate change skeptics, often backed by industry lobbyists and conservative think tanks, stoke the public's existing confusion about the phenomenon by trumpeting minor errors in the science and exposing supposed cover-ups on the part of scientists of disconfirming evidence against global warming.[22] In 2009, for example, skeptics attempted to drum up controversy over the leaked emails of climate scientists, which the skeptics claimed showed the researchers were dishonestly manipulating data (an investigation cleared the scientists of the allegations).[23] Of course, it does not help when the IPCC itself is the source of error. When it was discovered that a claim made in the 2007 assessment report about the Himalayan glaciers had not been properly checked and turned out to be unsubstantiated, skeptics again took it as evidence that the science of climate change is shaky and riddled with errors.[24] The IPCC immediately acknowledged the mistake and, along with many other scientists and scientific organizations, emphasized that such minor errors do nothing to undermine the overall evidence for global warming, but to many laypeople unaccustomed to the continuous process of revision and refinement of the scientific enterprise these minor mistakes are enough to cast doubt on the credibility of the organization.

The expert authority of the IPCC will become better integrated into a democratic political process, then, to the degree that it improves how scientific knowledge is communicated to lay audiences and strengthens its procedures. On this front, climate experts need to be able to explain just what is meant by the claim that there is a scientific consensus on global warming—that scientific knowledge is developed through gathering evidence, testing hypotheses, and continually reviewing and refining what we know. This also means fine-tuning how to characterize uncertainty in climate science. Like many realms of scientific inquiry, conclusions are framed in probabilistic terms. In lay terms, "uncertainty" can convey much more doubt than is meant when scientists assign probabilities to outcomes. Scientific uncertainty is not equivalent to saying "we're not sure," but rather is a way of communicating a range of likely outcomes. For instance, in the Fourth Assessment Report (2007), most measures for climate change phenomena are given as the predicted value, followed by a 90 percent uncertainty interval. The measure of the rise in global temperature over the last 100 years, for example, is 0.74 (0.56 to 0.92) degrees Celsius; the rise in sea level since 1993 is 3.1 (2.4 to 3.8) millimeters per year.[25] In order to foster better-informed debate over climate policy, these ranges of possible outcomes need to be made clear. Not only does reporting the range of likely outcomes better inform deliberation and policy making, but framing climate change issues in terms of their probability prepares the public for when the precise results differ from central tendencies, which could help to prevent further skepticism of the scientific consensus that does exist.[26]

A further step that could be taken to improve the communication of scientific knowledge to lay people is to make greater use of mechanisms for including laypersons in the process of producing and authorizing that knowledge. This of course would not amount to nonexperts actually writing reports and the like. Rather, the idea would be to create venues through which laypersons may observe the process of writing and reviewing reports.

Such mechanisms could also aid in publicizing and communicating IPCC reports to a lay audience. Upon the completion of an assessment report, a plenary panel of lay citizens, separate from the government delegations, could be convened to digest the central findings and issue its own report, akin to the citizen panels that have been developed in other areas of policy marked by significant scientific or technical issues.[27]

The UN has taken steps to address some of these challenges. In response to the problems posed by the errors revealed in the Fourth Assessment Report—and the broader popular backlash against climate science signified by the controversy over the leaked emails case—in March 2010 Secretary-General Ban Ki-Moon asked the InterAcademy Council (IAC), an association of national science academies, to undertake a review of the IPCC and to make suggestions for reform. In August 2010 the IAC offered its recommendations, which focused on creating more robust leadership in the form of an executive committee, tightening review procedures, better communication of uncertainty, and improving communication and transparency.[28] The IPCC made revisions to both its management structure and assessment practices in response.

THE IPCC AS A TRUSTEE FOR FUTURE GENERATIONS

The reforms made in response to the IAC recommendations will certainly improve the manner in which the IPCC undertakes its assessments and communicates them to policy makers and the public under the current climate change regime. However, in light of the significant challenges posed by climate change and the difficulties in realizing a successor agreement to the Kyoto Protocol, a different institutional model for integrating science into policy making is warranted. Policy-neutral knowledge assessment may have succeeded in convincing governments that a climate convention is necessary, as suggested by the UNFCCC. But the mixed success of Kyoto and the difficulties faced in negotiating a successor agreement suggest that the politics of policy-neutrality may have reached its limit. What the politics of climate change has taught us over the last three decades is that knowledge assessment is good at establishing the need to address the issue and sustaining issue salience, but that it is too passive and infrequent to respond to the rapidly changing political environment. Many scientists and policy makers have expressed frustration at the pace of producing the assessment reports, though defenders of the IPCC claim that maintaining the proper boundary between science and politics requires that the IPCC work essentially on its own clock, and that the time taken to produce reports is necessary to do good science.[29]

The larger problem, however, is that knowledge assessment, and the attendant aspiration to policy-neutrality, relies on the unfounded assumption that such activities can be apolitical in the realm of climate politics. When an issue has such profound implications for energy production and usage, industry, trade, economic development, and so on, it becomes exceedingly difficult to extricate the science from the politics. Indeed, many observers have found contradictions in the ostensibly policy-neutral process of producing the assessment reports—and these charges come both from politically interested parties, such as fossil fuel lobbies and conservative skeptics, and from more evenhanded critics interested in finding the most productive integration of science with the policy-making process.[30]

In addition to all of these challenges, the contemporary politics of climate change also suffers from an unaddressed democratic deficit.[31] The resolution that established the IPCC called for the "protection of global climate for present and future generations of mankind," but there is no mechanism in place to ensure that the interests of future generations are represented in the policy-making process. A primary reason that climate change is a troubling moral issue is because it amounts to a situation in which the decisions and activities of one powerful group—the present generation—substantially affect the interests of a group that is not included in the decision-making process that governs those activities.[32] Reframing the role of an expert body such as the IPCC as a trustee for future generations would be a way to remedy this deficit. In this capacity, the panel could be given a more robust and visible role in the process to replace the expiring Kyoto Protocol as an independent reviewing agency. This arrangement would allow the IPCC to act as an accountability mechanism on the COP process on behalf of future generations, and it would amount to a different method of drawing the boundary between science and politics than the current tenuous stance of policy-neutrality.

This model of expert authority is resonant with the trustee model of political representation, in which the superior knowledge, judgment, or virtue of the representative grants him or her authority to discern the interests of the represented. Critics of the trustee model charge that it implies an elitist, even antidemocratic view of the role of the representative, exemplified by Edmund Burke's conception of representation as, in the words of Hanna Pitkin, "an elite caring for others."[33] To be sure, casting scientific experts as guardian trustees along these lines would certainly undermine efforts to make the IPCC's role in climate change politics more democratic. However, the fact that contemporary expertise is granted via processes of education and training democratizes the idea of expert trustee representation in at least three ways. First, it constrains claims of expertise to those that are based in such processes. Second, because the training and education required to become an expert are in principle open to everyone, the aristocratic flavor of representative expertise is replaced with a more meritocratic one. Third, and most significant, is the fact that, as Mark Brown points out, the processes and criteria of professional training and certification are, in principle, open to regulation, providing a mechanism for some democratic control over the production of expertise.[34]

A critic might wonder, however, how it is that a panel of experts such as the IPCC could be conceived as a trustee agent for future generations. It seems clear that contemporary citizens can delegate authority to an expert body in this way, which is the conventional mode by which expertise is incorporated into politics in a democratic manner. But since future generations of necessity cannot do this, how can we credibly characterize an expert body acting on their behalf as a form of democratic trusteeship? Such a political relationship amounts to an instance in which the agent or representative is characterized by a tremendous amount of independence from the wishes or control of the represented. A consideration of Pitkin's treatment of this issue and how it informs the notion of trustee representation suggests an answer to this puzzle.

Pitkin addresses the trustee model of representation and the so-called mandate-independence controversy separately, but her analyses of these ideas are consonant with one another. The mandate-independence controversy revolves around the question of whether representatives should act strictly according to the wishes of the represented, or whether they should simply act in the interests of the represented, regardless of their expressed wishes.[35] Sensibly, Pitkin's answer is "it depends"—on such factors as why there might be conflict between the wishes of the represented and their interests as the representative sees them; whether the represented have preferences or opinions on the matter at all; whether there is conflict within the preferences of the represented group; and so on. Denying that the controversy is resolvable in the sense of deciding which side is right, Pitkin argues that the concept of representation is shaped by a continuum between these two poles, beyond which the purported representative becomes either an

oligarch (when he neglects or tramples the interests of the represented and/
or consistently and arbitrarily contravenes their wishes) or a tool, a passive
instrument for the often contradictory whims of the populace.

Where a representative arrangement falls on this continuum largely depends on the nature of the interests to be represented. Her analysis suggests
that greater independence for representative agents is called for when (1) the
represented have no opinion or preference on the matter at hand, (2) the
represented are incapable of expressing their opinions or preferences, (3)
the interests to be represented are more or less objective, and/or (4) representative agents have some expertise that enables them to claim some authority when they say what is in the interest of the represented. The first
three of these conditions are characteristic of future generations. Though it
makes little sense to say that future generations have opinions or preferences, much less that they can express them, what interests they do have
that can be known in the present will be more or less objective. Another
way of putting this is, while future generations are incapable of the subjec-
tive state of having an opinion or preference, there are states of the world
that are undoubtedly in their interest compared to others. We cannot know,
for example, what preferences future generations will have over, say, how
much state support there should be for the arts, but it is quite certain that an
environment suitable to the welfare of and able to meet the basic needs of
human life is in their interest. In sum, the interests of future generations are
well suited to representation via agents, institutions, and practices marked
by significant independence.

So much for the interests of the represented. The fourth condition describes the status of scientific experts and construes their representative role
as that of the trustee, the paradigmatic model of independent representative.
As Pitkin writes, the idea of the representative as a trustee is that "of freeing
the representative from the wishes or opinions of his constituents, while yet
regarding him as having an obligation to their welfare."[36] Often linked with
the idea that the represented is incapable of acting for themselves, the basis
of representative authority is often grounded in possessing special skill or
knowledge—that is, expertise.

Harnessing scientific experts as trustees of future generations on the issue
of climate change, then, is warranted by two factors. First, the kinds of interests affected by climate change are relatively uncontroversial. Basic human
needs, such as access to water, an adequate food supply, and a hospitable place
to live, are at stake. In order to act as a trustee on such issues, agents need not

be overly concerned with dominating those they act for or subverting their wishes, but rather should focus on discerning just what interests are at stake and how to protect them. Second, although there is some disagreement on some of the mid-level issues, there is a broad consensus among climate scientists about the basic hypothesis of anthropogenic climate change. An important corollary of this point is that while disagreement and uncertainty remain as to the precise method(s) that should be used to reduce GHG emissions, there is a scientific consensus that such reductions can and must occur. And it is in precisely these kinds of disagreements and debates—over, say, just how much GHG emissions must be reduced, and what kinds of adaptation and mitigation strategies should be considered—that experts are best positioned to participate as trustees of future interests.

This account of scientists and scientific organizations as trustee representatives of future generations suggests that they should be given a more prominent role in decision-making bearing on issues, such as climate change, that have significant implications for the future state of the planet. This perspective construes efforts to better inform decision-making processes with the available expertise as more than attempts to come to better decisions, but rather as enhancing the democratic legitimacy of such processes because of the position scientific bodies are in to act as trustees of future interests. However, to ensure that giving the IPCC more of a role in policy making does not turn into technocratic domination of the present generation, the authority granted needs to be situated within a broader institutional framework in which the IPCC (or some reformed successor body), as an independent agency, is in a position to review the policies produced by the COP process—and not to direct the process itself.

In this model, the IPCC would play a democratic role akin to what Philip Pettit describes as the contestatory function of reviewing courts and agencies.[37] On this view, the decisions of policy-making bodies—in this case, the COP process put into place by the UNFCCC—can be contested in reviewing institutions, such as administrative agencies, on the basis that they do not take into account the vital interests of a party affected by the policy. The contestatory interpretation of agencies is that they fulfill a crucial dimension of democratic decision-making by ensuring that political power is not exercised without being accountable to the interests of all affected by a decision. If the role of the IPCC were reoriented toward ensuring that the climate system will continue to sustain an environment suitable to the vital interests of future generations, those future generations may not be in a position to participate in the policy-making process, but there would be a trustee institution in place to review that process on behalf of their interests, a form of contestation that Pettit has characterized as "editorship" over policies in their application.

The challenge, then, is to incorporate the trusteeship of future generations to be held by a reformed IPCC within the broader institutional scheme in which governments, acting as representatives of the (contemporary) citizens of their countries, negotiate a framework to address the climate challenge as part of the COP process of the UNFCCC. To fulfill this role, the IPCC must transition away from policy-neutral knowledge assessment. I do not suggest, however, that the panel should take on the same kind of policy role considered for it in the 1980s. Rather, Pettit's account of the democratic-contestatory function of reviewing agencies suggests a third possible role for an expert body like the IPCC.

Just what kind of reviewing power should be granted is a difficult question to resolve. There is a continuum of possibilities. At one end, the reviewing power of the IPCC would amount only to providing analyses of the estimated impact of proposed measures to mitigate or adapt to climate change. An independent body charged with this task would serve as a check on the claims made by governments as to the effectiveness of their measures in responding to the climate change problem, and would be able to report on the likely range of outcomes for future human well-being in light of prevailing climate policy. This would be akin to the function of the Congressional Budget Office in the US government, a body charged with providing objective, nonpartisan assessments of legislation with budgetary implications. This is similar to how the IPCC currently functions, though with a closer link to the COP process. At the other end of the continuum, the IPCC would hold a form of review power over the climate policies of governments, akin to the judicial review power of a constitutional court. The former arrangement would depend too much on government officials and those they represent caring about the fate of future generations for the climate policy review body to have any real power; the latter risks granting a power to experts that goes beyond the bounds of their authority, threatening the domination of contemporary interests.

DEMOCRACY AND "SUCCEEDING GENERATIONS"

Between these two poles lies a role for a reformed IPCC to review climate change policies developed by governments in the COP process on the basis of how they affect the interests of future generations in light of the state of scientific knowledge on the subject. One possible arrangement would be for the IPCC to review the accord produced for its impact on the well-being of future generations. If it meets some minimum threshold set by the IPCC for mitigating and/or adapting to climate change, it could go into effect as written. If not, it could go into effect but trigger an earlier deadline for producing a new agreement. This modifies the role of the IPCC from only knowledge assessment, the work that is typically produced prior to and separate from the policy-making process, to that of a reviewing agency, whose capacity to act subsequent to the policy-making process allows it to shape that process.

Reorienting an expert body like the IPCC to be a trustee of the interests of future generations is consonant with other work in political theory concerned with what Dennis Thompson has identified as the presentism of democracy—that is, a bias in democratic politics in favor of the present generation over future generations.[38] From this perspective, treating climate change as only a global problem—and not also as an intergenerational problem—is not sufficient to satisfy the democratic principle that all whose interests are affected by a decision should be included in decision-making processes. This normative commitment should, as far as possible, shape the institutional response to the issue, and scholars are increasingly turning attention to institutional innovations to do just this.[39] Exploring such innovations in the context of the UN system would mark a significant step by the international community on behalf of succeeding generations.

Notes

1. United Nations General Assembly (UNGA), Resolution 43/53, "Protection of Global Climate for Present and Future Generations of Mankind," 1988, available at http://www.un.org/documents/ga/res/43/a43r053.htm (accessed July 15, 2013).

2. Naomi Oreskes, "The Scientific Consensus on Climate Change," *Science* 306 (2005): 1686.

3. See Gale E. Christianson, *Greenhouse: The 200-Year Story of Global Warming* (New York: Walker, 1999); and J. W. Anderson, "A 'Crash Course' in Climate Policy," in *The RFF Reader in Environmental and Resource Management,* ed. Wallace E. Oates (Washington, DC: Resources for the Future, 1999), 213–24.

4. See an image of the Keeling curve at http://earthobservatory.nasa.gov/IOTD/view.php?id=5620 (accessed December 14, 2012).

5. This, of course, simplifies a very complex process. For a more detailed description of Earth's climate system, see Richard Wolfson and Stephen H. Schneider, "Understanding Climate Science," in *Climate Change Policy: A Survey,* ed. Stephen H. Schneider, Armin Rosencranz, and John O. Niles (Washington, DC: Island Press, 2002), 3–51.

6. Intergovernmental Panel on Climate Change (IPCC), *Climate Change 2007: Synthesis Report. Contribution of Working Groups I, II, and III to the Fourth Assessment Report of the Intergovernmental Panel on Climate Change,* ed. R. K. Pachauri, A. Reisinger, and Core Writing Team, 30. The value of the 100-year rise marks an increase over the previous calculation of .6 degrees Celsius from the IPCC's previous assessment report of 2001.

7. Quoted in Shardul Agrawala, "Context and Early Origins of the Intergovernmental Panel on Climate Change," *Climatic Change* 39 (1998): 608.

8. Agrawala, "Context and Early Origins"; Clark A. Miller, "Climate Science and the Making of a Global Political Order," in *States of Knowledge: The Co-Production of Science and Social Order*, ed. Sheila Jasanoff (New York: Routledge, 2004), 46–66.

9. UNGA, Resolution 43/53, 1988.

10. Some observers, however, have criticized the IPCC of a bias for the natural sciences over the social sciences, which leads to less of an emphasis on the social and political impacts of climate change. See Mike Hulme and Martin Mahoney, "Climate Change: What Do We Know about the IPCC?" *Progress in Physical Geography* 34 (2010): 707–9.

11. Paul N. Edwards and Stephen H. Schneider, "Self-Governance and Peer Review in Science-for-Policy: The Case of the IPCC Second Assessment Report," in *Changing the Atmosphere: Expert Knowledge and Environmental Governance*, ed. Clark A. Miller and Paul N. Edwards (Cambridge: MIT Press, 2001), 237.

12. IPCC, "Summary for Policymakers." In *Climate Change 2013: The Physical Science Basis. Contribution of Working Group I to the Fifth Assessment Report of the Intergovernmental Panel on Climate Change* (Cambridge: Cambridge University Press, 2013), 2 and 15.

13. Oreskes, "Scientific Consensus."

14. See *States of Knowledge: The Co-Production of Science and Social Order*, ed. Sheila Jasanoff (New York: Routledge, 2004).

15. UNGA, Resolution 43/53, 1988.

16. Miller, "Climate Science," 60; Agrawala, "Context and Early Origins," 609–10.

17. UNGA, Resolution 45/212, "Protection of Global Climate for Present and Future Generations of Mankind," 1990. See Miller, "Climater Science."

18. Miller, "Climate Science," 53–55.

19. Shardul Agrawala, "Structural and Process History of the Intergovernmental Panel on Climate Change," *Climatic Change* 39 (1998): 621–42.

20. Daniel Bodansky, "The History of the Global Climate Change Regime," in *International Relations and Global Climate Change*, ed. Urs Luterbacher and Detlef F. Sprinz (Cambridge: MIT Press, 2001), 23–41. The UNFCCC calls for the parties to stabilize GHG emissions at levels that will prevent dangerous disruption of the climate system. The Kyoto Protocol commits countries to specific legally binding GHG levels. Only developed countries are required to limit GHG emissions, reflecting the principle of "common but differentiated responsibilities" recognized in the UNFCCC, which holds that developed countries have a greater responsibility for reducing GHG emissions in light of their historically greater industrial activity. This has been the primary reason cited for why the US did not sign the protocol.

21. For an analysis of public perceptions of global warming and climate science in the US, see A. Leiserowitz, E. Maibach, C. Roser-Renouf, and J. Hmielowski, *Global Warming's Six Americas, March 2012 and November 2011*, Yale University and George Mason University (New Haven: Yale Project on Climate Change Communication, 2012).

22. On the role of conservative think tanks in promoting environmental skepticism, see Peter J. Jacques, Riley E. Dunlap, and Mark Freeman, "The Organisation of Denial: Conservative Think Tanks and Environmental Scepticism," *Environmental Politics* 17 (2008): 349–85.

23. David Adam, " 'Climategate' Review Clears Scientists of Dishonesty over Data," *The Guardian*, July 7, 2010. Available at http://www.guardian.co.uk/environment/2010/jul/07/climategate-review-clears-scientists-dishonesty (accessed July 14, 2013).

24. Elisabeth Rosenthal, "U.N. Climate Panel and Its Chief Face a Siege on Their Credibility," *New York Times*, February 9, 2010, A1.

25. IPCC, *Synthesis Report*, 2.

26. For further discussion of this issue, see Stephen H. Schneider and Kristin Kuntz-Duriseti, "Uncertainty and Climate Change Policy," in *Climate Change Policy: A Survey*, ed. Stephen H. Schneider, Armin Rosencranz, and John O. Niles (Washington, DC: Island Press, 2002), 53–88.

27. For an account of how lay citizen panels may enhance the democratic legitimacy of expert advisory boards, see Mark B. Brown, "Citizen Panels and the Concept of Representation," *Journal of Political Philosophy* 14 (2006): 203–25.

28. Committee to Review the Intergovernmental Panel on Climate Change, "Climate Change Assessments: Review of the Processes and Procedures of the IPCC" (InterAcademy Council, 2010).

29. For a variety of perspectives from scientists on how to reform the IPCC, see "IPCC: Cherish It, Tweak It, or Scrap It?" *Nature* 463 (February 11, 2010): 730–32.

30. Agrawala, "Structural and Process History," 627; Daniel Sarewitz, "Curing Climate Backlash," *Nature* 464 (March 4, 2010): 28.

31. My treatment of this issue sets aside the question of just how democratic a global governance framework in which more or less sovereign states are the primary agents can be vis-à-vis present generations. I do not claim that the UNFCCC process or any other UN or international organization satisfactorily realizes democratic principles of legitimacy. Although the present generation affected by climate change is meant to be represented in the COP process via their state delegations, this makes climate change politics only as democratic as the international system, which of course is characterized by significant democratic deficiencies. The interests of present generations, however, are certainly included to a greater degree than those of future generations. On the question of global democracy, see, for example, David Held, *Democracy and the Global Order: From the Modern State to Cosmopolitan Governance* (Stanford: Stanford University Press, 1995), and James Bohman, *Democracy across Borders* (Cambridge: MIT Press, 2007).

32. For further discussion of the democratic principle of affected interest, see Ian Shapiro, *Democratic Justice* (New Haven: Yale University Press, 1999), 38–39; Robert Goodin, "Enfranchising All Affected Interests, and Its Alternatives," *Philosophy and Public Affairs* 35 (2007): 40–68.

33. Hanna Fenichel Pitkin, *The Concept of Representation* (Berkeley: University of California Press, 1967), 168–73.

34. Brown, "Citizen Panels."

35. Pitkin, *Concept of Representation*, 144–67.

36. Ibid., 128.

37. Philip Pettit, "Republican Freedom and Contestatory Democratization," in *Democracy's Value*, ed. Ian Shapiro and Casiano Hacker-Cordon (Cambridge: Cambridge University Press, 1999), 163–90.

38. Dennis Thompson, "Representing Future Generations: Political Presentism and Democratic Trusteeship," *Critical Review of International and Political Philosophy* 13 (2010): 17–37.

39. See, for example, Kristian Skagen Ekeli, "Constitutional Experiments: Representing Future Generations through Submajority Rules," *Journal of Political Philosophy* 17 (2009): 440–61.

Contributors

M. PATRICK COTTRELL, Department of Political Science, Linfield College

JAMES DOBBINS, United States Special Representative for Afghanistan and Pakistan

MICHAEL W. DOYLE, School of International and Public Affairs, Law School, and Department of Political Science, Columbia University; Assistant Secretary-General and Special Adviser for Policy Planning to United Nations Secretary-General Kofi Annan, 2001–3

OONA A. HATHAWAY, Yale Law School

JEAN KRASNO, International Security Studies, Yale University; Colin Powell Center for Policy Studies and Department of Political Science, City College of New York

JOSEPH LAMPERT, Division of Political Science, Hatfield School of Government, Portland State University

EDWARD C. LUCK, Joan B. Kroc School of Peace Studies, University of San Diego; Assistant Secretary-General and Special Adviser to United Nations Secretary-General Ban Ki-moon, 2008–12

SRINATH RAGHAVAN, Centre for Policy Research, New Delhi

STEPHEN SCHLESINGER, The Century Foundation

IAN SHAPIRO, Department of Political Science and MacMillan Center for International and Area Studies, Yale University

DEBRA SHUSHAN, Department of Government, College of William and Mary

Index

Abbas, Mahmoud, 166, 167, 168

Ad-Hoc Court for East Timor, 114–15

Advisory Group on Greenhouse Gases (AGGG), 227

Afghanistan, 200, 207, 212, 216

Africa Group, 178, 186

African Union, xviii, 111, 203, 204, 205–6, 209

Ahtisaari, Martti, xiii, 180, 183, 187–89, 191

Albanians, massacre of, 220

al Qaeda, 212, 215–16, 224n40

Alvarez, José, 68

Angola, 110, 185–86, 198

Annan, Kofi, 77, 80, 114, 117, 118, 202, 219, 221

antidiscrimination provisions. See human rights

Apartheid, xiii, 175, 183, 187

Arab Higher Committee, 160, 162

Arab League, 111

arbitration, mediation, and conflict resolution, 109

Argentina, 100, 170n9

arms inspections, 109, 222n12

Arrhenius, Svante, 226

Asiatic Land Tenure and Indian Representation Act ("Ghetto Act"), 150

Atlantic Charter (1941), 95, 144–45

Attlee, Clement, 146

Balfour Declaration (1917), 159

Ban Ki-moon, 137, 166, 169, 233

Belgian forces in Congo, 197

Ben-Gurion, David, 162, 163

Bernadotte, Folke, xii, 164

Better World for All: Progress Towards the International Development Goals (BWfA Report), 80

Bevin, Ernest, 147–48, 160

Bhagavan, Manu, 143–44, 151–52

Big Three/Big Four (US, Britain, USSR, & China), vii, viii, 121, 122. *See also* Permanent Five; *individual countries*

bin Laden, Osama, 212, 224n40

birth control. See reproductive health

Bolton, John, 79–80

Bosnia, 201, 204, 206, 207, 219–20, 224n32

Botha, P. W., 184, 186

Botha, Roelof (Pik), 179, 188–89

Boutros-Boutros Ghali, 114

Brachman, Jarrett, 215

Brazil, 123, 136

Bretton Woods institutions, 78, 80–81

Britain: in Bosnian conflict, 201; and British Empire's preservation, 112, 134, 144; and India's independence movement, 144–48; and Islamic relations, 154; and Palestine mandate, 157–58, 159; in Palestinian operations of UN, 165; and progressive provisions of UN Charter, 127; in Sierra Leone conflict, 202; in South West Africa, 175

Brown, Mark, 235

Bruce Report (1939), 131

budget of UN, 71–72. *See also* finances of UN

Bunche, Ralph, 164

Burke, Edmund, 234

Bush (G.H.W.) administration, 186

Bush (G.W.) administration, 80, 81, 88n39, 207, 213

Bush Doctrine, 213

Cambodia: conflict in, 198; peacekeeping operations in, 199; Special Tribunal for, 114; transition from conflict to peace, 199, 200
carbon dioxide emissions, 226
Carlsson, Bernt, 180
Carr, E. H., 103
Carter administration, 183, 184
"cascade effect," 138n13
Cecil, Robert, 91
Chamberlain, Joseph, 170n9
Chemical Weapons Convention, 110
China: and decolonization, 134; International Criminal Court (ICC), refusal to join, 115; negotiations to free captured US airmen (1950s), 75, 113; and progressive provisions of UN Charter, 125, 131; Roosevelt's insistence on including, 122–23; troops contributed to UN peacekeeping, 209
Churchill, Winston: and decolonization, 144–45; and founding of UN, 107; on General Assembly, 134; and India, 145; and USSR dealings, 124; and Yalta Conference/Statement, viii, 3–4
civil rights. See human rights
civil wars, 118
Claude, Inis, 93–94
climate change, xiv–xv, 225–41; challenges of, 231–33; communication about, 232–33; indicators of, 226–27; Kyoto Protocol, 231, 233, 234, 240n20; from scientific inquiry to institutional development, 226–28; and scientific uncertainty, 232, 237; UN involvement in worldwide campaign against, 117, 225. See also Intergovernmental Panel on Climate Change (IPCC)
Clinton administration, 207
coalitions of the willing, 73, 202, 206
code of conduct for UN operations, 190
Cold War: beginnings of, vii; end of, xviii, 137; peacekeeping during, 196–98; and Security Council, 108–9, 195; and UN endurance, 137; and UN institutional growth, 84; and UN voting provisions, 133

collective security, 97, 99, 103
Collier, Paul, 203
Commission on Human Rights, 114, 118, 128, 151
Commonwealth, 146, 149–50
Concert of Europe, 92–93
Conference of the Parties (COP), 231, 238, 241n31
conflict prevention, 110–11, 129
Congo, 119, 176, 181, 197–98, 201, 203
Connally, Tom, 124
Constitutional Court of South Africa, 68–69
constitutions, state: compared to UN Charter, ix, 67, 68–71, 83–84, 132; distinguished from league or treaty, 86n6
Conventions. See specific convention by topic or name
Coordinating Committee for the Liberation of Africa, 177
COP. See Conference of the Parties
costs of armed conflict, 203–4
Cottrell, M. Patrick, x, xv, 91
Council for Namibia (formerly South West Africa), xiii, 180–82, 184, 191
Covenant on Economic, Social, and Cultural Rights, 218
Croatia, 201–2
Cuban troops in Angola, 185–87
cyberattacks, 214
Cyprus, 109, 190, 197

Darfur, 119, 203, 206
deaths from armed conflicts, 203
Declaration of the United Nations (1942), 95, 134, 144
decolonization, 111–12, 134, 149–50, 197. See also India
de Klerk, F. W., 186, 189
delegation, 71
"democratic," not term used in Charter, 123
Department for International Development (DFID, UK), 80–81
Dieye, Binta, 189–90
disarmament and demobilization, 109, 110, 198–200
discrimination prohibitions. See human rights

Dobbins, James, xiii–xiv, xviii, 195
Dominican Republic, 109
Doyle, Michael, ix, xv, xvi, 67, 166
Dreyfus Affair, 158
drug control, 109, 115, 119
DTA (Namibia political party), 190
Duelfer, Charles, 223n13
Dumbarton Oaks Conference (1944), vii, 94, 123, 125

Eastern Slavonia, 201–2
East Timor, 110, 201, 202; Ad-Hoc Court for, 114–15
Eckhard, Fred, 189
Economic and Social Council (ECOSOC), 114, 116, 127, 128, 129, 130–31
economic and social initiatives: and League of Nations, 130–31; and progressive provisions of UN Charter, 129–30, 134; success of UN in promoting, xvii, 116–17, 199
Egypt, 163, 164
El Salvador, 110, 186, 198, 200
embassy bombings in Africa (1998), 216
enforcement actions, 109, 136, 201, 208
equality of UN members, xvi, 68, 76, 123
Ethiopia, 179
European Court of Justice (ECJ), 76, 83
European Union (EU): constitution of, 83, 84, 88n34; peacekeeping forces of, xviii, 204–6, 209; and Security Council resolutions, 76; and war on terror Security Council resolutions, 76
Expense Case, 71–72

fact-finding, 109
failed states, 197, 200–202
famine relief, 201
finances of UN, 71–72, 119, 168
Food and Agricultural Organization (FAO), 117
France: in Bosnian conflict, 201; and colonial preservation, 112, 134; failure to make UN payments, 71; as one of permanent Council members, 123;

recognition of Israel, 169n2. *See also* Permanent Five
Franck, Thomas, 69, 86n7
Franklin, Benjamin, 84
Freedom House, 115
freezing assets of suspected terrorists, 217

G-20, 117
Gandhi, Mohandas K., 145
GATT evolution to World Trade Organization, 84
Geingob, Hage, 176–77, 178, 181
gender discrimination, 127
General Assembly: and climate change, 225–26; compared to Security Council's conservative stance, 168; and Indian independence, 147; and Indian treatment in South Africa, 150–51; Nehru's views on, 150–51; and Palestine, 158, 162, 167, 168; resolution 43/53, 239n1; resolution 181, xii, 162, 163, 164, 166, 167, 171n30; resolution 194, 164; resolution 338, 178; resolution 1514, 185; resolution 2145, xiii, 180; role of, 134; voting procedures, 133
Geneva conventions, 218
Genocide Convention, 69, 218, 219, 221
genocides, 111, 118–19, 175. *See also* Bosnia; Kosovo; Rwanda genocide
Germany, 136, 175
Ghana, 176
Ghetto Act, xii, 150
Gildersleeve, Virginia, 126–27
Global Compact between business and UN, 117
global warming. *See* climate change
Goodrich, Leland, 98, 130, 131, 138n1
Gorbachev, Mikhail, 185–86
governance of UN, x–xi, 70, 73–74, 119. *See also* General Assembly; Secretariat and Secretary-General; Security Council
Great Britain. *See* Britain
Great Depression, 99, 116
greenhouse gases. *See* climate change
Grew, Joseph, 124
Gromyko, Andrei, 130

Guatemala, 110
Gurirab, Theo-Ben, 176, 177, 178

Habitat agency, 117
Haiti, 206, 207
Hamas, 167, 168
Hammarskjöld, Dag, 73, 74, 75, 83, 113, 166
Hathaway, Oona A., xiv, xvi, 210
Helfer, Laurence, 69
Herero, 175
Herzl, Theodor, 158, 170n9
Higgins, Rosalyn, 179
Hindus, 145–46, 152–53
historical institutionalist approach, 104n2
HIV/AIDS, 81
Hoeffler, Anke, 203
Hull, Cordell, 97, 124, 129–30
humanitarian intervention, 114, 118, 201
human rights: ability of UN to address
    abuses, 211, 217–22; missing in League of
    Nations' focus, 102–3; Nehru's views on,
    151–52; in South Africa, 183, 187; success
    of UN in, xvii, 114, 115; UN Charter
    provisions on, 125, 127–29, 134, 137, 218;
    Universal Declaration of Human Rights,
    114, 116, 127, 151, 218. See also Commis-
    sion on Human Rights
Human Rights Council, 114
Hussein, Saddam, 214
Hussein, Sharif, 158–59
hypocrisy, 93, 144

ICC (International Criminal Court), 115
ICJ. See International Court of Justice
ICSU (International Council of Scientific
    Unions), 227
idealism, viii–ix, xv, 97, 120, 144, 154
IDGs (International Development Goals),
    80–81
IMF. See International Monetary Fund
imperialism, 101–2
independence movements, 101, 112, 145,
    176–77
India, xi–xii, xvii, 143–56; emerging India
    in UN, 148–52; and Kashmir, 143,

153–54; and Pakistan, 152–53; and
    Security Council, 136; on Security
    Council resolutions' enforceability, 76;
    UN role in independence of, 144–48
Indian National Congress, 145
institutional autochthony, 86n7
Intergovernmental Negotiating Committee
    (INC), 230
Intergovernmental Panel on Climate Change
    (IPCC), xiv–xv, xvii, 225–41; Assessment
    Reports, 228, 231–32; bridging science
    and politics, 228–31; challenges of,
    231–33; founding of, 226, 227; future of,
    238–39, 241n31; influence of, 230–31;
    leaked emails over unsubstantiated
    claims, 231–32, 233; mandate of, 229;
    primary work of, 227–28; reviewing
    power of, 238; as trustee for future
    generations, 233–38
International Atomic Energy Agency,
    110
"The International Civil Servant" (Hammar-
    skjöld's "Oxford Lecture"), 73, 74
International Council of Scientific Unions
    (ICSU), 227
International Court of Justice (ICJ): *Expense
    Case*, 71–72; Indians in South Africa as
    issue for, 150; jurisdiction, 112; *Lockerbie
    Case*, 73; and Namibian independence
    movement, 178–80; *Reparations Case*, 71;
    replacing League's Permanent Court, 100,
    115; Statute of (text), 46–63
International Covenant on Civil and Political
    Rights, 218
International Criminal Court (ICC), 115
International Development Goals (IDGs),
    80–81
International Labor Organization, 116, 130
international law, 115–16, 218–19
International Monetary Fund (IMF), 117;
    and IDGs, 80; and MDGs, 80, 81, 82
international organizations, UN success
    requiring expertise of, 165–66
International Tribunals for Yugoslavia and
    Rwanda, 114

IPCC. *See* Intergovernmental Panel on
Climate Change
Iran: Russian troops' departure (1946), 113;
sanctions, 110
Iran-Iraq war, 113, 185
Iraq-Kuwait war (1990), 110, 113
Iraq war (2003), 204, 207, 213–14, 222n12
isolationism, 99
Israel, recognition of, xii, 162–64. *See also*
Jerusalem; Palestine/Israel

Japan, 136
Jerusalem, xii, 109, 170n11
Jinnah, M. A., 145–46
Jordan, 163, 164
Junagadh, accession to Pakistan, 152–53

Kashmir dispute, xii, 143, 153–54
Katangese rebellion, 197
Katjavivi, Peter, 176
Katjiuongua, Moses, 177
Kenya (Uganda), 170n9
Keohane, Robert, xixn4
Kerry, John, 169
Khama, Tsekhedi, 151
Khrushchev, Nikita, 73
Koevoet (South African special forces),
187, 191
Kosovo, xviii, 110, 206, 207, 220, 224n35
Krasno, Jean, xii–xiii, xvii, 174
Kutako, Hosea, 175
Kuwait war (1990), 110, 113
Kyoto Protocol, 231, 233, 234, 240n20

Labour Party (Britain), 146
Lampert, Joseph, xiv, xvii, 225
Latin American bloc, 111, 222n6
League Health Organization, 100
League of Nations, 91–106; compared to UN,
71, 93, 103–4, 131; Covenant Article 10,
133; Covenant Article 22, 159; economic
and social initiatives of, 130–31; Eurocentric
nature of, 102; failure of, x, 92, 94; and
hypocrisy, 93; multilateralist initiatives
expanded upon by UN, 99–101; origins

of, 92–93; and Palestine, 159; Permanent
Court of International Justice, 100,
106n28, 115; in realist narrative, 91–92;
reconciling power with principle, 96–99;
Secretariat, 100–101; and South West
Africa, 178; UN foundation from, 93–103,
122, 133; US failure to join, 123, 133; US
participation in activities of, 130
Lebanon, 109, 164; Special Tribunal for
Lebanon, 114; UN Interim Force in
Lebanon (UNIFIL), 172n46
legal personality of UN, 71
Legwaila, Joseph, 188, 190, 191
Lehi (Zionist militant group), xii, 164
Liberation Committee, 177
Liberia, 179, 202–3
Libya, xviii, 73, 206, 208
Lie, Trygve, xvi, 113, 160, 163, 165, 166,
170n23
Lippmann, Walter, 133
Lockerbie Case, 73
Luck, Edward C., x–xi, xvii, xviii, 121, 168
Lumumba, Patrice, 198
Lusaka, Paul, 184

Macedonia, 204
Madison, James, 86n6
Mandates Commission, 100
Mandela, Nelson, 186
Mazower, Mark, xixn3, 102, 126, 133, 143, 154
MCA (Millennium Challenge Account), 88n39
McHenry, Donald, 183
MDGs. *See* Millennium Development Goals
Mehta, Hansa, 152
Michelman, Frank, 69
Military Committee, 195, 196, 199
Millennium Challenge Account (MCA), 88n39
Millennium Declaration, 77, 80, 81, 82
Millennium Development Goals (MDGs),
ix–x, 77–82; creation and adoption of,
114, 117; as hardened soft law, 81–82; list
of 8 goals, 78–79; Road Map Report
(September 6, 2001), 78, 82; sources for,
80–81; and supranationality, 83; US views
on, 79–80, 82, 88n39

Miller, Clark, 230
Mitrany, David, 130
Mladić, Ratko, 220
Montreal Convention, 73
Montreal Protocol, 230
Moscow Conference (October 1943), 95
Mozambique, 110, 198, 200
multilateralism, x, xixn4, 92–93, 99–101
Muslim League, 145–46
Muslims, 148, 220

Nama, 175
Namibia, xiii, xvii, 174–92; attempts to
sabotage independence, 188–89; and
Carter administration, 183; Constitutional
Assembly, 182; Council for Namibia, xiii,
180–82; early history of, 175–77; first
elections, 187, 188–90; independence of,
190; and Reagan administration, 184–86;
success of peacekeeping operations in,
110, 191, 198, 200; UN individuals'
pivotal role, 189–90; UN resolutions for
independence of, 182–84; Western Five
Contact Group on Namibia, 183. *See also*
UN Transition Assistance Group for
Namibia (UNTAG)
National Party (South Africa), 185
nation building, 202–3; cost effectiveness of,
203–4; US missions of, 206–8
NATO, xviii, 111, 204–6, 209, 220, 224n35
Negroponte, John, 212
Nehru, Jawaharlal, xi, xvii, 143–44, 148–54
Netanyahu, Benjamin, 166–67
neutrality of Secretariat, 73–75
New Republic on League of Nations concept,
132–33
New Zealand delegation at San Francisco
Conference, 128–29, 139n28
Nicaragua, 198
Noel-Baker, Philip, 153–54
nonalignment, 152, 181
nongovernmental representatives, 125, 127
non-state actors as threats, 211, 215–16, 221.
See also war on terror
North Korea, 109, 110, 196

Nuclear Non-Proliferation Treaty, 110, 115
Nujoma, Sam, 177, 187–88

Obama administration, 214
observer status, 178
Office of UN High Commissioner for
Human Rights, 114
Oil-for-Food program, 118
Operation Deliberate Force, 220
Operation Enduring Freedom, 212
Organization for Economic Cooperation and
Development's International Development
Goals (IDGs), 80
Organization of African Unity (OAU), xvii,
177–78
Ottoman Empire, 158–59, 170n11
"Oxford Lecture" (Hammarskjöld), 73, 74

Pakistan, 146, 152–54, 216. *See also* Kashmir
dispute
Palestine/Israel, xii, xvi, 157–73; British
restraint with, 148; failure of partition
and UN recognition of Israel, 162–64;
Israeli settlements into predominantly
Arab territory, 169; Jewish migration
during British mandate, 159; lessons
learned from UN role in, 164–66;
Palestinian bid for UN membership,
166–69; partition recommendations,
160–62; peacekeeping operations in, 164,
166, 197; Peel Commission report (1937),
159–60; UN role in struggle over
Palestine, 157–60, 197
Palestine Commission, 162–63
Palestinian Authority, 166, 167, 168–69
Palestine Liberation Organization (PLO),
172n48, 178
Pandit, Vijayalakshmi, 150
Peacebuilding Commission and the
Democracy Fund, 117
peacekeeping operations, xiii–xiv; during
Cold War, 196–98; compared to other
international force providers, xiv, 201,
204–8, 209; cost effectiveness of, 203–4;
deficiencies in, 200, 202, 220; Department

of Peacekeeping Operations, 166;
enforcement actions differentiated, 201,
208–9; history of, 195–209; model of
Namibia, 191, 198; and nation building,
202–3; number of, 109, 196; post-Cold
War, 198–200; and Secretary-General's
powers, 114, 204–5; and Security Council's
role, 109, 136, 199, 204–5; soldiers and
officers involved in, 205; US and EU role
in, xviii, 204–8. See also specific countries
Peel Commission report (1937), 159–60
Pérez de Cuéllar, Javier, 113, 187, 189
Permanent Court of International Justice,
100, 106n28, 115
Permanent Five (US, USSR, Britain, France,
& China), 70, 72–73, 108, 122–23. See also
veto power; individual countries
Pettit, Philip, 237–38
Pharmaceutical, 68–69
Pienaar, Louis, 188
Pinsker, Leo, 158
Pitkin, Hanna, 234, 235–36
policing missions, 109, 166
Portuguese Goa, 154
post 9/11 era: and prohibition on use of
force, xiv, 211; and small footprint of US
forces, 207
Powell doctrine, 207
Preamble: authorship of, xixn3, 126;
principles articulated in, viii, xv, 68, 126,
131, 210, 218, 225; text of, 14
preemptive self-defense, 211, 213–14, 223n14
preventive self-defense, 223n14
Proposals for the Establishment of a General
International Organization (Oct. 9, 1944),
viii
pushback: to central authority's growth, 84;
and forces under Council's control, 73;
and MDGs, 82; powerful state exercising,
xvi; and Secretariat's independence, 74

"Quit India" movement, 145

Raghavan, Srinath, xi–xii, xvii, 143
Reagan administration, 184–86

realism, xv, 120, 123, 143, 154
regional banks, 117
regional bodies as part of UN, 111
Reid v. Covert, 76
reintegration of former combatants,
199–200
Reparations Case, 71
representation and transfer of authority,
72–73
reproductive health, 80, 81, 89n41
responsibility to protect, 118, 137, 221
Righter, Rosemary, 128
Road Map Report (Sept. 6, 2001), 78
Rome Statute, 115
Roosevelt, Eleanor, 218
Roosevelt, Franklin D.: Britain, relations
with, 144–45; and founding of UN, 96,
97, 99, 107, 122–23, 125; on need to end
all wars, 221; and progressive provisions
of UN Charter, 127; State of the Union
address (1945), 125; and Yalta Confer-
ence/Statement, viii, 3–9
Root, Elihu, 133
Royal Commission on Palestine report
(1937), 159–60
Russell, Ruth, 101
Russia: in Bosnian conflict, 201; Interna-
tional Criminal Court (ICC), refusal to
join, 115. See also USSR
Rwanda genocide, 110, 114, 119, 219;
International Tribunal for Rwanda, 114

sanctions, 109, 110
San Francisco Conference (1945): on
appointment and term of Secretary-
General, 74; attending countries, 134;
Indian representation at, 145; New
Zealand delegation at, 128–29, 139n28;
nongovernmental representatives at, 125,
127; political controversy over, 100,
111–14, 125; progressive views at, 125;
purpose and goals of, viii, 107, 116, 210;
on Security Council makeup, 122;
Truman's opening address, viii, 10–13
al-Saud, Faisal, 162

Saudi Arabia, 162

scandals, 114, 118

Schlesinger, Stephen, x, xv, 107

scientific uncertainty, 232, 237

SEATO, 111

Secretariat and Secretary-General: appointment and term of Secretary-General, 74; basis in League of Nations, 100–101; and MDGs implementation, 77; neutrality of, 73–75; and peacekeeping missions, 196, 199, 204–5; powers of, 113; Strategic Planning Unit, 78. See also specific secretary-generals

Security Council: binding decisions of, 70; and Bosnia, 220; and Cold War, 108–9, 195; and Congo, 197–98; and enforcement actions, 109, 136, 208; enlargement of, xviii, 119; flexibility and innovation of, 135–36; and Indian independence, 147–48; International Criminal Court (ICC), relationship with, 115; and Israeli independence, 165; jurisdiction of, 69; and Kashmir resolutions, 143, 153–54; and Korean War, 196; and Kosovo, 220; and Namibian independence, 182–83, 186, 188; and Palestinian state recognition, 167; and peacekeeping operations, 109, 136, 199, 204–5; permanent members of, 70, 72–73, 108, 122–23; post-Soviet era, 110, 185–86; purpose of, 107–8; resolution 385, 182; resolution 435, xiii, 174, 183, 191; resolution 566, 185; resolutions 628 & 629, 186; resolution 748, 73; resolution 781, 224n32; resolution 786, 224n32; resolution 816, 224n32; resolution 1368, 216; resolution 1373, 75, 76; resolution 1441, 222n12; resolution 1540, 75, 76; rotating members of, 108, 149; structural reform demands, 136; voting procedure, vii, 133, 138n13; and war on terror resolutions, 75–76. See also veto power

self-defense rights, xiv, xvi, 211, 212–15, 222n4, 223n14

self-determination, 101–3, 114

September 11, 2001, terrorist attacks, 212, 216, 222n3. See also post 9/11 era

Serbia, 201, 220

Shikaki, Khalil, 173n75

Shushan, Debra, xii, xvi, 157

Sierra Leone, 202–3; Special Court for, 114

small arms traffic, 115

Smuts, Jan, xixn3, 126, 127, 149, 150, 151

Somalia, 200–201, 206–7

South Africa: annexation of South West Africa, xii, xiii, 151, 175–77, 179, 183–84; and Ghetto Act, xii, 150; and Security Council, 136; and war in Angola leading to Namibian independence, 185–91

South Korea, 109, 196

South West Africa: Council for South West Africa, xiii, 180; early history of, 175–77; educational system in, 176; as German colony, 175; Katutura township, 175–76, 189; South African annexation of, xii, xiii, 151, 175–77, 179, 183–84. See also Namibia

South West Africa National Union (SWANU), 177

South West Africa People's Organization (SWAPO), xiii, xvii, 176, 177–78, 181–84, 187, 189–90

sovereign equality. See equality of UN members

sovereignty issues, xv–xvi, 102, 118–19, 128–29, 137

Soviet Union. See USSR

Special Court for Sierra Leone, 114

Special Tribunals for Cambodia and Lebanon, 114

spillover cooperation, 83

Srebrenica, 110, 114, 119, 220

Sri Lanka, 110

Stalin, Josef: and founding of UN, 107, 124; and progressive nature of UN Charter, 126; and Yalta Conference/Statement, viii, 3–4

Statute of International Court of Justice (text), 46–63

Stern Gang (Lehi Zionist militant group), xii, 164

Stockholm Conference (1972), 117

Strawson, John, 163, 170n9
successes of UN: buy-in from local
   stakeholders, 165; Congo as, 197–98;
   coordination with and cooperation of
   great powers, 164–65; East Timor
   operation as, 202; economic and social
   progress, xvii, 116–17; in human rights,
   xvii, 114, 115; Namibian independence as,
   110, 174, 191; organizational capacity
   required, 165–66
Sudan, 203, 216
Suez Crisis, 109, 113, 136, 166
supranationality: as constitutional element,
   82; and delegation, 71, 83; distinguished
   from sovereignty, xv–xvi; and financial
   matters, 72–73, 83; operation of, 69–70;
   state sovereignty favored over, 166;
   unique feature of UN Charter, ix; and war
   against terrorism, 75–76
SWANU (South West Africa National
   Union), 177
SWAPO. See South West Africa People's
   Organization
Sykes-Picot Agreement (1916), 159, 170n11
Syria, 162, 164

technological change, 215
Tehran Conference (1943), 95
terrorism. See al Qaeda; war on terror
Test-Ban Treaty, 110, 115
Texas v. White, 69
Thompson, Dennis, 239
Tjitendero, Mosé, 175, 176, 181, 182, 190
Tora Bora, Battle of (2001), 216
Torture Convention, 218
transfer of authority, 72
treaties compared to UN Charter, ix, 67, 69
Tripartite Accord (1988), 187
Truman, Harry: San Francisco Conference
   opening address, viii, 10–13; and veto
   power, 108
trusteeships and Trusteeship Council:
   continuing existence of, 119; and human
   rights, 128; in Jerusalem, 161; Mandates
   Commission of League of Nations

becoming, 100; purpose of, 112, 179; of
   South-West Africa, 151; use of term, 102

UN Charter: Article 1, 97, 106n37, 132;
   Article 1.3, 131; Article 1.4, 131; Article 2,
   132; Article 2.1, xvi, 68, 118, 123; Article
   2.4, xvi, 84, 214, 220; Article 2.7, 69, 84,
   118, 128–29, 148, 150; Article 4, 138n13,
   163; Article 4.1, 68, 133; Article 5, 138n13;
   Article 6, 138n13; Article 10, 102, 158;
   Article 13.1b, 127; Article 17, 71–72;
   Article 18, 71; Article 18.1, 123; Article 19,
   71; Article 24, 166; Article 25, 70; Article
   27, 138n13; Article 34, 129; Article 35,
   147–48; Article 39, 72, 75, 128; Articles
   43–47, 73; Article 48, 70; Article 51, xiv,
   xvi, 111, 211, 212, 214, 217, 222n4,
   223n16; Article 53.1, 138n13; Article 55c,
   128; Article 62.2, 128; Article 65, 129;
   Article 68, 127, 128; Article 71, 119;
   Article 76c, 128; Article 81, 161; Article
   97, 74, 138n13; Article 99, 75, 113; Article
   100, 70, 74; Article 101, 74; Article 103,
   69, 115; Article 108, 125; Article 109, 69;
   background of, vii–ix; British commentary on, 98; compared to Covenant of
   League of Nations, 131; compared to
   national constitutions, ix, 67, 68–71,
   83–84, 132; compared to other regional
   and international organizations, 86n11;
   compared to treaties, ix, 67, 69;
   conservative aspects of, 122–25, 136–37;
   early impact of, xi–xiii; flexible
   interpretation of, 70, 108–9; as global
   constitution, ix, 67, 68; origins of, x;
   perpetual nature of, 69; in practice,
   132–37; as precious institution, 85;
   progressive aspects of, 125–31, 134, 137;
   responsiveness of, 211; signing of, vii;
   standing force provision, 166; structure
   of, ix–x; text of, 14–45. See also Preamble
UN Conference on Succession of States in
   Respect of Treaties, 181
UN Conference on Trade and Development,
   81

UN Council for South West Africa, xiii

UN Development Program (UNDP), 79, 81, 82, 117; UN Development Assistance Framework, 82

UN Disengagement Observer Force (UNDOF), 172n46

UN Educational, Science, and Cultural Organization (UNESCO), 100, 168

UN Emergency Force in the Sinai, 71, 166

UN Environment Programme (UNEP), 117, 225, 227

UN Framework Convention on Climate Change (UNFCCC), 226, 231, 233, 240n20, 241n31

UN Fund for Namibia, 181, 191

UN High Commissioner for Refugees (UNHCR), 117

UN Institute for Namibia, 181, 191

UN Interim Force in Lebanon (UNIFIL), 172n46

United Kingdom. See Britain

United Nations: autonomous organizations and coordination within, 130, 134–35; in contemporary world, xiii–xv, xviii, 107–20, 134–36, 193–241; creation negotiated during World War II, 94–96, 122; governance of, x–xi, 70, 73–74, 119; legal personality of, 71; limitations of, 119; membership of, 134; name of, 105n12; reform of, x–xi, 114, 117–18; regional bodies as part of, 111; relevance in age of transformed warfare, 215–17; support and finances of, 71–72, 119, 168. See also General Assembly; Secretariat and Secretary-General; Security Council; UN Charter; headings starting with "UN"

United States: in Bosnian conflict, 201; and climate change, 227; Constitution compared to UN Charter, 68, 83, 84; and human rights provisions in UN Charter, 125, 127; ICJ jurisdiction as issue for, 112; International Criminal Court (ICC), refusal to join, 115; League of Nations experience as lessons for, 103; MDGs, views on, 79–80, 82, 88n39; multinational

forces led by, 200–201; nation-building missions of, 206–8; in Palestine/Israel dispute, 168–69; peacekeeping forces of, xviii; in planning process for UN creation, 122; recognition of Israel, 169n2; small-footprint approach as failure for, 207–8; stabilitization or reconstruction missions of, 207

Universal Declaration of Human Rights, 114, 116, 127, 151, 218

University of British Columbia report (2005), 111

UN Millennium Summit (September 2000), 77

UN Operation in the Congo, 71

UN Relief and Works Agency for Palestine Refugees in the Near East (UNRWA), 172n50

UN Special Committee on Palestine (UNSCOP), xii, 157, 160–62, 164–65, 170n23

UN Transition Assistance Group for Namibia (UNTAG), xiii, 174, 183, 187–88, 190

UN Truce Supervision Organization (UNTSO), 166, 172n46

Urquhart, Brian, 73, 157, 165

US embassy bombings in Africa (1998), 216

US National Security Strategy Memo (2002), xiv, 213

US National Security Strategy Memo (2006), 213

USS Cole bombing (2000), 216

USSR: and Cuban troops in Angola, 185–86; expulsion from League of Nations, 123; failure to make UN payments, 71, 72; and founding of UN, 97; and Indian independence, 147; and progressive provisions of UN Charter, 125, 127–30; recognition of Israel, 163, 169n2; San Francisco Conference controversy over Soviet bloc countries, 100; on Security Council permanent members, 123; seeking improved relations with the West, 185; and veto power, 108. See also Cold War

U Thant, 113

Vance, Cyrus, 183

Versailles Treaty (1919), 95, 104

veto power: Big Three views on, vii–viii, 123–24; continuing debate over, 108, 125; Nehru's views on, 149; rationale for, xv; in response to League of Nations' failure, 98; Security Council enduring despite of, 135; and supranationality, 70; Truman's role, 108; USSR views on, 108

Vienna Convention, 69

Villach conferences, 227

Waldheim, Kurt, 113

war crimes tribunals, 114–15

war on terror, 75–76, 212–17; freezing assets of suspected terrorists, 217. *See also* post 9/11 era

Warsaw Pact, 111

Wavell, Archibald, 146

weapons interdictions, 109, 115

weapons of mass destruction, xiv, 110, 213–14, 223n13

Webster, Charles, 103

Weiss, Thomas, 104

Western Five Contact Group on Namibia, 183

Williams, Abiodun, 78

Wilson, Woodrow, 92, 96

WMO/UNEP Task Force on a Convention on Climate Change, 229

World Bank: economic role of, 117; and IDGs, 80; and MDGs, 80, 81, 82; Poverty Reduction Strategy Papers, 82

World Food Programme, 117

World Health Organization, 81, 100, 117

World Meteorological Organization (WMO), 117, 225, 227

World Trade Organization (WTO), 78, 84, 117

World War II, creation of UN negotiated during, 94–96, 122

Yalta Conference/Statement, viii; Roosevelt's address to Congress on, 5–9; text of Statement, 3–4

Young, Andrew, 183

Yugoslavia: former Yugoslavia conflicts, 200, 201, 219–20; International Tribunal for Yugoslavia, 114

Zionist movement, 158, 167